STUDENT BOOK B
ETHICS AND RELIGIOUS CULTURE

LIVING in society

Secondary Cycle One

Denis Bélanger
Alain Carrière
Pierre Després
Catherine Mainville
André-Carl Vachon

Note to the reader:
There are other names for some of the terms specific to each religious tradition.

LES ÉDITIONS
CEC
A Quebecor Media Company

9001, boul. Louis-H.-La Fontaine, Anjou, (Québec), Canada H1J 2C5
Telephone : 514 351 6010 • Fax : 514 351 3534

ORIGINAL VERSION

Publishing Manager
Alexandra Labrèche

Production Manager
Danielle Latendresse

Coordination Manager
Rodolphe Courcy

Project Manager
Nicole Beaugrand Champagne
Koliny Chhim

Project Management Collaborators
Nicole Beaugrand Champagne
Koliny Chhim
Philippe Sicard

Linguistic Reviser
Monique La Grenade

Proofreader
Denis Desjardins

Graphic Design

Map Design
Claude Bernard

Iconographic Research
Nicole Beaugrand Champagne

ENGLISH VERSION

Translators and Linguistic Revisers
Rachel Alkallay
Donna Aziz
Fernanda Delgado
Alain Groven
Diane Lewis

Pedagogical Revisers
Kerry Ann King
Natalie Knott

Project Management
Patrick Bérubé
Rita De Marco
Valerie Vucko

The authors and the publisher would like to thank the following consultants for their contribution to this project.

Scientific Consultants
Mireille Estivalèzes, PhD, History and the Sociology of Religion, Professor of Religious Sciences at Université de Montréal.

Michel Langevin, Pedagogical Advisor, Or-et-des-Bois School Board.

Annie Laporte, M.Ed., M.A., Head of Professional Development, Faculty of Theology and Religious Sciences, Université de Montréal.

Benoît Mercier, Professor of Philosophy, Collège Montmorency.

Monelle Parent, Philosopher/Ethics specialist, Université de Sherbrooke.

Educational Consultants
Carole Bergeron, Collège Regina Assumpta

Nancy Gauvin, Saint-Paul Secondary School (Côte-du-Sud School Board).

Marie-Émilie Lacroix, Guillaume-Couture Secondary School (Navigateurs School Board).

René Thibault, École polyvalente de l'Érablière (Draveurs School Board).

Special thanks to Simon Duchesneau (Collège Durocher, Saint-Lambert) for his participation in the conceptual research for this book and to Albane Marret for her valuable contribution.

Authors
Denis Bélanger is a student in the Political Science undergraduate program at UQÀM.

Alain Carrière his teaching degree in Religious Sciences at UQÀM in 1990. Alain Carrière teaches at the International School (Des Patriotes School Board).

Pierre Després his PhD in Philosophy at UQÀM in 1994 under the direction of Georges Leroux. Pierre Després has been teaching at Collège Montmorency since 1977. He is the author of many books.

Catherine Mainville a degree in Communications, with a minor in Journalism, at UQAM in 2003, and a certificate in Communications from the Université de Montréal in 2000.

André-Carl Vachon a B.A. at Université de Montréal in 1996 (received certificates in Theology, Religious Sciences and Education). He received a teaching certificate for History and Adult Education at UQAM in 2006. André-Carl Vachon teaches at Collège Jean-Eudes in Montréal.

These programs are funded by Québec's Ministère de l'Éducation, du Loisir et du Sport, through contributions from the Canada-Québec Agreement on Minority-Language Education and Second-Language Instruction.

Living in Society, Student Book B
© 2009, Les Éditions CEC Inc.
9001, boul. Louis-H.-La Fontaine
Anjou, Québec, H1J 2C5

Translation of *Être en société, Manuel B, 1er cycle du secondaire*
(ISBN 978-2-7617-2580-4) © 2008, Les Éditions CEC Inc.

Legal deposit: 2009
Bibliothéque et Archives nationales du Québec
Library and Archives Canada

ISBN 978-2-7617-2893-5

Printed in Canada

1   2   3   4   5   13   12   11   10   09

Abbreviations
LAC: Library and Archives Canada

BANQ: Bibliothèque et Archives nationales du Québec

SHPFQ: Société d'histoire du protestantisme français au Québec (Society for the History of French Protestantism in Québec)

Table of contents

PRESENTATION OF THE STUDENT BOOK VII
INTRODUCTION X

Ethics 12

PRELUDE 14

Ethical reflection

CHAPTER 1 The influence of family and friends 16

1.1 **Individuals and their circle of family and friends** **18**
  The human being, a complex individual 18
  Individuals and their circle of family and friends 18
  TO KNOW MORE + Symbols 19

1.2 **Autonomy, a source of questions** **22**
  What is autonomy? 22
  Food for thought 23
  Some history Cyrano de Bergerac 26

1.3 **Freedom** **27**
  What is freedom? 27
  Issues related to freedom 28
  Some history Janette Bertrand and taboos in Québec 31

Culture and society Autonomy and freedom in recent centuries **32**

Here and elsewhere Autonomy and freedom today **34**

Synthesis **38**

CHAPTER 2 Society's influences 40

2.1 **Social order** **42**
  Types of power 43

2.2 **Protecting social values** **46**
  A look at the values in Québec society 46
  The protection of rights and freedoms 47

2.3 **Social norms** **50**
  Written and unwritten norms 50
  Social conventions 50
  Laws 51
  Codes 52
  Municipal regulations 52

2.4 **Individuals and the social order** **53**
  Autonomy and dependency in society 53
  Forms of obedience and disobedience of the law 54

Culture and society 56
    Ways of looking at freedom and social order 56
    The symbols of freedom 58
    Counterculture 59
Here and elsewhere   Law and order in Singapore 60
Synthesis 62

CHAPTER 3 The influences of the media 64
3.1 The media and social order 66
    The media, the individual and society 66
    The media and social change 67
3.2 The media and freedom 70
    The rights and freedoms of the media 70
    Some history 72
        Censorship and movies in Québec 72
        The first televised political debate 72
        The early years of Canadian television 72
    Responsibilities 73
    The issues 74
3.3 Individuals and the media 77
    Disinformation 77
    Autonomy 78
    Addiction 79
Culture and society 80
    Journalists and freedom of the press 80
    Poetry of commitment and censorship 81
Here and elsewhere   The Russian State and media control 82
Synthesis 84

Religious Culture 86

PRELUDE 88

The phenomenon of religion
CHAPTER 4 Influences on values and norms 90
4.1 The influence of religious institutions on the family 92
    A 400-year presence 92
    From religious tradition to family tradition 94
4.2 Religious traditions, values and norms 96
    Social rules, religious values 96
    Different values and common values 99
4.3 Prohibitions and taboos 100
    Beliefs and constraints 100
    Cursing, is it sacred? 100
    Beliefs and prohibitions 102
    Women and prohibitions 103

Culture and society Maria Chapdelaine **104**

Here and elsewhere Values and norms at the heart of our daily lives **106**

Synthesis **108**

CHAPTER **5** The influence of religious traditions on society **110**

5.1 **Religion's contribution to society** **112**

Religion and healthcare 112

Religion and education 114

Religion and values 115

Religion and economic life 117

Religion and heritage works 118

5.2 **Forms of religious expression in society** **120**

A diverse religious landscape 120

Places of worship of every denomination 120

A decor that is an expression of the divine 121

5.3 **Religious tradition and folklore** **124**

Legends and beliefs 124

Forms of religious expression in folktales 125

Far-reaching religious expressions 127

Superstitions 128

Culture and society The many representations of the world **130**

Here and elsewhere Mythical beings called gargoyles **132**

Synthesis **134**

CHAPTER **6** The diversity of forms of religious expression
in literature and the media **136**

6.1 **The diversity of representation of the divine in the media** **138**

Representations of the divine 138

The phenomenon of religion and the media 142

6.2 **The diversity of mythical and supernatural beings in literature and the media** **144**

Mythical and supernatural beings 144

Gods and mythical heroes 144

Some mythical animals 146

Supernatural beings 147

Angels, devils and spirits in the media 148

6.3 **The fundamental elements of religious traditions in literature and the media** **149**

Stories, rites and rules 149

Stories represented in literature and the media 150

Stories revisited in advertising 150

Culture and society The long-tailed beast **152**

Here and elsewhere **154**

Greco-roman mythology 154

The legend of King Arthur 156

The legend of Robin Hood 157

Synthesis **158**

Dialogue 160

Section 1

Forms of dialogue 162
Tool 1: Conversation 164
Tool 2: Discussion 166
Tool 3: Narration 168
Tool 4: Deliberation 170
Tool 5: Interview 172
Tool 6: Debate 174
Tool 7: Panel 176

Section 2

Means for developing a point of view 178
Tool 8: Description 180
Tool 9: Comparison 182
Tool 10: Synthesis 184
Tool 11: Explanation 186
Tool 12: Justification 188

Section 3

Means for examining a point of view 190
Types of judgments
Tool 13: Judgment of preference 192
Tool 14: Judgment of prescription 194
Tool 15: Judgment of reality 196
Tool 16: Judgment of value 198
Processes that may hinder dialogue created by appealing to others 200
Tool 17: 202

Personal attack	Conspiracy
Appeal to the people	Appeal to stereotype
Appeal to the crowd	Straw man argument
Argument from authority	

Processes that may hinder dialogue created through errors in reasoning 204
Tool 18: 206

Hasty generalizations	False dilemma
Appeal to prejudice	Causal fallacy
Two wrongs don't make a right	Slippery slope
False analogy	

Conditions that foster dialogue 209
Tool 19: 209

Attitudes that foster dialogue

GLOSSARY 211

Presentation of the Student Book

Living in Society is composed of three **COMPONENTS**, which correspond to the three subject-specific competencies of the *Ethics and Religious Culture Program*. These competencies are:

1. **REFLECTS ON ETHICAL QUESTIONS**
2. **DEMONSTRATES AN UNDERSTANDING OF THE PHENOMENON OF RELIGION**
3. **ENGAGES IN DIALOGUE**

The competencies relating to the **ETHICS** and **RELIGIOUS CULTURE** components of this *Student Book* have been presented separately. This is to ensure that **all of the points listed** in the Ethics and Religious Culture program are examined and to make it easier to further explore them in the activity sheets contained in the Teaching Guide and enable students to build on their knowledge. The **DIALOGUE** component of this *Student Book* presents descriptions within a context and provides strategies that facilitate the implementation of **learning and evaluation situations** proposed throughout the year.

INTRODUCTION TO EACH COMPONENT

Each component begins with a strong **illustration** accompanied by a **question** that sparks an initial reflection and opens dialogue.

A **PRELUDE** precedes the **ETHICS** and **RELIGIOUS CULTURE** components, thus providing a review of concepts that were introduced at the elementary level.

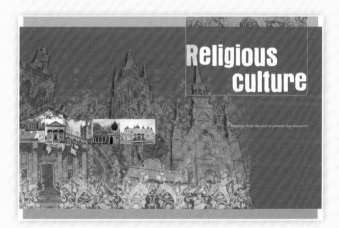

INTRODUCTION TO THE CHAPTERS AND THE SECTIONS OF THE DIALOGUE COMPONENT

Each chapter begins with an **INTRODUCTORY PARAGRAPH** connecting to the student's previous knowledge and experience, and is often presented in the form of a question that stimulates reflection on the concepts to be presented in the chapter.

A **SUMMARY** of the concepts to be presented provides an overview of the chapter.

A **CONNECTIONS** section points out ties to concepts in the other components.

The **DIALOGUE** component, divided into three sections, presents 19 tools relating to the different forms of dialogue, means for developing a point of view and means for examining a point of view.

CHAPTERS

The numbered sections of each chapter always begin with a question to capture the students' attention and guide their reading.

The more difficult expressions and words are written in blue in the text and defined in the margin. These expressions and words are presented once again, in alphabetical order, in the **GLOSSARY** at the end of this book.

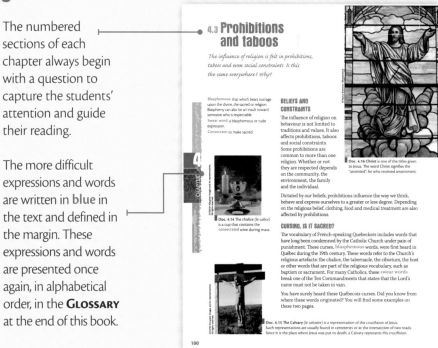

Numerous and varied **visual aids** and legends have been added to help explain the text.

TOOLS

Presented in the form of tools, the prescriptive contents for engaging in dialogue are divided into two-page blocks, facilitating an understanding of each tool and modelling a concrete application of each tool.

SYNTHESIS

At the end of each chapter, the **SYNTHESIS** section provides a review of the highlights of the chapter, as well as questions and exercises designed to promote better understanding of the concepts discussed so that they can be put into practice.

HEADINGS

TO KNOW MORE + is a sidebar that allows for deeper development of a subject or exploration of new aspects of concepts connected to ethics and religious culture.

SOME HISTORY provides historic facts related to the concepts being discussed. Topics vary from people who made a contribution, with a description of their actions and involvement, to the evolution of societal norms and values or rules that prevailed in social classes at other times in history.

The **CULTURE AND SOCIETY** section, which always appears after the discussion of the concepts, enables students to put the ideas into context by supporting them with concrete examples, connected to a society or culture. Many **cultural references** are addressed; these include symbols of commitment and freedom, key elements of different religious traditions or secular representations of the world.

At the end of each chapter is the **HERE AND ELSEWHERE** section, which allows for a look at the rest of the world. This section connects to the elements discussed in the chapter and allows students to explore different ways of living and of viewing society.

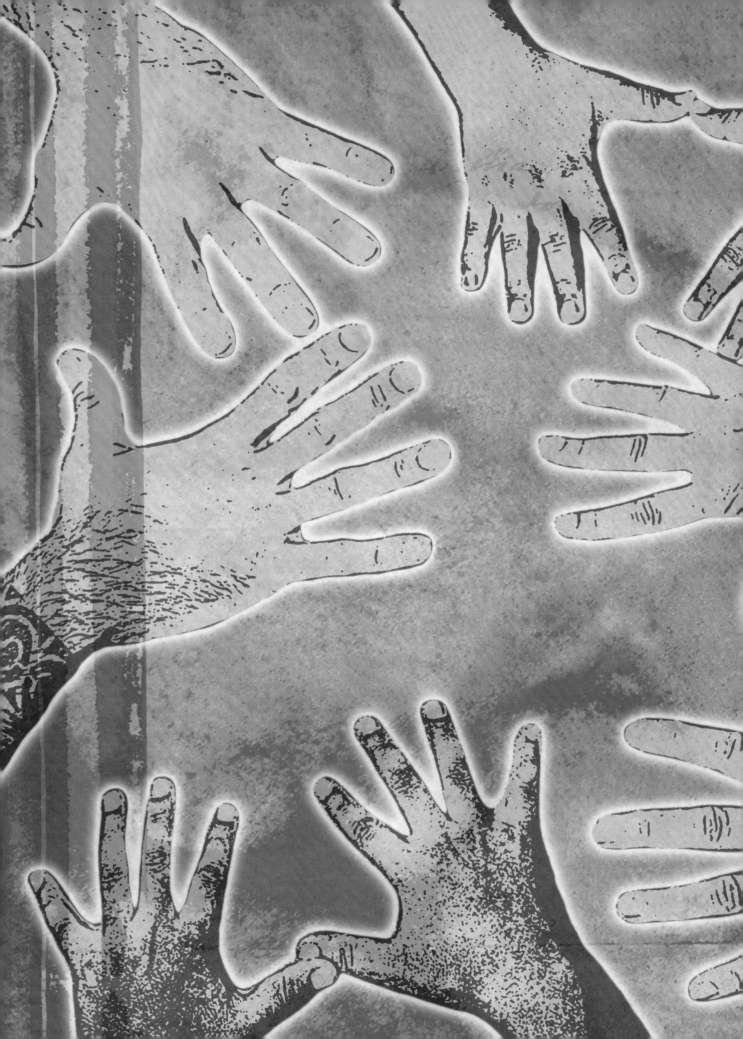

INTRODUCTION

SUMMARY

1. What is ethics?
What is religious culture?
What is dialogue? **2**

2. A constantly changing society **5**

3. Religions of the world **8**

4. Québec in the 20th century **10**

1. What is ethics? What is religious culture? What is dialogue?

This year, we will be talking about ethics, religious culture and dialogue. Do you know anything about these subjects?

ETHICS

Ethics is a critical reflection on the significance of behaviours, values and norms. It also involves questioning yourself on what is best to do, or not do, in a given situation. In some cases, it may be difficult to make the right choice, and that is why you need to reflect, ask yourself questions and analyze the situation.

You have personal values that guide you in your choices, but it is possible that laws or rules go against your values. It is even possible for some values to contradict other values.

Imagine that, according to your personal values, the students at your school would be able to dress as they like. However, the school administration is preparing to impose a rule that would force you to respect a dress code. Your freedom might be restricted by this rule.

Doc. 1
Dress code and freedom?

Doc. 2 Dress code and freedom?

2

When you think about a value that is very important to you, like freedom, for example, you realize that this value is often limited by certain rules both at school and at home. Why do officials want to establish a dress code at school? Which values would be favoured? Does the dress code respect students' freedom of choice?

If we checked with the students at your school to see what they thought of the dress code, we would probably find that they had many different points of view. As you listen to other people's opinions, you might decide to change your own opinion. You might also find that you believe they are right, but that you are also right. Furthermore, by reflecting and asking questions, you will be better prepared to make or not make a decision.

Doc. 3 Dress code and freedom?

RELIGIOUS CULTURE

Religious culture is the knowledge of the important elements of various religions. Religion is a set of beliefs and practices that, in a given culture, implies a representation of the world that includes all realities, both visible and invisible.

Key elements of religions are beliefs, practices, their way of organization, their images of the divine or Supreme Being, rites, celebrations, rules of conduct, places of worship and artistic expressions. All around you, on television and at school, you hear about people with values, beliefs and lifestyles that are different from your own.

Doc. 4 Orthodox Cross.

Doc. 5 The Christian Cross on Mount-Royal.

Doc. 6 Jewish Star of David.
© Odelia Cohen/Shutterstock

Doc. 7 Muslim Crescent Moon.

Doc. 8 Hindu symbol for the sound "OM".
© Oblong1/Shutterstock

Doc. 9 Buddhist Dharma Wheel.
© Thomas Lam/Shutterstock

Doc. 10 Sikh Khanda.
© Ajmone Tristano/ Shutterstock

Doc. 11 Dialogue is an effective interaction with others.

We can learn a lot from this wide religious diversity by being curious, interested and seeking to understand the meaning of all of these expressions of religious culture.

As you talk with other people, you will get to know them and yourself better. You will also discover the values that are associated with different religious cultures. Obviously, this means engaging in dialogue with others!

DIALOGUE

Dialogue is an effective interaction that aims to help people understand others and to be understood. Dialogue should be approached in a spirit of openness, tolerance and respect.

Your class is having a discussion on the new school dress code. During the discussion, the students refer to many values. Some talk about freedom while others talk about respect for others. This discussion allows you to make your ideas known and to criticize points of view that are different from your own. Yet sometimes, dialogues do not produce such good results. For example, if everyone talks at the same time, and no one is listening, then the dialogue cannot move forward.

To prevent this, we can learn to converse better so that we not only present our point of view but respect the points of view of others.

Discussing ethical questions and religious culture gives you the means for learning more about yourself and others. This, in the end, will help foster community life.

Doc. 12 It is hard to have a dialogue if everyone is talking at the same time.

Doc. 13 Understanding and being understood.

2. A constantly changing society

You may be wondering why you are studying a subject called Ethics and Religious Culture. What will you learn from this course? Why?

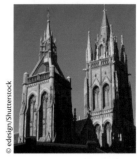

WHY ARE WE TAKING A COURSE ON ETHICS AND RELIGIOUS CULTURE?

It is not always easy to live in a pluralist society—one where people are free to express their political opinions, openly practise their religions, or live their lives according to their own customs and culture. It is even more difficult to live in such a society when we know very little about the people around us and when we sometimes have preconceived ideas about them. The unknown is always a bit scary.

To get along in a democratic and pluralist society, it is important that we develop attitudes of openness, tolerance and respect for others. The Ethics and Religious Culture program provides you with the tools you will need to better understand society and its cultural and religious background. These tools will help you to make decisions that are well thought out and take into account diverse points of view.

WHAT IS THIS COURSE ABOUT?

The Ethics and Religious Culture program is designed to provide you with three competencies: reflect on ethical questions, demonstrate an understanding of the phenomenon of religion, and engage in dialogue. These competencies are meant to be developed at the same time.

By engaging in dialogue, you will deepen your reflections on ethical questions, and you will increase your understanding of the phenomenon of religion.

Doc. 14 In a democratic and pluralist society, it is important to develop attitudes of openness, tolerance and respect for others.

Doc. 15 Schoolgirls in the 1950s.

BAC PA80937

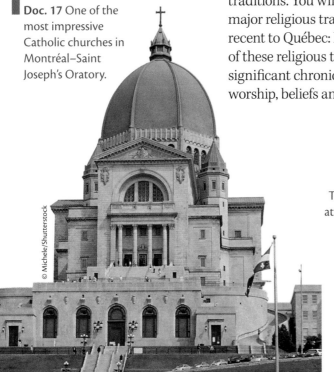

Doc. 16 Students in the new millennium.

© Lorraine Swanson/Shutterstock

Doc. 17 One of the most impressive Catholic churches in Montréal–Saint Joseph's Oratory.

© Michele/Shutterstock

THINKING THINGS THROUGH

Can you describe what values, norms and rules are, and where they come from? In this course, you will examine different values specific to various societies, here and elsewhere, and you will learn how to put them into perspective. You will discover the advantages and disadvantages of having laws, rules and codes of conduct that are required to live in society. You will learn about the requirements associated with the rights and duties of living in a democratic society. You will see that, depending on the place, time period or circumstances, norms and values are not always the same for everyone. In analyzing them, you will gradually be able to exercise personal judgment and say how people are influenced.

You will come to know the ethical issues involved in different situations; you will come up with possible options and see their consequences which will help you make more enlightened choices. Finally, you will become more aware of the impact of your actions on others.

LEARNING ABOUT THE PHENOMENON OF RELIGION

Did you know that the Catholic Church has existed in Québec for more than 400 years? Did you know that Protestants have been around since the early days of the colony, and that Jews have been here for 250 years? It is not surprising that the religious heritage left by our forefathers is considerable.

Forms of religious expression

Forms of religious expression include all of the elements that make up a religion. In this course, you will discover the important aspects of the Christian (Catholic and Protestant), Jewish and Amerindian traditions. You will also explore the elements that characterize the major religious traditions and movements in the world that are more recent to Québec: Buddhism, Hinduism, Islam and Sikhism. For each of these religious traditions, you will discover their origin, key figures, significant chronicles, rites, celebrations, symbols, rules, places of worship, beliefs and major values.

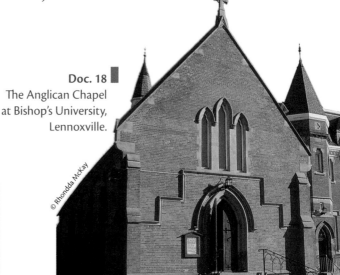

Doc. 18
The Anglican Chapel at Bishop's University, Lennoxville.

© Rhondda McKay

You will be able to analyze various depictions of the world and human beings as seen through the eyes of the major religions. You will understand how and why these images have an influence on people's lives. Finally, you will see that all of these values and concepts of life, which are often quite different from one religious belief to another, are worthy of respect and give meaning to life for those who believe in them.

■ **Doc. 19** The *Creation of Adam*, painted by Michelangelo in the 16th century on the ceiling of the Sistine Chapel in the Vatican.

Looking into the past helps us to better understand the present. Québec society, with its population of varying values and beliefs, faces a challenge with such diversity. As you seek a better and fairer life for yourself and society as a whole, you will someday need to make the most appropriate decisions. The ethical reflection being proposed in this book will be very useful to you in your approach in making appropriate decisions.

ENGAGING IN DIALOGUE

By engaging in dialogue with others, you will get to know them better and will be better able to get along with people who do not necessarily have the same values or culture as you, but who, like you, are interested in growing up in an open and tolerant society. Being in contact with people who have different opinions, values, cultures and religions is an enriching experience for everyone.

In this book, we will suggest tools that use dialogue to develop the ability to think and act responsibly for you and toward others. Engaging in dialogue is not always simple, so we have prepared a tool kit full of tips that will help you along the way. You will learn how to better state your own ideas and how to listen to others in a spirit of respect and openness that promotes community living.

Introduction

7

3. Religions of the world

Christianity

Judaism

Native Spirituality

Buddhism

Islam

Hinduism

Sikhism

Québec society has become more and more diversified in terms of culture and religion. However, what is happening here is far from unique. To a certain extent, the world's religious mosaic is reflected in our society: we meet people who feel passionate about values and convictions that are very different from our own.

If we were to take a snapshot of our planet, we would see that there are large pockets of religious beliefs. In Asia, the most populous area in the world, the religions with the most followers or members are Hinduism, Buddhism and Islam. There are close to 1 billion Hindus in the world, 750 million of whom live in India. There are approximately 350 million Buddhists in the world; they are spread out through the Asian continent. Of the 1.4 billion Muslims in the world, more than 600 million live in Indonesia, Pakistan, India and Bangladesh. Since the 1960s, many Hindus, Muslims, and Buddhists have moved to places like Europe and North America.

Let's head west to the Middle East and North Africa. The Middle East is the seat of three major religions: Judaism, which originated there more than 4000 years ago; Christianity, which originated there more than 2000 years ago; and Islam, which originated there in the 7th century. More than a third of the 14 million or so Jews in the world live in Israel. The number of Christians in this part of the world has been steadily dropping. There are Muslims in all Middle Eastern countries and in more than half of the countries in Africa; furthermore, the Muslim faith itself is present on all five continents. Each year, millions of Muslims make the pilgrimage to Mecca, their holy city. Nowadays, Québec welcomes more and more Muslims and there is a large Muslim community in Montréal.

Now let's head further north to Europe where Christians–Roman Catholics, Protestants, Orthodox and Jews have been living for centuries. With the expansion of large, colonial European empires, Christian religions spread from Europe to Africa, and of course, to North America.

This is how Québec society came to be developed by builders who brought their religious convictions with them into the New World.

Among the Christian denominations, Catholicism, which was practised by most of the European settlers who came to Québec, now has close to one billion members throughout the world. Rome, Italy, is the site of the Vatican, home of the Pope, who is head of the Catholic Church. However, did you know that close to half of all Catholics live in North and South America?

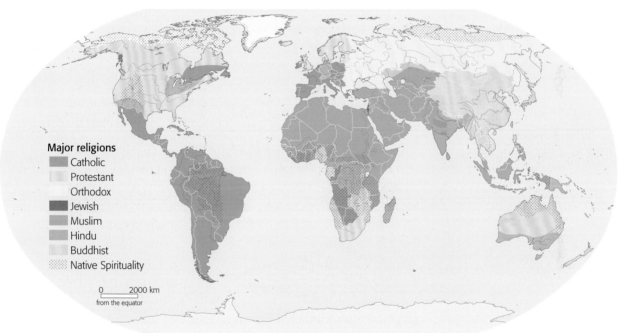

Major religions
- Catholic
- Protestant
- Orthodox
- Jewish
- Muslim
- Hindu
- Buddhist
- Native Spirituality

0 ──── 2000 km
from the equator

Doc. 20 Distribution of the major religions of the world.

We haven't quite finished our tour of the world. Look at the map above and take a close look at the continents of Australia, Africa, the Americas and the Arctic. Since ancient times, Aboriginals have had common religious beliefs. In Québec, for example, well before the arrival of the Europeans, there were Amerindians living here who were practising their own form of worship. Though they are fewer today, their religious traditions are still very much alive.

4. Québec in the 20th century

Let's travel back in time in Québec, to the beginning of the 20th century. This was long before you were born; in fact, your grandparents weren't even born yet. What do we see? We find a population that lives primarily in the country but is gradually moving toward the cities. It is a rural society that is centered around a community church. The church, most often of the Catholic denomination, oversees the daily lives of its members and watches over children's education. In the cities as well, churches rule life in their neighbourhoods. We can find similar communities in more Anglophone areas of Québec, but the religions tend to be Protestant or Jewish.

Doc. 21 Place des Nations, visited by more than 50 million people, was host to major ceremonies during Expo 67. The Expo 67 logo depicts friendship between peoples; it is in the shape of a circle to represent the world.

QUÉBEC IN TRANSITION

In the 1960s, while the Beatles were writing their first songs, Québec was changing with the times. Quebeckers gave up a more traditional lifestyle during the Quiet Revolution. Québec's population wanted more freedom to get out from under the wings of Christian churches in favour of a more secular lifestyle. Schools and hospitals, which had formerly been the responsibility of the churches, were now the responsibility of the Québec government.

An event symbolizes this change: Man and his World, the theme of Expo 67, was held in Montréal. Your parents or grandparents may have attended it. For the first time in its history, Québec opened its arms and welcomed millions of people from the four corners of the globe.

This openness to other ways of life continued as immigrants arrived regularly from all parts of the world. These newcomers brought with them the rich diversity of their cultures and beliefs.

THE NEW FACE OF QUÉBEC

Between the beginning and the end of the 20th century, there were many changes in the religious affiliation of Québec's population. The graphics and tables below illustrate these shifts.

DISTRIBUTION OF RELIGIOUS AFFILIATION–QUÉBEC 1901

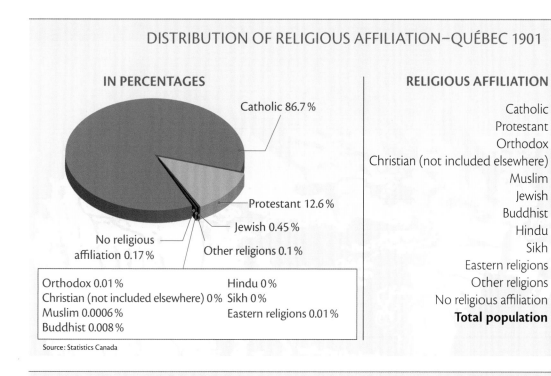

IN PERCENTAGES

Catholic 86.7 %
Protestant 12.6 %
Jewish 0.45 %
No religious affiliation 0.17 %
Other religions 0.1 %

Orthodox 0.01 %	Hindu 0 %
Christian (not included elsewhere) 0 %	Sikh 0 %
Muslim 0.0006 %	Eastern religions 0.01 %
Buddhist 0.008 %	

Source: Statistics Canada

RELIGIOUS AFFILIATION	POPULATION
Catholic	1 429 260
Protestant	207 122
Orthodox	215
Christian (not included elsewhere)	0
Muslim	10
Jewish	7498
Buddhist	141
Hindu	0
Sikh	0
Eastern religions	204
Other religions	1668
No religious affiliation	2780
Total population	**1 648 888**

DISTRIBUTION OF RELIGIOUS AFFILIATION–QUÉBEC 2001

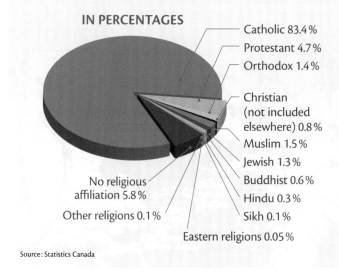

IN PERCENTAGES

Catholic 83.4 %
Protestant 4.7 %
Orthodox 1.4 %
Christian (not included elsewhere) 0.8 %
Muslim 1.5 %
Jewish 1.3 %
Buddhist 0.6 %
Hindu 0.3 %
Sikh 0.1 %
Eastern religions 0.05 %
No religious affiliation 5.8 %
Other religions 0.1 %

Source: Statistics Canada

RELIGIOUS AFFILIATION	POPULATION
Catholic	5 939 715
Protestant	335 590
Orthodox	100 375
Christian (not included elsewhere)	56 750
Muslim	108 620
Jewish	89 915
Buddhist	41 380
Hindu	24 525
Sikh	8225
Eastern religions	3425
Other religions	3870
No religious affiliation	413 190
Total population	**7 125 580**

At the beginning of the 20th century, Québec's population was nearly all Catholic or Protestant. One hundred years later, the population is still largely Catholic, but there is a wider diversity of religions being practised. Close to 5.8% of the population has no religious affiliation at all, and this group is the second largest. This means that we have a richer and more diverse set of values and beliefs that you will get to know better through *LIVING in society.*

Ethics

Reflecting to make better choices or making choices for better living?

ELEMENTARY CYCLE 1

THE NEEDS OF HUMANS AND OTHER LIVING BEINGS	• Myself as a unique living being (Chapter 1) • Shared and distinctive needs (Chapters 1, 3) • The diversity of interdependent relationships (Chapters 1, 3)
DEMANDS ASSOCIATED WITH THE INTERDEPENDENCE OF HUMANS AND OTHER LIVING BEINGS	• Responsibilities at home and at school (Chapter 2) • Appropriate and inappropriate actions (Chapter 2) • Values and norms that guide behaviour at home and at school (Chapter 2)

ELEMENTARY CYCLE 2

INTERPERSONAL RELATIONSHIPS IN GROUPS	• The development of personal identity and the groups to which people belong (Chapter 1) • The diversity of relationships between group members (Chapter 3)
DEMANDS OF BELONGING TO A GROUP	• Values and norms that guide group life (Chapter 2) • Roles and responsibilities of group members (Chapter 2) • Behaviours and attitudes that contribute or detract from group life (Chapter 3) • Conditions that foster or detract from the well-being of each member (Chapter 3)

ELEMENTARY CYCLE 3

DEMANDS OF LIFE IN SOCIETY	• Values, norms and responsibilities that guide life in society (Chapter 2) • The distinction between what is acceptable and unacceptable in society (Chapter 3)
INDIVIDUALS AS MEMBERS OF SOCIETY	• Young people as members of society (Chapter 1) • Differences as sources of enrichment and conflict in life in society (Chapter 1)

PRELUDE

- growth
- preferences
- interests
- physical, emotional and intellectual needs of human beings

- actions that satisfy needs
- the human being, an interdependent being
- interdependent relationships

- responsibilities
- roles
- rules of conduct
- values like cooperation, helping each other, sharing
- sources of values and norms: family, school, society, religion

- my preferences, my abilities, my qualities, my areas of interest
- my individual traits and traits that I have in common with others
- my needs
- harmonious, conflicting, controlling and power-based relationships

- rules of conduct or what is prohibited in different groups, the reason for these rules and the possible questioning of these rules
- values underlying group life
- roles and responsibilities in various groups
- behaviours, attitudes and actions that benefit or harm group life
- managing tension and conflicts

- rights and responsibilities
- references for taking action
- actions and attitudes that benefit or harm life in society
- appropriate and inappropriate behaviours toward others

- unchanged aspects of one's personality
- needs related to adolescence
- how adolescents fit into society
- the human being creates his/her own identity through contact with others

Ethical reflection

Summary

1.1 Individuals and their circle of family and friends	18
1.2 Autonomy, a source of questions	22
1.3 Freedom	27
Culture and society	32
Here and elsewhere	34
Synthesis	38

CHAPTER 1

The influence of family and friends

How do our family and friends influence our reactions and our decisions? How do we go about making choices? Are we free to act according to our own values? How much importance do we place on the expectations and demands of family and friends?

CONNECTIONS

■ RELIGIOUS CULTURE

- Moral codes such as catechisms or books of etiquette
- Rules with respect to behaviour in family situations and romantic relationships and practices related to food and clothing
- The influence of religious institutions on society and culture

■ DIALOGUE

- Forms of dialogue: conversation
- Means for developing a point of view: description
- Means for examining a point of view: processes that may hinder dialogue based on appeal to the crowd

1.1 Individuals and their circle of family and friends

Have you ever thought about where the values and norms you live by come from? What needs and what constraints help you to be yourself? Do your family and friends have an influence on who you are? Can human relationships be a source of tension?

Doc. 1.1 Individuals define themselves by their physical appearance, their relationships with others and their inner world.

Identity: all aspects of a person or group that give that person or group individuality, uniqueness.

Value: the importance attributed to things, to behaviours or to attitudes that are more or less highly regarded or desired by people or groups of people who use them to make judgments to base their conduct.

Norm: rules, laws or moral requirements that serve as criteria to define behaviour.

Need: a natural or social requirement that results in human beings performing actions that are necessary to them.

Constraint: that which obliges us to, or prevents us from, doing something.

Value system: a consistent and prioritized set of values.

Moral rule: a moral norm that indicates how a moral principle or value must be applied in a given situation.

THE HUMAN BEING, A COMPLEX INDIVIDUAL

Every human being is unique. A person's **identity** can be defined by three things: their physical appearance, their relationships with others and their inner world. Thoughts, feelings, **values**, **norms**, **needs** as well as **constraints** are all part of this world. These are some of the elements we will be looking at more closely.

Values and norms

Each person adopts values according to various reference indicators, namely education, family, and life experiences. When values are shared and prioritized by a group of people, they make up what we call a **value system**, in other words, family values, social values and other values.

Norms are **moral rules** and laws that control our behaviour within a group or a society. For example, software pirating laws are an application of the moral rule according to which we do not steal from our neighbour. Norms may have been established by the government, society or even by the different groups that make up our circle of family and friends.

Needs and constraints

Fulfilling our basic needs creates desire. To live, human beings need to eat, sleep, clothe themselves and be in contact with others. Fulfilling other types of needs helps us to develop our personal plans; wanting to attend a show, undertake some activity or play a sport are examples.

Needs vary little from one person to another; it is the way of fulfilling these needs that differ. For example, eating is a universal need, but what we eat differs from one person to another.

Sometimes constraints keep us from fulfilling our needs. Some of these obstacles include time constraints, money and space issues as well as age. For example, everyone needs to eat a healthy diet, but due to a lack of money or education, some people can't seem to adequately fulfill this need.

Needs and constraints, like values and norms, influence attitudes, behaviours and ways of perception. As such, they help to create a person's identity.

Doc. 1.2 Sometimes a lack of money prevents us from fulfilling our needs.
© Natalia Siverina/Shutterstock

INDIVIDUALS AND THEIR CIRCLE OF FAMILY AND FRIENDS

We've seen that each of us has our own identity. Since individuals have relationships with their family and friends, a dynamic is created: each person influences the other. The values, norms, needs and constraints that define a person are influenced by the environment around them.

Family

An identity, which is what characterizes a person and convinces them of who they are and makes them unique, is acquired over time through life experience. Family is a major influence in building a person's identity. It is family that provides that person with their initial set of values and norms, some of which are accepted and some of which are rejected. For example, your parents may encourage you to be honest and respectful of others because these are important values for them. If you also consider them important, you will adopt them as well.

As such, the family establishes norms according to the values it upholds. In some families, working together is an essential value that can show itself as a norm: the members of a family must help each other when there is a need. For example, children help their parents to prepare meals.

Finally, family can also influence the way needs are fulfilled. As such, some parents encourage their children to eat certain foods or to dress in a particular way. The family dynamic is such that we experience fulfillment as well as disappointment as we go about fulfilling our needs. That said, because needs are generally the same for everyone, conflicts related to needs do occur in exceptional and rather rare circumstances. For example, if a parent has a sudden urge to eat when the child needs to sleep, the two needs can't be fulfilled at the same time. Since there is no food in the house, the adult would have to go out to get some food, and because the child can't be left alone, the parent and the child have a conflict of needs.

© Cathleen Clapper/Shutterstock

Doc. 1.3 Family life has an influence on an individual.

© Monika Wisniewska/Shutterstock

Doc. 1.4 Family influences the ways in which needs are met.

The influence of family and friends

19

Doc. 1.5 Families are constantly changing.

Doc. 1.6 Friends have an influence on a person's values and needs.

Finally, the family manages behaviour by setting limits. These limits provide a framework for behaviour. For example, your parents may tell you to be home at a certain time or not to spend the entire evening in front of your computer. Are there times when you don't agree with the constraints they impose on you? This is quite possible because constraints can also be a source of tension in a family.

At the age you are now, your parents don't treat you the same way they did when you were a child. The influence your family has on you changes throughout your life.

Despite the importance you give it, family is not the only group that influences the values, norms, needs and constraints that make you who you are. Your social environment is also a major contributor in your development.

Social environment

As a teenager, groups of friends, neighbours, sports teams and school make up a large part of a social environment. This environment has some bearing on our identity at this stage of life.

Like family, your social environment passes on values to you. Also, your neighbours may influence you to be more open-minded and helpful with others.

The social environment also provides norms. At school, you have to abide by norms, a code of conduct. The same principle applies to team sports. There are regulations to follow.

Our social environment also influences the tastes and choices that we make in how we fulfill our needs. In a group of friends, everyone in the group may listen to the same type of music or wear a similar style of clothing.

Finally, a social environment may also pressure us to yield to certain constraints. At school, for example, if there are not enough lockers, you may have to share yours with someone else.

Doc. 1.7 A person's social environment imposes rules that must be respected.

Doc. 1.8 The relationship that individuals have with their social environment can be a source of tension.

Our contact with our social environment may cause tension because not everyone holds the same values and norms. In addition, how well personal needs are met may be limited by the constraints of family and friends. Like family, your social environment is always changing. As a result, your relationships with your family and friends change as you change.

TO KNOW MORE +

Wearing a school uniform

Many schools require their students to wear uniforms. This requirement is not always welcomed by all including the students themselves, their parents or their teachers. There are several reasons for this. The following example is related to freedom that illustrates two positions:

For: The uniform forbids students from wearing clothing that is too tight, but doesn't forbid them from expressing their individuality by using different accessories and hairstyles. As such, it doesn't stifle their freedom of expression.

Against: All students have to wear the uniform, even those who dress appropriately. As such, it impinges on their freedom of action.

Some schools have taken the concept of a uniform and adapted it so that not everyone has to wear the exact same clothing. The students have to wear a white shirt or sweater and navy blue or black pants. This compromise imposes fewer constraints. What do you think?

The influence of family and friends

1.2 Autonomy, a source of questions

*What are the questions that really concern a human being? Is it important to succeed on a social level? To work at becoming independent? To have a healthy level of self-esteem? What about pressures from family and friends? And what about love and relationships? What do **autonomy** and dependency have to do with these questions?*

Doc. 1.9 Our autonomy affects the autonomy of others.

Autonomy: the possibility of making decisions without going to an authority, to decide independently which rules to follow.

Common good: the material and spiritual conditions which provide a group's well-being and which help in the development of individuals making up the group.

WHAT IS AUTONOMY?

Being autonomous means being able to make responsible choices and being able to face the consequences of these decisions. Autonomy can only be exercised if certain conditions are met: being able to pass critical judgment, making good sense, being sincere and taking moral responsibility.

Autonomy is the capacity to cope in different situations. Autonomous people rely on good judgment and make informed decisions. They thus exercise their critical judgment and good sense. They are sincere in making decisions, and base their decisions on the values and norms that are relevant to the situation. They must accept responsibility for their decisions which means assuming responsibility for the consequences that these decisions may entail.

Are there limits to autonomy?

Individuals exercise their autonomy within a society where they are in contact with other people. We've already seen that our values, the norms we hold, our needs and the constraints we are placed under, can all have an effect on others. The same applies to autonomy.

Exercising one's autonomy may be a source of conflict. One person may be autonomous and decide to act according to his or her needs, but this may not always be compatible with the **common good**.

Let's imagine the following situation to understand properly what's at stake here: Benjamin and Saïd are sitting on a park bench. Benjamin is drinking juice from a glass bottle that he throws on the ground when he's finished. Saïd tells him not to leave the bottle on the ground because the glass might break and hurt someone.

Doc. 1.10 Autonomy can only be exercised if certain conditions are met.
© Yuri Arcurs/Shutterstock

© Andrey Shadrin/Shutterstock

Benjamin replies to him, "We each do what we want. Since I'm the one who paid for the bottle, I can do what I want with it. What's more, there are people who are paid to pick up trash." And Saïd replies, "Can you imagine what would happen if everybody thought the way you do?"

FOOD FOR THOUGHT

All through life, we ask ourselves questions about ourselves and about others. Some of these questions have a lot to do with autonomy: social success, dependency on others, self-esteem, pressure from family and friends, love and relationships. Now, let's look at these questions. The goal is not so much to provide answers but rather to think about the conditions and the tension associated with them. In everyday life, these questions can be answered by looking at our own values and life experiences. Everyone reacts differently to this type of reflection according to individual identity and life experiences. For example, a person can be autonomous at one point in life but dependent on others at some other time; in the same way someone can be autonomous in certain situations and dependent in others.

Social success

Human beings constantly worry about **social success**. Most people want to be accepted and acknowledged by their **peers**. This issue is related to autonomy and dependency. To succeed socially one must be autonomous, but we also need others. Therefore, there is a tension between autonomy and dependency.

Social success: a person's success in their relationships with others.

Peer: a person in the same social situation; having the same standing.

Let's look at a concrete example. Justin considers himself to be an autonomous person because his choices are based on critical judgment and good sense. He also strives to be sincere and accepts responsibility for his choices. On the other hand, for Justin it's important to be socially successful. He needs to be around his family and friends and, to some extent, depends on them to be happy.

Doc. 1.12 Social success is part of a human being's concerns.

The influence of family and friends

Doc. 1.13 When we're teenagers, we sometimes depend on our friends.

© Yuri Arcurs/Shutterstock

Doc. 1.14 Sometimes a lack of self-esteem leads to dependency.
© Jose AS Reyes/Shutterstock

Dependency on others

Have you noticed that the people around you are not always completely autonomous? Some of them are very self-sufficient because they have the skills to behave that way. Then again, there are people who always depend on others. They're unable to decide for themselves or to make a choice without first asking someone else's opinion. In itself, dependency is not necessarily negative. During our teenage years, we continue to depend on our parents to some extent and sometimes also on our friends. Being dependent poses a problem when a person depends completely on others. This type of attitude can become a contributing factor to a lack of self-esteem.

Self-esteem, a fragile concept

Self-esteem can be defined as the perception a person has of themselves. Someone with a healthy level of self-esteem has confidence in their abilities. But someone with low self-esteem may feel inferior or awkward. Such people think poorly of themselves and may begin to doubt their abilities and their skills. Let's take Maria's case: she is very talented but she doesn't have any confidence in her skills. She is terrified to have to speak alone in front of a class. Yet, when she makes an oral presentation as part of a team, she is not as shy because she feels the support of her friends. Thus, her lack of self-esteem causes her to depend entirely on others to feel at ease.

TO KNOW MORE +

Tarnished victories

Some athletes have had their medals taken from them after failing a drug test. Such is the case for Geneviève Jeanson who used performance-enhancing drugs to boost her endurance. In 2007, she admitted having used such drugs from the age of 16. According to Geneviève, it was her trainer who encouraged her to take the substance. Can the desire to be the best justify cheating? Can cheating be acceptable in certain circumstances?

Doc 1.15 Cyclist Geneviève Jeanson

Pressure from family and friends

It can happen that the people around us exert pressure on us. Sometimes, it can come from an authority figure: a parent, teacher or coach. Some parents push their children to perform well in school. Pressure can also come from peers. Perhaps a friend is pressuring you to copy a music album for them even though it is illegal. There are various ways of reacting to this type of pressure. Some people aren't affected but others are very susceptible. They do what others expect of them because they believe this will satisfy or please them. They can't live without the approval of the people around them. In other words, they are dependent.

Does love conquer all?

The search for love can also lead to autonomy or to dependency on others. The following is Naomi's story: she meets Joel and falls in love, but after a few weeks of dating, she realizes that their values are incompatible. Naomi respects others while Joel pokes fun at everybody. For her, helping others is important while he thinks only of himself. The difference in their values spurs Naomi to end her relationship with Joel. In your opinion, is Naomi being autonomous or dependent? Why?

Thinking about whether we are self-sufficient or dependent in our attitudes, our behaviour and our way of thinking brings us back to the question of freedom. Therefore, it is important to ask ourselves whether or not we are able to exercise this freedom.

Doc 1.16 Love is also related to autonomy and dependency.

The influence of family and friends

Some history

CYRANO DE BERGERAC

Do you know about the play *Cyrano de Bergerac*? Cyrano was a poet and fencer who, because of his big nose, had low self-esteem where love was concerned. One day, he fell in love with the beautiful Roxane but didn't dare tell her for fear of rejection. Since he was talented with words, Cyrano wrote love letters to Roxane pretending they came from his friend Christian. Roxane was charmed by the letters that she believed were written by Christian and fell in love with him. Christian was killed during the war, but Cyrano decided not to tell Roxane that he was, in fact, the author of the letters. His deception wasn't discovered until 15 years later, when the dying Cyrano admitted his love to Roxane. That is when Roxane realized that throughout the years it was Cyrano's soul that she loved and not Christian's beauty. Cyrano died in her arms, happy to have shared his love, if only for a moment.

Doc. 1.17 A dying Cyrano reveals his love to Roxane.
© Robbie Jack/Corbis

The play *Cyrano de Bergerac* was written in 1897 by Edmond Rostand (1868-1918), a French poet and author. Cyrano is not only a character in a play, but also a real French poet who was born in Paris (1619-1655). Rostand used the life and works of this author as the inspiration for his play.

We have seen that the attitudes of human beings, their behaviour and their way of perceiving things are all influenced by their values, the norms of their environment, their needs and the constraints they are under. In this context, what freedom do we have to think and to act? What does freedom mean to you? What kind of freedom do you have at your age? What are the limitations? What questions does freedom raise?

WHAT IS FREEDOM?

Freedom exists when people have the power to think, to act or to choose for themselves. It is freedom that places the responsibility for decision-making on the individual who makes the decision, rather than on their family or friends. When we act freely, we can accept or reject values or norms by relying on our judgment. However, since our freedom can affect others, it is important to think about its implications.

There are limits to freedom

"The freedom of one individual begins when the freedom of another individual ends." This proverb means that freedom has its limits. If we were all free to do as we please all the time, it would not take long before no one would be free. This is why our behaviour is bound by moral rules and laws. These contribute to the respect for the rights of individuals and the maintenance of social order. Individuals are thus free to act and decide for themselves but only within the confines of certain legal limits. This topic will be covered in more detail in the next chapter.

A person's freedom is also limited by the norms and constraints imposed by that person's family and friends. For example, some parents require that their children do their homework before playing video games. Sometimes, teenagers themselves impose limitations on themselves. Such limitations can take many forms: promises, pacts, commitments and other forms. To better understand how freedom can or cannot continue to exist within such a framework, let's look at Kevin's case. Kevin is on a hockey team. He and his teammates have made a pact not to use violence while practicing their sport. During a match, Kevin gets angry and insults an opponent. The team captain, who witnessed the altercation, asks the coach to bench Kevin for the rest of the match. The violence, in this example, is verbal violence. Kevin did not honour the commitment he made to his team. His teammates therefore expect him to get a penalty. Do you feel that someone who doesn't honour his commitments should have the same freedom as someone who does? Why or why not?

Doc. 1.18 An individual's freedom must take into account the freedom of others.
© Mandy Godbehear/Shutterstock

© Junial Enterprises/Shutterstock

Doc. 1.19 Limitations on freedom can cause tension.

The influence of family and friends

Doc. 1.20 Individuals exercise their freedom according to their values and their view of the world.

World view: the way that individuals perceive themselves and those around them and that which guides their attitudes and actions.

ISSUES RELATED TO FREEDOM

We now know that freedom is limited by a structure that governs behaviour. Within that structure, people are free to act as they see fit. They can make choices according to their values and their **world view**. As such, exercising freedom differs from one person to the next and from one situation to another. The following are some of the issues related to exercising our freedom.

Privacy

Most people want to keep certain thoughts and facets of their life to themselves. They want to maintain their privacy. There is a fine line between what is private and what is not. The freedom of some may infringe upon the privacy of others.

Eva's situation is a good example of this problem. Eva considers her bedroom as her private world. She's decorated it the way she likes it, hung pictures she cherishes, and she shares secrets with her friends in it. Her room is her domain and she forbids her brother from entering it because he goes through her things. For this reason, she asked her parents to have a lock installed on her door. In other words, she's asking for more privacy. Her parents don't accept this because it limits their access to their daughter's room. In fact, it limits their access in their own home. Do you think her parents are justified in limiting their children's privacy?

Doc. 1.21
Eva considers her bedroom as her private world.

Confidentiality

Confidentiality is also related to the boundary between the freedom of some and that of others. Keeping information confidential means keeping it secret and not divulging it. Everyone has a specific idea of what must remain confidential. For example, some people display their personal information on their website: their first and last names, age, telephone number and more. Others consider such information confidential, so they don't display it publicly.

Confidentiality forces us to ask various questions about freedom: Do I have the right to keep certain information confidential? Can others have access to it by invoking their right to freedom of information? Let's take a concrete example to illustrate this issue. Nathan is a teenager who has questions about his body. He'd like to have answers, but he doesn't want to ask his parents or any of his friends. He intends to discuss this with his doctor next time he sees him, but he's worried that the doctor will tell his parents. He'd like his concerns to remain confidential.

Doc. 1.22 Confidentiality sets limits on freedom.

TO KNOW MORE +

Confidentiality and young people

From the age of 14, teenagers have the right to confidentiality when they consult a healthcare professional whether it's a doctor or a psychologist. In fact, according to the law, at 14 years of age, an individual has the maturity and intellectual capacity to make informed decisions. Doctors and psychologists must respect the confidentiality of the information shared with them by their patients. This is part of the rules of their **code of ethics**. However, there is a limit to confidentiality. When the health of a teenager is at risk, the health professional must advise the parents. They must also contact the parents if the teenager remains in a health or social services establishment for more than 12 hours.

Doc. 1.23
Doctors must often face issues of confidentiality.

Code of ethics: the rules and duties imposed on the members of a profession.

Doc. 1.24 Voyeurism is the result of a more or less unhealthy curiosity.

Voyeurism

Voyeurism consists of looking at or listening to something that we shouldn't be looking at or listening to. It stems from a more or less unhealthy curiosity.

There's a difference between voyeurism and simple curiosity. For example, a curious person might, in going by a house where a party is underway glance inside without stopping. This gesture stems from curiosity. On the other hand, an individual who stops to observe people who are enjoying an intimate moment without their knowledge would be considered a voyeur.

Certain acts of voyeurism infringe upon the right to privacy and to intimacy. Taking a picture of someone or filming them without their consent are examples of voyeurism. Voyeurs may say that they are free to photograph what they want. But what about the person being photographed? Doesn't that person have the right to a private life?

TO KNOW MORE +

Criminal voyeurism

The Canadian justice system considers certain acts of voyeurism as criminal acts. Sexual voyeurism is one example. People who look at, photograph or film other people for sexual purposes without their consent are liable to imprisonment.

Doc. 1.25
Taking pictures without prior consent can infringe on the freedom of others.
© Ronen/Shutterstock

Some history

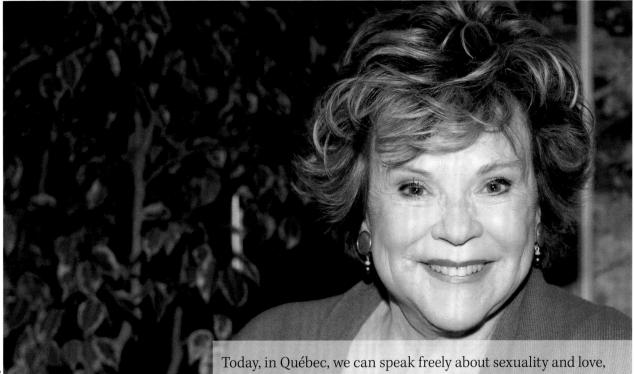

Doc. 1.26 Janette Bertrand helped free Quebeckers from certain taboos.

Today, in Québec, we can speak freely about sexuality and love, among other topics. This was not always the case. Your grandmothers and grandfathers probably didn't talk about certain subjects because they were taboo, that is, it wasn't acceptable to discuss them. A woman named Janette Bertrand, a public figure, played an important role in ridding the province of some of these taboos. Janette Bertrand was born in 1925. Through her work as an author and journalist, she contributed greatly to modernizing Québec society. During the 1950s, she worked on a weekly paper, *Le Petit Journal*, and answered questions from the general public in a column called *"Courrier du Coeur."* People wrote in to ask advice on topics that were not often discussed in those days, for example: love, personal relationships, sexuality, homosexuality and infidelity.

In 1970, after a stint as a radio moderator, she became very popular on television. During the 1980s and 1990s, she pursued her educational role by covering new and very delicate topics that affected individuals, their families and their friends; topics like HIV-AIDS, suicide, violence and compulsive gambling. In addition to her role of moderator on many shows, she wrote several plays and films for television.

In 1990, Janette Bertrand was chosen "Woman of the Century" at the *Salon de la Femme*, and in 2000, she received the Governor General's Performing Arts Award for her exceptional contribution to the cultural life of Canadians.

Culture and society
Autonomy and freedom in recent centuries

Teenagers' identity and the limitations on their autonomy have changed a great deal over the course of history. Your view of the world is very different from what it was for teenagers in the past. Let's take a look at what life was like for young people your age in Québec in the 19th and the middle of the 20th centuries. When you compare your life to that of these young people, what strikes you most?

Doc. 1.27 Two brothers photographed in 1863.

© McCord Museum I-7007-1

THE 19th CENTURY

During the 19th century, the roles and responsibilities of young people were very different from those of today. Young men and young women lived in completely separate worlds. In wealthier circles, boys attended schools (collèges) run by religious communities. When they turned 12, they were sent away by their families and boarded at the schools; in other words, they were housed and fed there. At the schools, discipline was very strict and individual freedoms were almost non-existent. Often, the effects of this discipline created very strong bonds among the young boys and sometimes it caused them to rebel against authority. On the other hand, in poorer communities, adolescent boys led a very different life. For example, the boys had to work on a farm or in a factory.

Young girls of that time lived an entirely different life. Adolescence was a period of transition that prepared them for marriage. Their world centered on domestic life. Their education was mainly provided at home by their mother. So very early on, they learned to assume the responsibilities of a homemaker: cooking, cleaning and taking care of children. The family and the social environment of these girls encouraged them to be submissive, modest and polite.

© McCord Museum I-3235.1 (detail)

Doc. 1.28 In this photograph from 1862, these two sisters are dressed quite differently. The older sister is wearing a rather modest dress with a buttoned-up collar, long sleeves and a skirt down to the ground. In the 19th century, as soon as a young girl was of marrying age, she had to dress very modestly. On the other hand, her sister's dress is less serious. It has an open collar, short sleeves and a skirt that is several centimetres from the ground. These clues tell us that she is between 12 and 14 years old.

THE 1960s

Following education reform, the 1960s marked a turning point in the lives of young people, and attending school became compulsory until the age of 15. Integrated classes were now the norm which was something new for the time. Boys and girls now attended the same classes, ate in the same cafeteria and had recess in the same schoolyard.

Yet, at the beginning of the decade, the roles of boys and girls had not really changed. Boys were oriented toward a trade or university studies. Most girls followed a general course of study that included classes in the domestic arts where they learned to cook, sew and knit. Nevertheless, some of the girls did manage to attend university.

Early on, adolescents still had two separate views of the world: the girls' view and the boys' view. Their responsibilities and their rights were different. But these differences faded over the course of the decade, especially under the influence of the feminist movement and the social upheaval that marked the late 1960s.

Doc. 1.29 A family portrait from the 1960s.

Doc. 1.30 Music played an important role in young people's lives in those days.

Doc. 1.31 Expo 67 was a world fair that took place in Montréal in 1967. Its theme was Man and His World. People could visit some 100 national or thematic pavilions that focused on technology, art and religion. In six months, some 50 million people visited Expo 67. For Quebeckers, the event opened new horizons on the diversity of life experiences that existed all over the world.

The influence of family and friends

Here and elsewhere
Autonomy and freedom today

In your opinion, are your values, norms, needs and constraints the same as everyone else's? What about the autonomy and freedom of young people in other parts the world?

Collection particulière

Doc. 1.32 Cambodian family at the dinner table. In Asia, it is common for grandparents, parents and children to live together under the same roof.

Every culture has its own values and its own norms; each has its own perception of autonomy and freedom. Everywhere in the world, young people hope for self-realization, but many others are mainly concerned with meeting their basic needs, like finding food and lodging. Let's look at some of the aspects that influence the autonomy and freedom of young people elsewhere in the world.

FAMILY

There are many ways of looking at family and, consequently, at looking at autonomy and freedom within the family. In some cultures, various members of the family live together under one roof, that is, grandparents, parents, children, uncles, aunts and cousins. How do you think such a situation affects the freedom of young people?

In some countries, notably Jordan, young people rarely get to discuss matters that affect them directly with members of their family, for example, career choices or even marriage. Such decisions are often made by other members of the family without even consulting the young person.

On the other hand, children throughout the world live outside the family framework or have very little contact with their family. This is true of street kids who often have no ties whatsoever. Can it be said that homeless kids have more freedom than children who grow up within a very strict family framework?

TO KNOW MORE +

Street kids

The Canadian International Development Agency estimates the number of homeless children in the world at 100 million. Approximately 60% of them work on the street but have a roof over their heads or a place to sleep while the other 40% are homeless. To survive, they sell small items, perform manual labour or prostitute themselves. Nearly 90% of these young people have alcohol or drug problems. There are many reasons why young people end up on the street, notably due to wars, natural disasters, drug addiction and abuse.

BY002174| Standard RM| © Barry Lewis/Corbis

Doc. 1.33 Homeless teens taking refuge next to Bucharest's main train station in Romania. Every day, some 60 young people use the station as a place to sleep.

Doc. 1.34 In 2007, following a major flood, the Tumha village school in India was forced to close. Rupesh Kumar and his brother had to wait for the village to be cleared before going back to school. In many regions of the world, natural disasters jeopardize children's access to education.

Doc. 1.35 Many organizations struggle to promote access to education for the young. This photo shows a classroom at the school in Rabour, a village in Kenya, which welcomes orphans whose parents have died of HIV-AIDS.

EDUCATION

In many countries, education is not accessible to everyone. In many cases, parents don't have the money to pay education-related costs (school fees, supplies, transportation, etc.). Often, the older children in the household have to stay home to work so that the younger children can attend school. As well, in some countries, girls are not considered as needing an education. Do you think that children who can attend school have more freedom than those who can't? Are they more self-sufficient?

Doc. 1.36 The Taliban, who held power in different regions of Afghanistan, imposed many human rights abuses. Among other things, they forbade girls from attending school and female teachers from practicing their profession. Nowadays, the Taliban are no longer in power, but Afghanistan is still being repressed by this extremist group. This photograph, taken in 2006, shows a class of young girls in Kabul. On many occasions, schools for Afghan girls have been the targets of attacks and arson.

TO KNOW MORE +

- According to UNICEF, 110 million of the world's children do not attend school; two thirds of them are girls.

- In 2001, in Gambia, only 19% of girls attended school. UNICEF introduced a program, known as the Mothers' Club, to motivate mothers to promote school access and attendance, as well as praise their daughters for their achievements. This initiative proved to be very successful. In 2003, the rate of girls attending school rose to 34% and very few girls were forced to leave school to get married.

Doc. 1.37 Certain types of work do not negatively affect children's development. Here, a teenager is selling olives in a Marrakesh market in Morocco.

© Owen Franken/Corbis

WORK

According to the Canadian International Development Agency, some 130 million children are working throughout the world. Some of them work to meet their own needs while others work to help their families. In general, girls are not paid as much as boys for the work they do because often it's housework. Sometimes, the work that children do does not negatively affect their development, for example, selling products in the market. However, some types of work do negatively affect the health and development of children: weaving wool in a plant, spreading pesticides, mining, prostitution or the armed services. What consequence does child labour have on their autonomy and their freedom? Does working necessarily make them freer? Does it make them more self-sufficient?

Wikipedia

Doc. 1.38 In Bangladesh, many of the children and adolescents work in vermilion plants. This bright red, powdery substance is very toxic. Any contact with the skin should be avoided.

TO KNOW MORE +

Child soldiers

Using children as soldiers in armies probably goes all the way back to antiquity. The Canadian International Development Agency estimates that 300 000 girls and boys under 18 are now taking part in armed conflicts in some 30 different countries. Some children join the army voluntarily to escape poverty or to find a new "family" after losing theirs to war or natural disaster. Others don't have a choice; they are kidnapped by these armies. Child soldiers perform various tasks: they transport ammunition, act as messengers, detect mines or are armed soldiers. They are recruited by the army because, being small, they can get around easily, eat less and can be intimidated more easily than adults.

Doc. 1.39 A 12-year old soldier in the Vietnamese Republican Army poses for an American photographer in 1968. He is armed with a grenade-thrower.
Wikipedia

SPORTS AND LEISURE ACTIVITIES

Did you know that a child's right to rest, play and enjoy leisure activities is included in the United Nations Convention on the Rights of the Child which was adopted by the United Nations General Assembly in 1989? This organization recognizes the importance of sports and leisure activities in the physical development of young people. As well, the UN believes that practising such activities allows young people to develop the values and skills they need to live in society; these include learning cooperation, conflict resolution and learning how to win or lose while respecting others. What might be the influence of sports and leisure activities on the autonomy and freedom of young people throughout the world?

Doc. 1.40 A breakdancing class in Bedzin, Poland. This dance style was created in the Bronx, in New York, in the 1970s. A former gang leader wanted to channel the energy of young people in his neighbourhood toward artistic activities rather than violence. Inspired by various African dances, he invented breakdancing.

© Andrzej Grygiel/PAP/Corbis

TO KNOW MORE +

The most popular sport in the world

Soccer, as it is called in North America and "football" everywhere else, is admittedly the most popular sport in the world. Its popularity is due to the fact that soccer doesn't require much in the way of equipment. It can be played with a ball or any other similar object. The sport is suitable for people from all walks of life.

42-16725017| Standard RM| © Joao Luiz Bulcao/Corbis/Corbis

Doc. 1.41 Soccer is Brazil's national sport. This photograph shows young people from a poor neighbourhood in Rio de Janeiro. Many organizations, keenly aware of the role soccer can play in self-esteem, encourage young people to play the sport. Most young players dream of one day following in the footsteps of their idols, Pelé, Romário, Rivaldo, Ronaldo and Ronaldinho by becoming professional players. They also dream of having a chance to play in Rio de Janeiro's Maracanã stadium, the world's largest soccer stadium.

Sources: Canadian International Development Agency, 2008, United Nations Organization, 2006 and UNICEF, 2008.

Doc. 1.42 A group of navy cadets in St. Petersburg, Russia. The cadets are not part of an army; rather, they participate in programs that allow them to find out more about naval and aviation traditions, among other things. These programs also help develop self-esteem, discipline and awareness of the importance of personal and collective community involvement.

© Catherine Karnow/Corbis

The influence of family and friends

Synthesis

- A person's identity is defined by his or her physical appearance, relationships and inner world.

- Each individual's inner world is shaped by the values and norms, needs and constraints that affect them.

- The family and the social environment have the greatest influence on an individual.

- Needs are generally the same for everyone; however, the ways in which these needs are met can differ from person to person.

- The dynamic that binds individuals to their family or their social environment can be a source of tension.

- Exercising our autonomy can have consequences for the people around us and can also be a source of tension.

- It is in exercising one's autonomy that individuals are able to act when presented with certain situations.

- Autonomy and dependence are linked to issues like social success, dependence on others, self-esteem, pressure from family and friends, love and relationships.

- An individual responds differently to issues such as social success, dependence on others, and self-esteem in accordance with their identity and experience.

- Some situations may force us to act contrary to our own values.

- Freedom is the capacity for one to think, to act and to choose for oneself. Exercising this freedom involves taking other people's freedom into consideration.

- The law protects our right to privacy and to intimacy, but these rights can limit the freedom of others.

1 What is the basis for adopting certain values?

2 What is a norm?

3 In your circle of family and friends, which people or organizations set the norms?

4 What makes it possible for us to fulfill our essential needs?

5 How can our needs create tension in our circle of family and friends?

6 Can you name three constraints that keep an individual from fulfilling their needs?

7 What group provides us with our first set of values?

8 What does it mean to "be autonomous?"

9 How can our autonomy bring about conflicting situations? Justify your answer.

10 What is dependence?

11 How can dependence become a problem?

12 What is low self-esteem?

13 How can pressure from family or friends make a person dependent? Why?

14 In your own words, define freedom.

15 What limits an individual's freedom?

16 How can young people set limits for themselves?

17 How can exercising freedom cause tension? Why?

18 How can one person's desire for privacy infringe on another person's right to freedom?

19 How is confidentiality a freedom-related issue?

20 Does everyone see confidentiality in the same way? Justify your answer.

21 Is curiosity necessarily unhealthy? Justify your answer.

22 What is the difference between voyeurism and simple curiosity?

23 How can voyeurism constitute a criminal act? Why?

Ethical reflection

SUMMARY

2.1 Social order   **42**

2.2 Protecting social values   **46**

2.3 Social norms   **50**

2.4 Individuals and the social order   **53**

Culture and society   **56**

Here and elsewhere   **60**

Synthesis   **62**

CHAPTER 2

Society's influences

We live in an organized society. What is social order? How does the existing form of power in our society influence our actions? Are we really aware of the values conveyed by our society? Do we have the power to act within this organized society?

CONNECTIONS

RELIGIOUS CULTURE

- The organization of Québec's religious institutions
- The influence of religious traditions on values and norms
- Rules with respect to behaviour in family situations and romantic relationships and practices related to food and clothing

DIALOGUE

- Forms of dialogue: debate
- Means for developing a point of view: justification
- Means for examining a point of view: errors in reasoning

2.1 Social order

What is social order? What type of society do we live in?
What are the various forms of power that govern society?

TO KNOW MORE +

The structure of Québec's governmental apparatus

In industrialized countries, the governmental apparatus is generally complex. In Québec, it consists of some 20 government departments (or ministries) and approximately 200 public corporations and agencies. Some of them concern teenagers directly. This is the case with the Ministère de l'Éducation, du Loisir et du Sport whose mission includes promoting and developing the three above-mentioned domains. There is also the Youth Council, an organization that champions the needs and interests of young people.

In the preceding chapter, you saw that your circle of friends is governed by norms, laws and moral rules. In other words, you are growing within the framework of an established order. In this chapter, we will see that this framework of order also exists on a social level.

In general, a country is managed by a government body, that is, a group of people who hold power. It is the government in power who makes the laws and sees that they are enforced over the entire territory. The government also makes the necessary decisions to ensure the country is run properly.

However, the notion of government is not limited only to a country. For example, Canada is managed by the Canadian Parliament, but it is also a **confederation**. In effect, the country is managed by a central government, but each province also has its own government and **governmental apparatus**. Some departments, like the postal service, are run by the central government; others, like education, report to the provinces. In Québec, the National Assembly manages the affairs of the State. Finally, in each city, a local council makes decisions regarding **municipal** regulations and administers various services to the population. For example, it is responsible for drinking water, road maintenance, snow removal and the collection and disposal of waste. The local council also administers recreational sports and cultural activities.

Other types of groups, institutions and organizations are also governed by a social order. This is also true for industry.

Confederation: the association of several states that maintain a certain degree of autonomy in relation to a central government.

Governmental apparatus: a combination of institutions, structures and mechanisms held by a government to fulfill its functions.

Municipal: that which concerns a given city or territory.

In Québec, debates on the matter of laws and their implementation take place in the National Assembly. The ministers and deputies of the party in power, along with the deputies of the opposition, discuss the bills that are proposed. As well, this is where commissions–groups mandated by the government to examine specific questions–present their reports and make their recommendations.

The National Assembly is where important decisions are made regarding the running of the affairs of the State. How can we protect the environment? How will we structure the teaching of ethics and religious culture in primary and secondary schools? There is no lack of questions–or answers.

Doc. 2.1 The Debating Chamber of Québec's National Assembly.

© Pierre McCann/La Presse

TYPES OF POWER

Do you think that all groups, institutions and organizations resort to the same types of power and organization? The types of political organizations, the ways to assume power, and the methods of organizing work are very diverse. Below are some examples.

Democratic power

You've certainly often heard that we live in a **democracy**, or that it's important to preserve our democratic values.

A democratic society is based on respect for liberty and equality for each person in society. When a society works in this way, government members are elected by all the citizens who have the right to vote. Elected officials are expected to make decisions that improve the living conditions, the well-being of each and every citizen, and the respect of human rights.

In a democratic society, people are free to express their opinions, and they can disagree with the decisions made by the government. Each person has the right to defend an idea or value.

Doc. 2.2 In a democracy, we are free to vote for the people and political parties whose values we share and are in accordance with our views of society.

Doc. 2.4 A modern peace symbol at the entrance to the United Nations headquarters.

> **Democracy:** a type of political organization where the people hold the power and freely elect representatives to exercise it on their behalf.

Doc. 2.3 The United Nations headquarters is located in New York City.

TO KNOW MORE +

The United Nations

Many international institutions, like the United Nations (UN), are founded on democratic values. The UN's main objectives are to promote peace throughout the whole world and defend human rights.

Doc. 2.5 German dictator, Adolf Hitler (1889-1945), started World War II.

Repression: using violence to stop protests and revolts.

Dictator: a leader who seizes power and exercises it in an authoritarian manner.

Charisma: the quality that gives an individual a great deal of influence, a magnetic power over others.

Authoritarian power

We often contrast dictatorship and democracy. A dictatorship is an authoritarian political system where the people don't really have a voice. In general, with this type of government, the people in power have very little concern for the well-being of the population and provide it with very few services.

An authoritarian government often seizes power through a coup d'état. The leaders of a dictatorship do not tolerate protests from the population. The opinion of the citizens means very little to them. **Repression**, assassination and violations of human rights are commonplace.

We often associate this type of government with the following people:

• The German **dictator**, Adolf Hitler, who started World War II.

• General Francisco Franco who ruled Spain from 1939 to 1975.

• General Augusto Pinochet who held power in Chile from 1973 to 1990.

The power of charisma

Some people are said to have **charisma**. Their very presence inspires and energizes the people around them. In politics, this type of person can bring crowds around to their way of thinking, fill them with passion and even lead them to war. These are said to be "charismatic leaders." In Canada, two such charismatic leaders impacted our history: Pierre Elliott Trudeau (1919-2000) and René Lévesque (1922-1987). Trudeau, who was Prime Minister of Canada, defended the unity of the country. Lévesque, who was Premier of Québec, campaigned for Québec's sovereignty.

Doc. 2.6 René Lévesque was Premier of Québec from 1976 to 1985.

Doc. 2.7 Pierre Elliott Trudeau was Prime Minister of Canada from 1968 to 1979 and from 1980 to 1984.

Cooperative power

Cooperative power is based on the association of people who share a common goal. These people share project management, resources, responsibilities and tasks that are related to their goal. The benefits are divided proportionally according to the work each person has accomplished. This type of power is very prevalent in the economic world. For example, there are many types of cooperatives: farmers' co-ops, credit co-ops and housing co-ops.

Doc. 2.8 In a cooperative, it is the members who hold the power.

Partnerships

A partnership consists of two or more interested parties. The purpose of this type of power is to realize a project by pooling material, intellectual and financial resources. Partnerships can involve governments, businesses or individuals.

Some history

QUÉBEC'S HOUSING COOPERATIVES

Québec's first housing cooperatives were created in 1940 by the Catholic clergy. At the time, when a housing co-op was set up, the members combined their efforts to build houses for each member, one after the other. Once all the houses were built, the co-op was dissolved.

The housing co-op movement has grown since the 1940s and has disassociated itself from the Catholic clergy. Nowadays, a housing co-op is a building or residence where people live. Individually, they rent their apartment, but collectively, they own the building. These same residents manage and help maintain the co-op and the quality of life in it.

At the present time, the *Confédération québecoise des coopératives d'habitation* has 50 000 members. This group is founded on the values of equality, equity, solidarity and transparency. The federation also advances various principles like democracy, autonomy and commitment to the community.

TO KNOW MORE +

Fair trade

Fair trade is a form of economic partnership. Its purpose is to give producers and craftspeople in developing countries a fair price for their products. This type of partnership is based on dialogue, transparency and respect between producer and consumer. There are many fair trade products available in the marketplace: coffee, tea, sugar, fruit and vegetables, rice, cotton and others.

In Canada, fair trade is not government controlled. However, a few associations do play a monitoring and certification role. The fair trade logo guarantees that the products are fairly traded.

Many consumer groups would like to see a fair trade law, one similar to that regulating organic produce which has been in existence in Canada since 2006. Such a law would help prevent abuse and misleading practices.

Doc. 2.9 This is the symbol applied to pruducts that have been independently certified to conform with international Fair Trade standards.
© TransFair Canada

2.2 Protecting social values

All societies are founded on values. What do you know about the values our society embraces? Do you agree with them?

Doc. 2.10 The National Assembly represents Québec's democratic values.

Wikipedia

Abolish: putting an end to a custom or practice.

A LOOK AT THE VALUES IN QUÉBEC SOCIETY

Collective values vary from one society to another. They are linked by many historical factors, such as the system of government, language, culture and religion. These values are usually respected in all institutions within the society. In fact, they are protected by laws respecting fundamental rights. In Québec, for example, each citizen is free to choose their own lifestyle, to act according to their own values, to have their own opinion and to practise the religion of their choice. Did you know that in almost all democratic societies, most people consider freedom as the most fundamental of all values? There are many definitions of freedom. However, nearly all of these definitions support the idea that freedom has to be limited in its exercise. Personal freedom is not absolute; it exists only in relation to the freedom of others.

Doc. 2.11 Even today in various parts of the world, 27 million slaves are forced to work as servants, prostitutes or soldiers.
© Vladimír Radosa/Shutterstock

Some history

SLAVERY OR THE COMPLETE LACK OF RIGHTS AND FREEDOMS

Slavery consists of forcefully taking individuals and forcing them to work. In antiquity, this practice was standard in many societies. When America was discovered by the Europeans, the African slave trade grew by leaps and bounds. Wanting cheap labour, the European colonists started what came to be called the "Black Trade." At the beginning of the 19th century, many countries officially **abolished** slavery.

Yet human trafficking still exists. Only now, it is done in a different way. It is estimated that on all continents, there are over 27 million victims of modern slavery. Most of the victims are women and children who are used for labour or prostitution. UNESCO, like other international organizations, is fighting against these new forms of slavery.

Fundamental freedoms

In the preceding chapter, you saw that freedom can take on different forms in your daily life. You also saw that exercising your own freedom may conflict with other people's freedom. On a social level, freedom can be defined as being able to decide one's own actions while respecting the rules of the society in which one lives. So-called "fundamental freedoms" are the freedoms that are protected and defended by law and deemed essential by the individuals who live in a given society. Laws also put limits on fundamental freedoms. For example, the right of association does not include the right to take part in a criminal organization, the same way the right to free speech does not give someone the right to say whatever they want.

Freedoms in Québec

According to the Québec Charter of Human Rights and Freedoms, everyone has the following basic rights:

- Freedom of conscience
- Freedom of expression
- Freedom of religion
- Freedom of peaceful assembly
- Freedom of opinion
- Freedom of association

THE PROTECTION OF RIGHTS AND FREEDOMS

In our society, the protection of rights and freedoms is an essential value. The governments of Québec and Canada have passed basic laws in this regard. In Québec, this is called the Québec Charter of Human Rights and Freedoms, and in Canada, the Canadian Charter of Rights and Freedoms. The main purpose of these charters is to ensure that every person is equal before and under the law, has the right to life, the right to vote, the right to privacy and all other forms of freedom discussed previously.

Consumer protection

When a person earns a salary or income and abides by the law, they have the right to spend their money to purchase the products and services they desire. There are also laws to protect consumers against dishonest merchants, defective products or other similar problems. In Québec, the purpose of the *Office de la protection du consommateur* (Consumer Protection Bureau), a government body, is to inform and educate citizens and ensure consumer laws are enforced. This bureau processes the complaints of people whose rights regarding the purchase of goods or services have not been respected.

TO KNOW MORE +

Doc. 2.12 Inside the *Grande Bibliothèque du Québec*.
Wikipedia

The Grande Bibliothèque du Québec

The *Bibliothèque et Archives nationales* is a Québec government agency. Part of its mission is to provide free access to its collections in an effort to promote the cultural development of citizens.
At the *Grande Bibliothèque*, the agency's main location, we can have access to over 4 million documents. The building opened its doors to the public in 2005 in downtown Montréal.

Doc. 2.13 Consumers are protected by laws in Canada.
© Andresr/Shutterstock

Commission of inquiry: a commission mandated by the government to seek the opinion of the public on a given topic or to shed light on a specific event. Most of the time, the name of such a commission is abbreviated by giving them the name of the person in charge, for example, the Gomery Commission or the Bouchard-Taylor Commission.

Sponsorship: financial support given to an organization or an event.

Public funds: sums of money belonging to the State and subject to specific laws (income taxes, etc.).

The right to information

In our society, everyone has the right to receive and disseminate information. For example, citizens have the right to clear and concise information on the functioning of the State. The quality of a government is often measured by its transparency, that is, the accurate nature of the information passed on to the population.

The right to privacy

Everyone has the right to privacy. For example, a person's love life, sexual life and family life, as well as that person's state of health are no one else's concern. The right to privacy, like the right to information, is protected by law. That is: the Act respecting access to documents held by public bodies and the protection of personal information. However, if the public interest is threatened, authorities are not bound to protect this right. This is the case, for example, if there is fear of a terrorist attack or if someone's behaviour is presumed to be that of a pedophile.

© CHRISTINNE MUSCHI/Reuters/Corbis

Doc. 2.14 Judge John Howard Gomery was born in Montréal in 1932. He received his law degree from McGill University and specialized in family law and commercial litigation. In 1982, he was appointed Justice of the Québec Superior Court. From 1999 until 2004, he was President of the Copyright Board of Canada, after which he presided as head of the 2004 public inquiry into the federal government's sponsorship and advertising activities. Mr. Justice John H. Gomery retired in 2007.

TO KNOW MORE +

The right to information: the Gomery Commission and the sponsorship scandal

In 2004, the Liberal Party, which was in power in Ottawa, created the **Commission of Inquiry** into the **Sponsorship** Program and Advertising Activities. Initially, a newspaper article raised the issue of **public funds** that might have been spent without respecting government rules. The Liberal Party was allegedly involved in the operation. The Gomery Commission lasted for nine months and heard testimony from 184 witnesses. According to a report by the Auditor General, the total amount of money spent for the Sponsorship Program was $250 million and, of this amount, $100 million was allegedly misappropriated. This was a huge scandal! Ministers were involved and people from the advertising world were fined and jailed. The right to information had a price tag: experts estimate that this Commission directly or indirectly cost some $75 million in public funds. When the Commission's report was released, elections were called and the Liberal Party lost power.

Doc. 2.15 Although protecting the right to privacy is important in Québec, public safety sometimes requires the use of surveillance cameras in public places.

19075540 © Jupiter Images and its representatives. All rights reserved.

Personal duties

Rights, freedoms and protection are not the only thing in a democracy. Individuals also have duties. Among other things, they must adequately inform themselves and respect the opinions of others.

The opinion you have on a certain topic mostly depends on the accuracy of the information you have. You can't really comment on what you don't know much about or know nothing at all about. The phrase "Ignorance of the law is not a defence" doesn't constitute a legal obligation to be informed, but remember that it is our duty to know the law, and that this duty has consequences. In fact, we may not be aware of certain laws, but if we violate them, we cannot invoke this ignorance in our own defence. No one will go to prison for not knowing the law. Jail time is reserved for those who disobey the law. But, in the end, it is a citizen's fundamental duty to obey the law which doesn't necessarily involve knowing what it is. Obviously, knowing the law can only help but in itself, it is not an obligation.

Respecting the opinions of others doesn't necessarily mean agreeing with them. Rather, it means letting others express themselves freely while expecting them to let us express ourselves just as freely. Such tolerance encourages dialogue between people.

Personal obligations

In all organized societies, individuals must obey the laws and the regulations that are in force. Every day, life provides us with many opportunities to fulfill our obligations in regards to the law. Below are a few examples.

- A person who gets a ticket must pay it.

- A young person must attend school until the age of 16.

- A person who borrows money, whether by written **contract** or verbal agreement, must reimburse the lender.

Contract: agreement between individuals.

TO KNOW MORE +

To be or not to be politically correct?

Political correctness, i.e. the fact of being politically correct, means having an attitude where words and actions that might be interpreted as being offensive by some are avoided. There's no shortage of delicate subjects: ethnic origin, sex, sexual orientation, religion and the handicapped are just a few examples.

Political correctness provokes all sorts of reactions. Some see it as an obstacle to freedom of expression. In their opinion, always being aware of the sensitivities of others is like not being able to think, say, or write what they would like. Others see it as a gesture of politeness and respect for people's sensitivities.

Doc. 2.17 Political correctness: a violation of freedom or respect for others?
© Kirsty Pargeter/Shutterstock

© Liv Friis-larsen/Shutterstock

Doc. 2.16 In all societies, individuals must respect certain obligations.

2.3 Social norms

For a society to function as it should, it relies on norms. What do you know about social conventions? How are laws applied in our society?

Some history

THE HISTORICAL EVOLUTION OF WOMEN'S SWIMSUITS

Morals are a part of social conventions. As society changes, so do its morals. Fashion is a phenomenon that closely follows the evolution of morals. Let's look at women's swimsuits. If, in the early 20th century a woman had worn a bikini on the beach, she would have been cited for indecency and condemned for improper morals. At the time, swimsuits were considered acceptable if they covered most of the body. Over the century, swimsuit design evolved with modern thinking and covered less and less of the body. The bikini, invented during the 1940s, only became popular in the 1950s.

Doc. 2.18 A swimsuit that was in fashion in 1916.

© Bettmann/Corbis

Doc. 2.19 As morals changed, the bikini gained popularity in the late 1950s.

© Bettmann/Corbis

WRITTEN AND UNWRITTEN NORMS

Social norms refer to behaviours that are considered appropriate within a given society. They are different in different countries and among different peoples, and they change over time.

Among other social norms, there are rules of conduct specifying what we must do and not do in a society. Some norms are more or less implied: these are social conventions. Others are clearly written down: they are laws, codes and regulations.

SOCIAL CONVENTIONS

In our society, there are many levels of etiquette that generally frown on things like putting your finger in your nose, making obscene gestures and swearing.

Social conventions and the degree to which its rules are respected vary greatly in different social circles and circumstances. In general, ignoring social conventions doesn't result in any harsh consequences. Rather, one runs the risk of being considered as a person "who has no class" or who was raised badly. Not respecting convention might result in being excluded from a group. However, the same behaviour might be tacitly accepted in another group.

Morals: customs and codes of behaviour common to a society, a people and an era.

Circumstances and the individuals concerned play an important role in deciding whether or not a gesture is appropriate. Tapping your index finger against your temple to indicate to a friend that you consider them to be crazy can be funny in certain situations. The same gesture under different circumstances may provoke an entirely different reaction. Look at the following examples and see for yourself.

- A teenager on the street makes this gesture to a policeman after he is told not to disturb the peace.

- In the National Assembly, one deputy makes this gesture to another deputy in front of television cameras.

LAWS

Laws guarantee that a society's members' rights and freedoms will be respected. At the same time, laws restrict the rights and freedoms of others as these same rights are respected. It's a matter of social balance.

In a democratic society, the government is elected by the people. As such, we believe that it is mandated to act according to the interests of the community. With this in mind, government passes laws and ensures compliance.

The legal system

What we call "the law" is a complicated set of rules established by our political leaders. In fact, in Canada for example, there is not just one law but hundreds, even thousands if we consider all levels of government. In addition, laws might include regulations that lead to their implementation. The purpose of the legal system is to provide citizens with a framework for functioning properly in all areas of activity, notably agriculture, health, the environment and the economy.

© Lisa F. Young/ Shutterstock

Doc. 2.20 An example of changing values and norms. In the early 20th century, attending school was not compulsory in Québec. Today, young people must attend school until the age of 16 (Education Act).

Consent: to accept that something should take place.

Discrimination: the act of separating one group of human beings from another and treating this group differently.

Ban: to exclude permanently.

Some history

HOMOSEXUALITY AND THE LAW

All societies change over time. The reasons for this are many: influence from other cultures, level of education, social awareness and technological advances, etc.

These changes are reflected in the laws and in the recognition of individual rights. The following are historical dates related to the recognition of the rights of homosexuals in Québec and in Canada.

1969: The Parliament of Canada decriminalizes homosexual relationships between **consenting** adults.

1977: The Government of Québec includes sexual orientation in the Charter of Human Rights and Freedoms as an illegal motive for **discrimination**.

1996: The Canadian Human Rights Act **bans** discrimination on the basis of sexual orientation.

2005: Canadian law allows two people of the same sex to marry.

Every level of government passes laws according to its **legislative competence**. Canada has laws that apply to its entire territory, including Québec. Québec's laws concern the province's territory. In turn, municipal regulations are used to administer the territory of a city. The laws in each jurisdiction must be in line with and respect those of the higher level. For example, at the municipal level one cannot allow something that contravenes the Civil or Criminal Codes.

CODES

Codes are collections of legal texts that deal with a specific area. In Canada, the Criminal Code consists of a description of acts that are forbidden as well as the punishments they entail: for example, theft, fraud, mugging, homicide, drunk driving.

In Québec, the Civil Code applies to people, social relationships, and property: the rental and sale of goods, the sale of services, marriage and divorce. The Highway Safety Code specifies the regulations motorists must respect; these include obtaining a driver's licence, following road signs and obeying speed limits.

MUNICIPAL REGULATIONS

Each municipality establishes a set of rules and regulations to manage its territory. These include various domains such as traffic circulation, construction and renovation, public behaviour and noise.

Doc. 2.21 The minimum wage is set by the Québec government.

© PhotoCreate/Shutterstock

Legislative competence: an authority's power to make laws in a given area.

Infrastructure: the large-scale public systems, services and facilities that are necessary for economic activity (e.g. power and water supplies, roads, telecommunications, schools).

Doc. 2.22 Codes are a collection of laws on a specific subject.
© Rafa Irusta/Shutterstock

Doc. 2.23 The maintenance of certain **infrastructures** falls under municipal jurisdiction.
© Julie Ten Eyck (JTeffects)/Shutterstock

2.4 Individuals and the social order

Do autonomy and dependency exist at the social level? How are they expressed? Can they be a source of tension? How can we react to social order?

AUTONOMY AND DEPENDENCY IN SOCIETY

In the first chapter, we saw how autonomy and dependency come into play in a person's relationships with their circle of family and friends. This is also true for a society. Following are two examples.

Emancipation

Emancipation consists of freeing oneself from the authority or power exercised by an individual or group. It can take various forms; it can be political. For example, the Parti Québécois has been advocating sovereignty for Québec for many years. The party has long been arguing for Québec's emancipation and complete autonomy. There is also social emancipation. At the beginning of the 20th century, women depended entirely on men. They were subject to their father's authority and also to that of their husband's. After decades of struggling and advocating for their rights, women saw the laws that made them legally dependent abolished.

Doc. 2.24 Idola St-Jean (1880-1945) is known for her contribution to the **suffragette** movement. In 1927, she founded the Canadian Alliance for Women's Votes. Three years later, she ran as a candidate in the federal elections. She was not elected but did garner 3000 votes.

© Bibliothèque et Archives nationales du Québec's digital collection

Doc. 2.25 In 1961, Marie-Claire Kirkland-Casgrain (1924-) was the first woman to be elected as a member of the Québec government. In 1962, she became the first female minister. She is responsible for the law that put an end to the judicial incapacity of married women.

© Bibliothèque et Archives nationales du Québec

Suffragette: someone who fought for women's right to vote in the early 20th century.

Senate: assembly where senators sit in the Parliament of Canada.

Judicial incapacity: the inability of a person to exercise his or her rights.

Some history — THE RECOGNITION OF WOMEN'S RIGHTS

The emancipation of women in Québec did not take place overnight. It is the result of a struggle that began a long time ago. Below are some of the events that marked this evolution.

1911: The police arrest 223 women who demonstrate on Parliament Hill in Ottawa to get the right for women to vote.

1919: Women are granted the right to vote in federal elections.

1929: Women became "persons" under the law.

1930: A woman is appointed to the Canadian **Senate** for the first time.

1940: Women in Québec are granted the right to vote.

1941: Women can now become lawyers.

1947: Women who marry foreigners can now keep their Canadian citizenship.

1961: Marie-Claire Kirkland-Casgrain is the first woman to sit in the Legislative Assembly.

1964: A law is passed ending the **judicial incapacity** of married women in Québec.

1972: The Québec government sets up the Council for the Status of Women.

1975: The Québec Charter of Human Rights and Freedoms bans discrimination on the basis of gender.

1981: Equality is recognized between spouses. Women now keep their maiden name and can give it to their children.

Some history

STALIN'S RULE IN THE USSR

■ Joseph Stalin imposed a totalitarian regime in the **USSR** through dominance over the political, economic, social and cultural life of its citizens. They were forced to submit to the established order. Stalin's regime, founded on terror, banned any form of opposition.

Doc. 2.26
Joseph Stalin (1879-1953).

Order: that which has been specified.

Reprisals: violent measures taken against someone because of their acts of retaliation.

USSR: the Union of Soviet Socialist Republics, a state whose territory extended to Europe and Asia from 1917 to 1991. The USSR has since been divided into several countries, including Russia.

Doc. 2.27 Compliance with the law can take many forms, namely respect, conformity and submission.

Struggling against dependency

Many people are plagued with problems of dependency. They suffer a pathological, physical or psychological need for someone or something. Such people may be dependent on love, sex, drugs or something else. Dependency entails severe consequences for the individual. Some also suffer social consequences. Governments are currently trying to prevent, reduce and treat gambling and alcohol dependency. Yet, these same governments promote games of chance and the sale of alcohol.

FORMS OF OBEDIENCE AND DISOBEDIENCE OF THE LAW

Earlier, we saw that society is governed by social conventions, rules and laws. How do citizens behave in the face of social order? Are they always compliant? How is a lack of compliance with the law expressed? There are many factors that influence people's behaviour as it relates to social order. These include: education, family values, the forms of social power, and belonging to a group. Following are some examples of behaviour with respect to the law.

Respecting the law

Obeying the law means obeying what is **ordered**. People who obey the law do not commit illegal acts. The values that induce people to behave this way are many, and include, for example, a sense of duty and responsibility, or respect for authority. This said, some people obey the law simply because they are afraid of being punished.

Conformity

A conformist models their behaviour by going along with the majority. They don't ask questions and they don't criticize society.

Submission

Submission to the law is a form of obedience without protest. A person may submit to the law without protest all the while believing that it is unfair. Another will do so while believing that the law is just and fair. Often in a totalitarian regime, the majority of the population submits to power through fear of **reprisal**, including the risk of being jailed, tortured or killed.

Crime

The term "crime" encompasses all the criminal acts committed within a society, a group or a city. A criminal act or behaviour is one that seriously and adversely affects the fundamental values of the society, its social order and safety. In most cases, such acts are covered in the Criminal Code. Some values can induce individuals to commit crimes, and include, for example, loyalty to a group, the belief that personal interest comes before the common good, and the refusal to compromise.

Civil disobedience

Civil disobedience consists of refusing to comply with a law or regulation in order to protest against authority or a specific action by this authority. Generally, civil disobedience involves a non-violent act carried out in public in an effort to raise public awareness of the importance of changing a specific norm. People who use this form of disobedience run the risk of being punished. Sometimes, the power of civil disobedience does result in laws being changed.

Protest

In a democracy, when social conventions, rules or laws are not in line with our own values, they can be called into question through various forms of protest: press campaigns, speeches, petitions, street demonstrations, seeking legal recourse in the courts and other forms. Boycotts are also a form of protest. An individual, group or country can boycott an event by refusing to attend it. One can also protest by refusing to maintain a relationship with other people.

TO KNOW MORE +

Civil disobedience

Anti-globalization groups often use civil disobedience to be heard. José Bové is a French anti-globalization protestor known for his radical activities. This man opposes the use of genetically modified organisms (GMOs). On many occasions, Bové and other activists destroyed GMO crops. Bové's disobedience of the law has cost him dearly in fines, lawsuits and even jail time.

Wikipedia

Doc. 2.28 José Bové (1953-) commits acts of civil disobedience to affirm his convictions.

Anti-globalization: term used to describe opposition to economic neo-liberal globalization where the state intervenes very little.

Doc. 2.29 In 1976, 28 African countries boycotted the Olympic Games in Montréal. They did this to protest New Zealand's presence at the Games because this country maintained relations with South Africa which at the time was under apartheid rule. Apartheid was a regime that practised the strict and regulated separation of white people and people of colour, which was contrary to the values of the African countries that boycotted the Games.
© Bettmann/Corbis

Society's influences

Culture and society
Ways of looking at freedom and social order

Freedom has always inspired individuals, whether they are politicians, thinkers, scientists or artists. It has also induced groups to question social values and norms. This section will include some famous quotes that deal with freedom. We will then look at a monument dedicated to freedom. Finally, we will see three examples of social groups that have used freedom to question the established social order.

Doc. 2.30 Abraham Lincoln.

Abraham Lincoln (1809-1865)

Lincoln was the 16th President of the United States. His name is associated with the abolition of slavery in that country.

> "We here highly resolve...
> that government of the people,
> by the people and for the people,
> shall not perish from the earth."

(Excerpt from the Gettysburg Address, 1863)

Doc. 2.31 Oscar Wilde.

Oscar Wilde (1856-1900)

A British writer of Irish origin known for his **non-conformity**.

> "Democracy: the oppression
> of the people, by the people
> for the people." (Reference unknown)

Non-conformity: an attitude that is opposite to established norms.

Simone de Beauvoir (1908-1986)

French philosopher, author, and the face of modern feminism. Her contribution to the fight for equal rights between men and women is famous worldwide. She is the author of: *Le deuxième sexe (The Second Sex)*.

"Wanting to be free is also wanting others to be free."

(*The Ethics of Ambiguity*, 1947)

Doc. 2.32 Jean-Paul Sartre and Simone de Beauvoir.

Jean-Paul Sartre (1905-1980)

French philosopher and novelist who was a leading figure of his era. His thinking is at the root of existentialism. He was awarded the Nobel Prize for Literature in 1964.

"Freedom is not being able to do what we want, but wanting what we can do."

(*Situations I*, 1947)

Sir Winston Churchill (1874-1965)

British politician and author. Prime Minister of Great Britain during World War II. He was awarded the Nobel Prize for Literature in 1953.

"Democracy is the worst system of government known to man, except for all the others that have been tried."

(Excerpt from a speech made to the House of Commons, London, 1947)

Doc. 2.33 Winston Churchill showing the V for Victory sign.
© Bettmann/Corbis

Society's influences

Culture and society
The symbols of freedom

CHAPTER 2

■ **Doc. 2.34** *The Statue of Liberty Enlightening the World*, sculpture by Frédéric Auguste Bartholdi.

■ **Doc. 2.35** The light from the torch symbolizes the Age of Enlightenment.

© Jolamay/Shutterstock

© SVLumagraphica/Shutterstock

© Amy Nichole Harris/Shutterstock

Doc. 2.36 The date of the United States Declaration of Independence, July 4, 1776, is engraved on the statue's tablet.

Age of Enlightenment: intellectual, cultural and scientific movement dating back to the 18th century.

Freedom is not always easy to come by. The monument shown in the adjacent photo evokes memories of the armed confrontations linked to the conquest for freedom in the United States: the War of Independence (1775-1782) and the American Civil War (1861-1865).

LIBERTY ENLIGHTENING THE WORLD

You may know the Statue of Liberty. It stands proudly on a small island called Liberty Island, at the entrance to the Port of New York. The statue's real name is "Liberty Enlightening the World." It was created by the French sculptor Frédéric Auguste Bartholdi (1834-1904). A French engineer, Gustave Eiffel (1831-1923), who designed the famous tower that bears his name, helped Bartholdi to sculpt this statue. In total, the sculpture measures over 90 metres high.

France presented this statue to the United States as a gift to commemorate the 100th anniversary of its Declaration of Independence and to show its patronage to the country. Since 1984, the monument has been on the UNESCO World Heritage List.

Because of what it represents, the Statue of Liberty has become a symbol, par excellence, for the United States, a country which the Americans themselves love to call "The Land of Liberty."

THE SCULPTURE'S SYMBOLISM

Liberty is personified by a woman holding a torch, the symbol of the **Age of Enlightenment**. The tablet in her left hand bears the date of the United States Declaration of Independence. The broken chains at the foot of the statue are a symbol of the end of oppression and slavery in the United States.

Counterculture

Doc. 2.37 The hippies questioned traditional differences between men and women. Both sexes had long hair, wore loose clothing and sandals or went barefoot.

The term "counterculture" was first introduced in the early 1970s. It stood for the values and lifestyle that opposed the dominant culture of a given society. A counterculture is initially created by young adults and teenagers who use their freedom to put the social order into question. One of several countercultures may emerge at any given time. Depending on the situation, a counterculture can be identified by its ideology, mode of clothing, music, social behaviour or other characteristics. Often, counterculture currents eventually become a part of our consumer society.

THE LATE 1960s: THE HIPPIE ERA

The hippie movement was born in North America. This movement represented the systematic rejection by young **baby-boomers** of the values they considered as being those of their parents: a consumer society, materialism, marriage and family, professional success, conformity...Among the new values put forward were the following: sexual freedom, universal peace, the rejection of religious traditions, the importance of a spiritual life and a back-to-earth movement. During the 1980s, most hippies came back into society. Even today, we talk about this movement as one of *peace and love*.

THE 1970s: THE PUNK ERA

The punk movement first made its appearance in Great Britain. More than a simple rejection of established values, the movement was actually a revolt. Far from the *peace and love* of the hippies, punks were agitators and their movement has continued to grow throughout the decades. They do not offer just one ideology, but several, often difficult to separate.

THE 1980s: THE GOTH ERA

The Gothic movement (or Goth) also originated in Great Britain. Influenced by the punk culture, it continues to grow and to intermingle with various ideologies.

Doc. 2.38 The punk style is recognized by torn clothing, extreme haircuts, tattoos and piercings.

Baby-boomer: generation of people born after World War II (1945-1964).

Doc. 2.39 The Goth style was characterized by dark-coloured clothing and extravagant accessories.

Society's influences

59

Here and elsewhere
Law and order in Singapore

In this chapter we saw that there are different types of societies.
Let's look at a society that is very different from ours, the Republic of Singapore.

Doc. 2.40 The flag of the Republic of Singapore.

Doc. 2.41 "Danger–Keep Out." In Singapore, signs in the four official languages are commonplace.

AN OVERVIEW

The Republic of Singapore is in Asia. It consists of one big island and dozens of smaller islands. The capital is also called Singapore. Its population is approximately 5 million and its area covers 700 km². In comparison, its population is approximately 65% that of Québec's, and its area is one and a half times that of Montréal's. There are four official languages in Singapore: English, Mandarin, Malaysian and Tamil. Nearly 75% of the population is of Chinese origin. Various religions are practised there: Buddhism, Taoism, Islam, Christianity and Hinduism.

Singapore's government is often considered to be an authoritarian democracy. The Republic is known for its severe application of its laws and regulations and for its exceptionally low rates of corruption and crime.

Doc. 2.42 Singapore is a modern city whose streets are known to be safe even late at night.
© Ng Wei Keong/Shutterstock

Doc. 2.43 The durian is a fruit native to Asia. It is flavourful and very well-liked but very smelly. In Singapore, it is forbidden to bring this fruit on public transportation.

PUBLIC ORDER

In public, it is important to mind one's manners toward women. Men who do not respect a woman's modesty risk being beaten.

In public places, smoking, spitting, chewing gum and littering are forbidden. Individuals who disobey are fined and sometimes have to perform community services.

Eating or drinking on public transportation is punishable by a fine. Shoplifting carries very stiff fines.

Contrary to other countries, many regulations are very strictly enforced and include for example, crossing on a red light or somewhere other than at a crosswalk.

Doc. 2.44 Owning firearms is forbidden in Singapore, even if it's a collector's item or…a toy.

THE USE OF DRUGS

All types of drugs are forbidden in Singapore. Drug possession, even small amounts, may be considered as trafficking which could lead to the death penalty for the offender. According to some sources more than 400 people have been hanged in Singapore over the past 20 years, most for drug trafficking. Authorities can have new arrivals to the country submit to drug-screening tests. If someone tests positive, the offender is considered as having taken drugs on the country's territory.

Censorship: control exercised by a government or other authority over the press, among others.

CENSORSHIP

Censorship is commonplace in Singapore. Pornography is forbidden, erotic displays are very rare, and the import of numerous foreign publications is not allowed. Going on strike is also illegal.

Doc. 2.45 Singapore's symbol is the statue of Merlion, half lion, half fish.

Society's influences

Synthesis

- Society is governed by a social order.

- In Canada, there are several levels of political power: the federal government, the provincial governments and the municipal councils.

- Groups, institutions and organizations use different forms of power in regards to politics, society and the economy.

- Canadians live in a democracy which is a society where citizens who have the right to vote elect the members of the government.

- Québec set up a Charter of Human Rights and Freedoms that protects the following freedoms: freedom of conscience, religion, opinion, expression, peaceful assembly and association. For its part, Canada adopted the Canadian Charter of Rights and Freedoms.

- Individuals have duties to fulfill. Among other things, they must adequately inform themselves about and respect other people's opinions.

- Social conventions are norms that indicate ways of behaviour that are considered appropriate in a society.

- A law is a written rule of conduct that must be obeyed to avoid punishment. In Québec, there are many laws for many areas of activity.

- Individual behaviour may also be governed by codes and regulations.

- Autonomy and dependency also exist at the social level–especially where it concerns emancipation and certain struggles against dependency.

- Individuals and groups may act differently in the face of social order. They might obey the law or disobey it by committing crimes through civil disobedience or through protests.

1 What responsibilities do municipal leaders assume?

2 On what elements is democratic power based?

3 Why is it said that authoritarian power interferes with people's freedom?

4 Is being a head of state enough to be considered a charismatic leader? Justify your answer.

5 In which of society's sectors of activity is cooperative power usually found?

6 What is a partnership?

7 What is the most fundamental value in a democracy?

8 What are the six fundamental freedoms listed in the Québec Charter of Human Rights and Freedoms?

9 What is "government transparency?"

10 What is the purpose of the Consumer Protection Bureau?

11 Under what circumstances can a person's right to privacy be infringed upon?

12 When someone disobeys the law, can that person avoid the consequences of their actions by saying that they were ignorant of the law in question? Why or why not?

13 What are the consequences for not respecting a social convention?

14 How can the same gesture produce different reactions?

15 Why does the government change its laws over time?

16 What level of government is responsible for the Criminal Code?

17 What is the Civil Code?

18 What is emancipation?

19 What motivates someone to obey the law?

20 What is the difference between respect for the law and conformity?

21 Why are the people who live under totalitarian rule forced to submit to authority?

22 What values can lead an individual to commit a crime?

23 What can incite people to commit acts of civil disobedience?

24 What is boycotting?

Ethical reflection

SUMMARY

3.1 The media and social order	66
3.2 The media and freedom	70
3.3 Individuals and the media	77
Culture and society	80
Here and elsewhere	82
Synthesis	84

CHAPTER 3

The influences of the media

Every day, the media comes into our lives through television, Internet, movies and other entertainment and information sources. How does the media influence our attitudes, our behaviour and how we see things? Is it concerned with ethical questions? If so, which ones?

CONNECTIONS

■ RELIGIOUS CULTURE
- Catechisms, prohibitions and taboos
- Stories: origins, characteristics and roles
- The influence of religious institutions on society

■ DIALOGUE
- Forms of dialogue: interview
- Means for developing a point of view: synthesis
- Means for examining a point of view: judgment of reality and value

What is media? How can it influence social order?
Can it bring about social change?

TO KNOW MORE +

Below are a few figures that show how much time Québec's 12 to 17 year olds devote to television and the Internet.

How many hours a week do young people spend watching TV?

- Ages 2 to 11: 16.3 hrs.
- Ages 12 to 17: 15.4 hrs.

What do young people do on the Internet?

- On average, boys surf the Internet nine hours a week, while girls devote seven hours to this activity.
- On average, two hours a week are spent on homework.
- 78% of young Internet users search for information.
- 72% exchange e-mail messages.
- 70% listen to music online or download it.
- 66% chat.
- 56% play online games.
- 54% visit sites related to their leisure activities.

Do you recognize yourself in this picture?

Reference: *Le Quotidien*, Chicoutimi, October 23, 2001 and April 5, 2003.

THE MEDIA, THE INDIVIDUAL AND SOCIETY

Every day, different types of **media** come into our lives and provide us with information. The best known and most widely-used media are the press, radio, television and Internet. They surround us everywhere in our daily lives whether at home, in transit, at school or in public places.

The media has many purposes. Some, like newspapers, radio and television serve as means of conveying daily news and keeping us informed and up-to-date on what is happening in the world. Others, like books or websites, serve to educate us. Finally, all media may also serve some entertainment purposes.

Because it is present in our daily lives, the media can have a major influence on both individuals and the society in which it exists.

Doc. 3.1 The media plays an important part in most people's daily lives.

Doc. 3.2 Teenagers devote much of their free time to the media.

Media: a collection of means for distributing information to the public (press, radio, television, movies, advertising, notices, the Internet).

THE MEDIA AND SOCIAL CHANGE

The media can bring about social change because it is a reference point. It can change our attitudes, our behaviour and our way of seeing things because it conveys values and norms. Therefore, it can influence our individual and collective identity. Let's look at a few examples that show the media's influence on individuals and society.

Stereotypes

There are times when the media creates or reinforces social stereotypes. A stereotype is an idea or opinion that is formed without question or forethought about a person or group without considering their individual characteristics. All social groups are subject to stereotyping, namely men, women, Aboriginals, **ethnic groups** and homosexuals.

Sometimes, the media conveys images and messages that have nothing to do with reality. Such pictures can contribute to reinforcing stereotypes.

For example, let's look at a stereotype of women. The women we see on television, in movies, in magazines and on the Internet are often beautiful, young and slim. Since young girls and women are bombarded daily by such images, they end up believing they should look like these models.

This is what happened to Joanne, a 14-year-old teenager who was ready to sacrifice everything to look like her feminine **ideal**. Since she really wanted to look like the women she saw on television, Joanne watched her weight. She didn't go out because she wanted to save her money to buy fashionable clothes. She also spent a great deal of time on her hair and makeup. Why did Joanne feel she had to make sacrifices to look good?

Doc. 3.4 Teenagers are also influenced by the media.

Ethnic group: a group of people who speak the same language and share the same culture.

Ideal: a model of perfection toward which we strive.

Doc. 3.3 The media influences how young girls perceive themselves.

The influences of the media

67

Doc. 3.5 Since May 31, 2006, the law has banned smoking in public places, including shopping centres and restaurants.
© Marc Dietrich/Shutterstock

© Rob Byron/Shutterstock

Doc. 3.6 The media can raise public awareness about certain social problems.

Slogan: a short phrase used to spread an idea.

Influencing values and norms

The media, be it the press, the Internet, advertising or television, can also contribute to certain changes in a society. By disseminating information, the media influences social norms by reinforcing certain ways of doing things or suggesting that citizens adopt new ones. The media may contribute to society's rejection of a certain type of behaviour by demonstrating why it is unacceptable. It can also raise public awareness about various issues. Let's look at three examples that illustrate this: smoking, drinking and sexuality.

Smoking

The Québec government has made health a priority. Since 2006, it has been battling for a smoke-free province with its *Le Québec respire mieux* campaign. Québec's anti-tobacco legislation was amended to protect non-smokers, prevent nicotine dependence in young people and reduce smoking among Quebeckers. To reach these goals, ads were published in all the media in an effort to reach as many people as possible. This issue was talked about everywhere, including in articles, on radio call-in shows, on educational programs, and on online forums. All this media coverage, along with a ban on smoking in public places, helped reduce the number of smokers.

Drinking

With the help of the media, the government and various organizations can also raise public awareness about responsible alcohol consumption. These groups also remind us of the severe penalties imposed for alcohol abuse. You have probably seen the billboards that advertise **slogans** against drinking and driving, or public affairs programming that show victims of drunk driving telling their stories. By spreading such messages, the media is helping to show how irresponsible drinking goes against social norms.

TO KNOW MORE +

Drinking and driving

The media publishes various messages related to the dangers of drinking and driving. Yet the problem persists. Below are some statistics on drinking and driving in Québec between 2002 and 2006:

- Drunk driving was the cause of 32% of all road-related deaths, 16% of serious injuries and 5% of minor injuries.

- 33% of all 16 to 24 year olds who died on the road had a blood alcohol content of more than 80 mg/ml.

Today, along with speeding, alcohol is still the cause of most traffic deaths in Québec.

Reference: *Société de l'assurance automobile du Québec*, 2008.

Sexuality

Many organizations use the media to educate the public on matters of sexuality. Radio and television broadcast regular information campaigns that address both teenagers and adults mainly on contraception and sexually transmitted diseases (STDs). Several websites also deal with these subjects. The media makes it possible for organizations considered to be experts in the field, for example, the Society of Obstetricians and Gynaecologists of Canada, to reach the public at large. The messages they transmit help eliminate certain sexual behaviours that are harmful to people and to the society in which they live.

Does all the media play an equal role in social change? You need to know that there is a difference between privately-owned media and Crown corporations. The principal mandate of a Crown corporation is to educate the public, that is, to disseminate content that is educational and of public interest. On the other hand, the mandate of privately-owned media is to make a profit. However, this does not prevent certain specialty channels from broadcasting educational programs.

The above examples on smoking, drinking and sexuality show that the media can influence social order by communicating values and norms. To do this, the media must have a certain amount of freedom.

TO KNOW MORE +

Organizations that help and support young people

The media helps advertise the organizations and services that work closely with teenagers. Below are a few of these organizations and the areas of expertise each deals with:

- **Tel-Jeune:** (hot line and website): bullying, violence, sexuality, suicide, addiction.
- **STOP** and **PASSAJ:** programs on violence and sexual harassment, love relationships, **abusive control**.
- **Canadian Association for Adolescent Health:** sexuality, communication, health, psychological help.
- **V• Go ahead, do it for yourself!:** nutrition, exercise, health.
- **Gay Line:** sexual orientation.
- **S.O.S. Pregnancy:** sexuality, contraception, pregnancy.

Abusive control: excessive control that is likely to cause harm to someone.

Doc. 3.7 The media can educate us on social norms, for example, with respect to health matters.
© Miodrag Gajic/Shutterstock

The media and freedom

Can the media publish anything they want? How do they exercise their freedom? What is the limit of this freedom? Do the media have any responsibilities? Are certain ethical issues of concern to it? Is there any tension between individual rights and the rights of the media?

Doc. 3.8 Internet usage raises many issues related to freedom of expression.

TO KNOW MORE +

Hate propaganda on the Web

In 2002, German-born Ernst Zundel, then living in Canada, used his website to spread hate propaganda against Jews. When brought to court, Zundel defended himself by stating that freedom of expression gave him the right to express his opinions. The Canadian courts ordered him to shut down his website. In defiance of the law, Zundel used a U.S.-based server to host his website. He was able to continue to spread his propaganda for many years. In 2007, having been found guilty on 14 counts, including inciting hatred and denying the **Holocaust**, he was finally convicted by a German court and sentenced to five years in prison.

Defame: to discredit someone's reputation by saying or writing things that are unfounded.

Propaganda: an action taken to provoke the public to adopt certain ideas.

Holocaust: the systematic extermination of Jews by the Nazis.

THE RIGHTS AND FREEDOMS OF THE MEDIA

The rights and freedoms of the media are closely related to the type of government in power in a given society. In a country under authoritarian rule, the media has very little freedom. They are subject to the ruling authority. However, in democratic societies, the media has a great deal of freedom. This freedom brings up many ethical issues.

Freedom of expression

The Universal Declaration of Human Rights includes the following article: "Everyone has the right to freedom of opinion and expression; this right includes freedom to hold opinions without interference and to seek, receive and impart information and ideas through any media and regardless of frontiers."

Does this freedom have limitations? Of course. Canada's Supreme Court recommends finding a proper balance between freedom of expression and the protection of human rights. For example, we must not **defame** anyone, or court proceedings may be initiated against us. This said, there is a fine line between rights and freedoms and sometimes tensions arise. Let's take hate propaganda as an example. Should the media's freedom of expression be limited to protect the public's right not to be exposed to hatred? In this regard, the Supreme Court found that democratic societies have the duty to restrict hate **propaganda** so that everyone can live freely.

The question arises: how can this norm be enforced with the proliferation of information such as blogs and forums where anything can be written?

Freedom of the press

Freedom of the press means being able to freely report and comment on events, without **interference** or fear of reprisal. The expression dates back to the time when the only means of rapidly communicating one's ideas to a large number of people was through print media. Nowadays, this freedom applies to all media.

Freedom of the press is often considered one of the cornerstones of democracy especially since it promotes **transparency** and facilitates the exchange of ideas. In Canada, the media has a great deal of freedom. For example, political commentators can criticize the government and question its decisions without fear of imprisonment. In contrast, in an authoritarian regime, this freedom is often non-existent and censorship is prevalent at almost all levels of society.

As with all freedoms, freedom of the press has its limitations. The media cannot use this freedom indiscriminately. Yet, there are times when pressure groups, individuals or businesses try to manipulate the media to their advantage. In the next section, we will see that the media, like individuals and groups, have responsibilities toward society.

Interference: an obstacle that prevents something from taking place.
Transparency: the quality which expresses reality without changing it.

The UNESCO/Guillermo Cano prize

Since 1997, the UNESCO/Guillermo Cano prize has been awarded to a person, organization or institution that defends and promotes freedom of the press. It is awarded each year on May 3, which is also World Press Freedom Day. The prize was named in honour of Guillermo Cano Isaza, director of a Colombian newspaper who was assassinated in 1986 in front of the building where he worked. Cano was targeted by the Colombian mafia for denouncing drug trafficking in his country. In 2008, the UNESCO/Guillermo Cano prize was awarded to Mexican Lydia Cacho Ribeiro, who denounced political corruption, organized crime and violence in her country.

Doc. 3.9 In Québec, the media enjoys extensive freedom of the press.

Some history

CENSORSHIP AND MOVIES IN QUÉBEC

For a long time, movies were censored in Québec. In 1913, the *"Bureau de censure des vues animées de la province de Québec"* was set up. This agency, which banned the showing of numerous films that were considered immoral, was very effective. At the time, Québec rejected more films than England, the United States and the rest of Canada combined. The Catholic Church, which was extremely influential at the time, applied a great deal of pressure on the censorship bureau. It considered movies to be a source of **corruption** for young people. Moreover, according to the Church, since movies were shown in the dark, cinema led young people into sin. In the 1940s, the government became yet another source of influence for the censorship bureau. The government censored films that dealt with political issues, all the while pursuing its **crusade** against so-called immoral films. In 1967, the censorship bureau relaxed its rules considerably. The *Régie du cinéma* is still in charge of approving films and classifying them by age. It rejects some 50 films every year.

Doc. 3.10 All media, including movies, is susceptible to censorship at some time.

Corruption: the means taken to provoke individuals to act contrary to their conscience or duty.

Crusade: a campaign undertaken to mobilize public opinion on a specific subject.

THE FIRST TELEVISED POLITICAL DEBATE

Doc. 3.11 The first televised political debate took place in the United States on September 26, 1960, pitting Senator John F. Kennedy (1917-1963) opposite Vice President Richard Nixon (1913-1994). Nearly 70 million American viewers watched the debate. This event had a major impact on politics. For the very first time, the public had a chance to see the candidates interact with each other. In Canada, the first such debate took place in 1962, pitting Daniel Johnson (1915-1968) and Jean Lesage (1912-1980) against each other during the Québec provincial elections. Since then, live televised debates have become commonplace. Politicians confront each other on live television and debate various issues. The discussion is led by a moderator, that is, a person who is in charge of moderating the debate.

THE EARLY YEARS OF CANADIAN TELEVISION

Doc. 3.12 The beginning of Canadian television took place in September 1952 when the Canadian Broadcasting Corporation broadcast its first program. Colour television first appeared here in 1967. According to the *Institut de la statistique du Québec*, in 1972, 24.2% of Canadian homes owned a TV. In 2005, the number had climbed to more than 99.0%.

Reference: *Institut de la statistique du Québec*, 2005.

RESPONSIBILITIES

Since democracy is founded on the free circulation of ideas and information, the media has a major responsibility toward its public. Also, since it has a great deal of influence on individuals and groups, it cannot publish or broadcast just anything it likes. According to the Human Rights Council, directed by the UN, the media plays a major role in promoting values such as tolerance, respect, and freedom of religion or belief. Several of the media acknowledge the importance of their responsibilities toward the public. In an effort to properly fulfill their role, they have adopted a code of ethics that stipulates that they must obey the law and any related regulations.

Codes of ethics

In Chapter 1, we saw that certain professions are governed by a code of ethics, that is, a collection of rules and duties imposed on each member of a profession. In Canada, many organizations establish codes of this type to set guidelines with respect to the freedom of the press. For example, the Canadian Association of **Broadcasters** (CAB) has established a code of ethics that defines various norms regarding, among other things, stereotypes, advertising and human rights. In addition, the CAB oversees the administration of other codes of conduct that broadcasters can comply with on a voluntary basis:

- violence in television programming
- stereotyping in television and radio programming
- advertising to children

In addition to respecting the above-mentioned codes, broadcasters can develop their own code of ethics. In fact, the Canadian Broadcasting Corporation, Canada's national public broadcaster, has established its own code of ethics which states that they are fully committed to providing information that is fair, accurate, comprehensive and balanced.

TO KNOW MORE +

Journalistic values in Québec

© Florian ISPAS/Shutterstock

In 1966, in an effort to correctly position the role of journalists, the *Fédération professionnelle des journalistes du Québec* adopted their own code of ethics. This collection of rules is based on the following fundamental values: critical viewpoint, impartiality, fairness, independence, respect for the public, compassion, honesty and open-mindedness.

Reference: *Fédération professionnelle des journalistes du Québec*, 2008.

Broadcaster: an organization that transmits television programs or radio shows.

TO KNOW MORE +

Children's advertising

The Québec Consumer Protection Act prohibits commercial advertising directed at children under the age of 13. The law also prohibits advertising of certain products (toys, candies and foods) in children's programming.

The law

Although the media voluntarily subscribes to codes of ethics, the same does not apply with respect to the law. The media must obey the law or be penalized with sanctions. Laws regarding various fields related to the media have been passed by either the federal or provincial governments. Below are some examples:

Federal laws

- Broadcasting Act
- Telecommunications Act
- Access to Information Act

Provincial laws

- Educational Programming Act
- Press Act
- Consumer Protection Act

The laws and responsibilities concerning the media are constantly changing. They take the evolution of society into account.

Doc. 3.13 Freedom of information and respect for privacy are two issues related to freedom of the press.

THE ISSUES

The media does not enjoy absolute freedom because it has certain responsibilities to assume. Its freedom is constantly confronted with such limitations, and this can cause tension and conflict. Following are two examples of issues that limit the media: freedom of information and respect for privacy.

Freedom of information

One of the media's fundamental roles is to disseminate information. On the one hand, people have the right to know what's going on in their society and elsewhere in the world. This said, should the media disseminate all the information to which they have access? Do individuals have the right to access such information?

In a democracy, access to government information is very much a fundamental right. In Canada, the State is considered to be at the service of its citizens, and as such, it is accountable to them. This was the mindset of the Gomery Commission's mission which was discussed in the previous chapter. In contrast, in other societies, access to government information is not an established right.

In our society, some information is considered confidential, that is, the media cannot disseminate it and the public does not have access to it. For example, by virtue of the Youth Protection Act, any adolescents involved in court proceedings, whether they are the accused, the victims or the witnesses, have the right to **anonymity**. However, the media sometimes has the right to circumvent this law, namely when the individual concerned is a danger to society.

This kind of situation can cause tension or conflict. For example, some people may think that they are free to access information though the latter is not considered to be in the public interest.

Doc. 3.14 In Canada, there is a law that protects the identity of young people under 18 who are involved in legal proceedings.

Anonymity: the state in which a person's identity is not made public.

TO KNOW MORE +

Identifying sex offenders

Since 2004, the government has maintained a registry of Québec's sex offenders. This registry is not available to the public. In November 2007, a petition bearing 62 000 names was submitted to the National Assembly in an effort to obtain the right for the population to have access to the information contained in this registry. The government denied this request. According to the Minister of Justice, information related to sexual offenders must only be accessible to the courts and the police. The purpose of this measure is to prevent certain people from taking the law into their own hands. Therefore, the government considered that such information is not in the public interest.

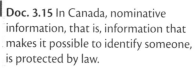

Doc. 3.15 In Canada, nominative information, that is, information that makes it possible to identify someone, is protected by law.

The influences of the media

75

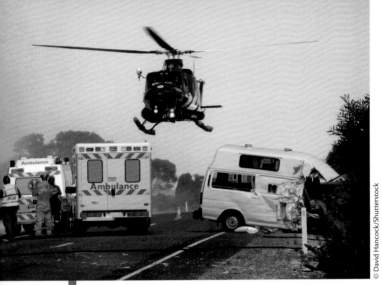

© David Hancock/Shutterstock

Doc. 3.16 Under some circumstances, the media may decide not to disclose information.

TO KNOW MORE +

The paparazzi

© Vladimir Mucibabic/Shutterstock

The term "paparazzi" comes from Federico Fellini's 1960 film *La Dolce Vita*. In this film, the main character is often accompanied by a young photographer called Paparazzo. Later, his name became synonymous with photographers who take pictures of the private lives of famous people.

Respect for privacy

Respect for privacy is also an issue related to freedom of the press. In our society, everyone has the right to have their privacy respected. However, the public has the right to be informed. So, where do we draw the line between personal information that can be divulged to the public by the media and information that should not be divulged?

Most media make the distinction between information that is of public interest and information that is simply a matter of public curiosity. For example, before publishing the details of a human tragedy (suicide, mugging, or serious accident), journalists must first ask themselves if identifying the people concerned is really necessary. Divulging the names of the victims or their loved ones might lead to unnecessary trouble.

Some media, especially those that cover famous people, is not too concerned about respect for privacy. In these situations, reporters don't hesitate to cause problems for famous people by publishing spicy details about their private lives. This is the case of the paparazzi, those photographers who hunt down stars to invade their privacy. Tabloids love this type of information. Some people are simply curious, while others feel they have the right to know what their favourite star is doing. What about the respect for privacy and freedom of the famous people being photographed?

Some history

PRINCESS DIANA'S AND DODI AL-FAYED'S ACCIDENT

In 1997, Princess Diana and Dodi Al-Fayed were killed in a car accident in France. The paparazzi that were chasing them were accused of having violated the couple's right to privacy by taking pictures of them in their car. They were also accused of photographing the car's occupants after the accident that had cost them their lives. In 2006, the French Court decided that three of the paparazzi were guilty of having violated the couple's right to privacy. The photographs taken at the time were immediately seized by the police and have never been published.

DISINFORMATION

Is the content to which you have access through the media always reliable? Do you believe everything you read on the Internet or see on television? There is a great deal of misinformation floating about, especially on the Internet, where the authors don't necessarily want to deceive anyone. Sometimes, this can simply be unintentional due to ignorance. Nevertheless, every day questionable information comes our way that is not based on actual facts and that is disseminated with the intention to deceive the public. This is called disinformation.

This phenomenon is rather rare in some types of media, as in televised newscasts, because journalists, researchers and writers verify their information. Some inaccurate information may slip by but the journalists' code of ethics prohibits them from intentionally deceiving the public.

There are many forms of disinformation but one thing never changes: that is, the authors try to pass off lies or inaccurate information as the truth. Disinformation is very prevalent on Internet hate sites, certain commercial sites, personal pages and in email. For example, you have probably received an email message that contains a virus scam or an ad for a miracle product. How do we determine the credibility of the sometimes contradictory information we receive?

Do individuals have responsibilities with respect to the media? Should we believe everything we hear or read? Can individuals exercise their autonomy where the media is concerned? Can we become dependent on the media?

Doc. 3.17
Disinformation circulates in the media, especially via the Internet.
© Jerome Scholler/Shutterstock

Some history

THE INTERNET

The Internet made its first appearance in 1969 as the U.S. Department of Defense was trying to link up the computers of the army's research centres. At first, the Internet was mainly a strategic military tool: if a war erupted and one section of the network was destroyed, it would not affect the system's overall operation. But nowadays, the Internet is an integral part of our lives. When you write a message to your friends, either through email or instant messaging, you probably use a language that is completely different from the one you use in school. This language, called SMS (short message service), was standardized in the 1990s to facilitate communication between two cellphone users. To avoid exceeding a maximum number of characters, users abbreviated words, used their **phonetic** equivalent or created word **puzzles**. Following are a few examples:

Abbreviation: ttyl = talk to you later

Phonetics: W8 = wait

Puzzle: <3 = love

Phonetics: a written representation of the sound of a word.
Puzzle: a series of words, signs or drawings that evoke the sound of a word or an expression that the recipient must guess.

TO KNOW MORE +

Counter-publicity

With the advent of the Internet, a phenomenon called counter-publicity began. An increasing number of people use cyberspace to complain about various products and services. Some people use their websites to describe their bad experiences in certain restaurants, and actually name the businesses in question. Is this legal? In 2002, Canada's Supreme Court ruled that freedom of expression authorizes citizens to use counter-publicity on the Internet and in other media.

The influences of the media

AUTONOMY

Can a person be autonomous where the content disseminated by the media is concerned? Of course! An autonomous person applies critical judgment with regards to whatever is said or written in the media. Autonomous individuals also show common sense with respect to both media content and its use. These same people can use the media to promote their own values and to make enlightened choices.

The example below is a good illustration of an individual's autonomy with regards to the media. Mark receives an email that contains an ad for a meal replacement drink that claims to dramatically increase muscle mass. According to the ad, muscle size will increase in no time and without any effort. There are several photographs of people before and after taking the advertised product. The results are spectacular! Mark is interested, but since his health is important to him, he wonders if the claim is too good to be true. On the Internet, he finds several sites where people are complaining about being deceived by this company, and when he consults the Canadian Food Guide, he realizes that the drink in question doesn't contain nearly enough of the nutrients needed for good health. Mark decides that this is a case of false advertising.

Doc. 3.18 A person can be autonomous with regards to the media.

Doc. 3.19 If individuals use critical judgment, they can be autonomous with regards to the media.

ADDICTION

Did you know that people can become addicted to the media? Previously in this chapter, we saw that television and radio can be very attractive to some people. Sometimes these people reach a point where they can't do without them. Media addiction can be even more harmful. Let's look at cyber-addiction, for example.

Cyber-addiction

Cyber-addiction consists of an excessive dependence on the Internet. It's not simply liking to surf the Internet; it's also not being able to get along without it, and eventually not having enough time for loved ones. It's feeling empty or depressed when deprived from using the computer, lying about activities to keep this addiction from being discovered, or even going as far as neglecting your health. People can become dependent on the Internet because they abuse it in various ways, especially with online games, auction sites or virtual communities.

Cedric's case is an example of addiction to virtual communities. This young boy lacks self-confidence. He's shy and doesn't know how to approach others. He spends his evenings in front of his computer and lives an online social life that he doesn't have in the real world. He has created a very confident character for himself and writes to people on several different sites. His life on the Internet occupies so much of his time that he never wants to go out. When he doesn't have access to his computer, Cedric gets depressed. He develops physical symptoms such as a sore back, dry eyes, and insomnia because he is in front of his screen for so long. His mother believes his obsession is unhealthy because it helps him escape reality. In contrast, Cedric believes that the Internet allows him to be more self-sufficient because he doesn't need people around him to have a social life. What do you think about all this?

© Killroy Productions/Shutterstock

Doc. 3.20 Cyber-addiction can lead to isolation and cause people to neglect their health.

TO FIND OUT MORE +

Cyber-addiction

Cyber-addiction is not well known in Québec. According to the *Centre québécois de lutte contre les dépendances*, this problem is growing very rapidly. In 2008, an estimated 6% of the 4 million Quebeckers who use the Internet were cyber-addicted. Cyber-addiction mainly affects single men in their thirties. According to a study by the University of Pittsburgh, cyber-addicts spend an average of 38 hours per week on the Internet while other users spend only eight hours on the same activity. In some countries, like the United States, France and Holland, the government has opened rehabilitation clinics for cyber-addicts. In Québec, there are currently no such clinics.

References: *Le Devoir*, Montréal, November 3, 2006 and *Banque de terminologie du Québec de l'Office québécois de la langue française*, 2008.

Culture and society

Freedom of expression, information and the press are not respected in all circumstances. Sometimes, freedom of the press and freedom of expression are blatantly disregarded. The two examples that follow concern the written press, that is, journalists and poetry.

Journalists and freedom of the press

Freedom of the press is not respected everywhere in the world. According to the UN, the 10 countries in which the press is most censored are: North Korea, Burma, Turkmenistan, Equatorial Guinea, Libya, Eritrea, Cuba, Uzbekistan, Syria and Belarus. In many countries, the price for freedom of the press is very high. According to Reporters Without Borders–an organization which defends freedom of the press everywhere in the world–between 2003 and 2007, 209 media professionals (journalists, photographers and others) were assassinated in Iraq; two disappeared and 14 were kidnapped. Do you think Canadian journalists are sheltered from threats? Below are the stories of three Canadian journalists who suffered reprisals because of their work here or in another country. Note that assassination attempts on journalists don't have the same impact if they are perpetrated by criminals rather than by the State. Because Jean-Pierre Charbonneau and Michel Auger were being threatened by criminal elements, they were protected by the police. But Zahra Kazemi fought against the Iranian governmental apparatus.

Jean-Pierre Charbonneau (1950-   )

During the 1970s, journalist Jean-Pierre Charbonneau, who was then investigating organized crime, published several shocking articles denouncing the activities of certain criminal groups. On May 1, 1973, a Montréal Mafia sympathizer shot him in the arm in the newsroom of the French newspaper *Le Devoir*. Despite this attempt on his life, Jean-Pierre Charbonneau continued his investigation of organized crime and also pursued a career in provincial politics before returning to the media where he continues to work.

David Boily/La Presse

Michel Auger (1944-   )

In the 1960s, journalist Michel Auger covered legal affairs and the crime world for the French newspaper *Le Journal de Montréal*. On September 13, 2000, he was struck by six bullets as he walked through the newspaper's parking lot. His injuries were very serious, but he survived. This attempt on his life urged him to pursue his unrelenting struggle to bring down organized crime. Michel Auger retired in 2006.

Photo Le Journal de Montréal/Pascal Ratthé

Zahra Kazemi (1948-2003)

While working in Iran, this Iranian-Canadian photojournalist was imprisoned, beaten, and finally murdered. She was arrested for taking pictures of families of detainees being held in Iran's Evin Prison. In 2005, a collection of photos taken by Zahra Kazemi was shown at the *Contre l'oubli (Lest We Forget)* exhibit presented at Montréal's Côte Saint-Luc library. Just a few days later, the people in charge of the exhibit decided to close it because they felt it included controversial images.

© Reuters/Corbis

Poetry of commitment and censorship

Do you think that freedom of expression only concerns the mass media? You should know that some authors have also been victims of censorship. This is especially the case with poets. In many countries, poets are arrested, imprisoned or exiled because of their controversial writings.

■ Frankétienne (1936-   )

"I have always expressed myself freely because, at the risk of losing my life, I have chosen to let others know what I have to say."

This Haitian poet, playwright and professor has published some thirty poems in French and in Creole. He was under house arrest in his own country for 20 years for denouncing the Duvaliers' political regime. His play, *Pèlin-Tèt*, contributed greatly to freedom of speech in Haiti.

■ Henri Lopès (1937-   )

"There are two sayings from home that I like to repeat to myself: When you talk too much, no one listens and when you speak, take pity on those who are listening."

Henri Lopès is a poet, writer and Métis diplomat originally from the Republic of Congo, a country where freedom of expression and freedom of the press are often disregarded. Lopès is a distinguished figure in contemporary African literature. He has written extensively about the Métis identity, a subject that is taboo in Africa:

■ Tahar Bekri (1951-   )

"My most recent book is a denunciation of the denial of freedom and of art in the world. It's a poetic statement because I have no other language."

Tunisian poet, Tahar Bekri writes in French and in Arabic. He has been in exile in France since 1976. Bekri is considered one of the important voices of the **Maghreb**. His work has been translated into several languages, including Russian, English, Italian and Turkish.

References: Interviews with Michel Morin and Frankétienne, Henri Lopès, and Tahar Bekri, *Chez nous le matin*, Canadian Broadcasting Corporation, May 2008.

Some history

THE DUVALIERS' REGIME IN HAITI

François Duvalier (1907-1971) was President of Haiti from 1957 to 1964 and dictator from 1964 to 1971. When he died, his son, Jean-Claude, took power, which he held until 1986. The Duvaliers' regime was marked by violence and repression.

Maghreb: The Maghreb is made up of various countries in northwest Africa: Libya, Tunisia, Algeria, Morocco and Mauritania.

Doc. 3.21 Poets can also be victims of censorship.

The influences of the media

The Russian State and media control

Under some governments, the media has a great deal of freedom. But this is not the case in all countries, as seen in places such as the Russian Federation, a state that calls itself democratic.

The Russian Federation in a nutshell

Population: 143 221 000

Currency: Ruble

Area: 17 075 400 km²

Capital: Moscow

Language: Russian

Head of State: Dmitri Medvedev has been President since March 2008.

© argus/Shutterstock

Doc. 3.22 The Russian flag.

Back in the days of the USSR when the people lived under a dictatorship, the media was all under government rule. In principle, the Russian Federation has since become a democratic regime, but the situation with the media has not changed much. Admittedly, its people now have access to foreign media, which was not the case under the old regime, but the government still controls most Russian media. In fact, several organizations, for example, Reporters Without Borders, have accused the Russian government of bullying the press.

THE RUSSIAN MEDIA EMPIRE

Two of the three press agencies in the country are controlled by the state: ITAR-Tass, which now has the status of Crown Corporation and RIA Novosti, an information agency managed by the Russian Press and Information Ministry. The government also owns three television stations: Channel One, TV Centre (TVC) and VGTRK which has approximately 80 million viewers.

THE GAZPROM MEDIA EMPIRE

Russia's natural gas production and transport company, Gazprom, owns numerous media. This giant monopoly is privately owned, but 50.1% of its shares are held by the State. Gazprom owns three newspapers, a television company and a 66% share in a radio station.

Doc. 3.23 The Kremlin is Russia's political headquarters. Located in the heart of Moscow and enclosed by a brick wall, the Kremlin includes many historical monuments, among them a theatre as well as a number of cathedrals and palaces.

© AKV/Shutterstock

LAWS THAT IMPOSE CENSORSHIP ON THE MEDIA

Over the past few years, the Russian government has passed several laws that censor the media. One media-related law that went into effect in 2002 bans any media that is deemed to be extreme. Another law, passed in 2003, bans the media from voicing their opinion of the candidates during an election period.

CLOSURE AND CENSORSHIP

In 2002, the Russian State shut down an independent television station, TV6, for being very critical of the government in power. That same year, the Press and Information Ministry allegedly prevented another station from broadcasting an interview with a member of a Chechen commando group. The Ministry banned the interview because Chechnya is a region of Russia that was torn apart by civil war when Chechen rebels tried to achieve independence through armed combat.

THE BESLAN HOSTAGE CRISIS

In September 2004, a Beslan school was taken hostage by Chechen rebels. A few days later, Russian security forces stormed into the building, causing the death of some 350 hostages, 185 of them children. According to Reporters Without Borders, the two Russian journalists who were experts on the Chechen issue were deliberately kept away from the school. Anna Politkovskaya was poisoned and had to be hospitalized for several days. Andreï Babitski was jailed because the police suspected him of transporting explosives. Following an investigation, he was released but when he left the prison, a fight broke out, and Babitski was arrested again. Anna Politkovskaya was assassinated in 2006.

© Alex Kapranoff/Shutterstock

Doc. 3.24 The Ostankino television tower is 540 metres high and after Toronto's CN Tower, is the second tallest self-supporting tower in the world.

© EDUARD KORNIENKO/Reuters/Corbis

Doc. 3.25 The media covered the trial of the terrorists responsible for the Beslan hostage crisis. In this picture, a child testifies in the Vladikavkaz court under the watchful eye of the cameras.

Synthesis

- Every day, the media comes into our lives and provides us with information.

- By communicating values and norms, the media can influence people's attitudes, behaviour and ways of seeing things.

- The media can create, destroy or reinforce stereotypes.

- A stereotype is an idea or an opinion formed without question or forethought about a person or group without considering their individual characteristics.

- The media can have an influence on how people perceive themselves.

- The media can contribute to social change, particularly in regards to smoking, drinking and sexuality.

- In Canada, the media enjoys a great deal of freedom of expression.

- Freedom of expression has its limitations: there must be a balance between freedom of expression and the protection of human rights.

- In Canada, the media enjoys freedom of the press which means the media can freely report and comment on events without hindrance or fear of reprisal.

- The responsibilities of the media are defined in the codes of ethics it adopts and the laws with which it must comply.

- Certain ethical issues are of concern to the media. Freedom of information and respect for privacy are two examples.

- Media-related issues can be a source of tension.

- Disinformation can sometimes be found in the media.

- An autonomous person applies critical judgment and common sense to what is disseminated by the media.

- Some people develop an addiction to the media. For example, a cyber-addict is excessively dependent on the Internet.

1. What are the four main types of media found in society?

2. Do stereotypes reflect reality? Justify your answer.

3. Why are some people influenced by the stereotypes found in the media?

4. How can the media influence a society's values and norms?

5. What was the media's role in the government's *Le Québec respire mieux* campaign?

6. What is the message behind advertisements that deal with impaired driving?

7. What is the relationship between a society's form of government and the rights and freedoms of the media?

8. Does freedom of expression allow the media to defame someone? Why?

9. What is hate propaganda?

10. In a democratic society, what freedom makes it possible for the press to report and comment on events without fear of reprisal?

11. According to the UN, what values must the media promote?

12. On what values is the code of ethics of the *Fédération professionnelle des journalistes du Québec* based?

13. Is the federal government the only government to pass laws regarding the media? Justify your answer.

14. What law prohibits commercial advertising directed at children under the age of 13?

15. In Canada, does the public have access to government information? Why?

16. What is the difference between information that is of public interest and information that is simply curiosity on the part of the public?

17. Do the media always release the names of the people involved in human tragedies? Why?

18. What are paparazzi?

19. Are the paparazzi allowed to infringe upon someone's right to privacy? Why?

20. Is disinformation prevalent in television newscasts? Why?

21. What makes it possible for individuals to exercise their autonomy where the media are concerned?

22. What is the term used to refer to Internet addiction?

Religious culture

Heritage from the past or present-day treasure?

ELEMENTARY CYCLE 1

FAMILY CELEBRATIONS	• Celebrations (Chapter 4) • Rituals associated with birth (Chapter 5)
STORIES THAT HAVE TOUCHED PEOPLE	• Stories that have a major influence (Chapter 6) • Stories about key figures (Chapter 6)

ELEMENTARY CYCLE 2

RELIGIOUS PRACTICES IN THE COMMUNITY	• Places of worship where religious practices take place (Chapter 5) • A time for celebrations (Chapter 4) • Places of worship, religious objects and symbols (Chapter 5) • Practices of prayer and meditation (Chapter 4)
FORMS OF RELIGIOUS EXPRESSION IN THE YOUNG PERSON'S ENVIRONMENT	• The physical environment (Chapter 5) • Cultural forms of expression (Chapters 5 and 6) • Stories about the origin of the world (Chapter 5)

ELEMENTARY CYCLE 3

RELIGIOUS VALUES AND NORMS	• Values and norms (Chapter 4) • Exemplary individuals and their works (Chapter 5) • Practices related to food and clothing (Chapter 5)

- Easter, Christmas, Thanksgiving, Passover, Sukkot, Eid al-Fitr, Hanukkah, birth of Guru Nanak, New Year's Day, birthday
- Baptism, naming a baby girl, circumcision, characteristics of the name given by a shaman, horoscope

- stories related to religious holidays (Three Wise Men, Maccabees, sacrifice of Ishmael), foundational texts (Noah and the Flood, the Beaver Who Steals Fire, Muhammad's first revelation), cultural references related to influential stories (Noah's Ark, menorah)
- Annunciation, birth of Jesus, birth of Moses, birth of Siddhartha Gautama

- mosque, temple, church, synagogue, pagoda, chapel, cathedral, Buddhist temple
- Mass, First Communion, Divine Service, funerals, Sabbath, Friday prayer
- the Cross, the Star of David, the Crescent, the menorah, calligraphy of the name Allah, eight-spoked wheel, the kirpan, the khanda

- names for the divine (God, Adonai, Allah, Brahma, Shiva, Vishnu)
- Scriptures (the Bible, the Torah, the Koran, the Tripitaka, the Vedas)
- ablutions, prayer positions, contemplation, rosary, drum, prayer rug, prayer wheels, the Lord's Prayer, reading the Bible, Shema Yisrael, giving thanks

- monuments, buildings, toponymy
- works of art, community works, cultural events related to religion
- symbols and images representing the creation of the world, stories about the creation of the world, cultural references associated with representations of the creation of the world

- parables, the two most important commandments, the norm associated with love for others, the Ten Commandments, the Five Pillars of Islam, Dharma, the sacred character of the individual, the individual as the strength of a group
- Vincent de Paul, helping the less fortunate; Mother Theresa, helping the less fortunate; Martin Luther King Jr. and the fight for civil rights; Henri Dunant, founder of the Red Cross; Gandhi and the Dalai Lama and the use of passive resistance to achieve independence for their countries; and Elie Wiesel and human rights
- symbolism associated with certain food-related practices (fasting, Lent, Ramadan, Christmas Eve), food-related rules (fat and lean days, Kosher laws, vegetarianism, halal), dress-related practices, symbolism and rules associated with those practices (colour, baptismal clothing, mourning clothing, pastor's robe, kippa, turban, veil, tilak)

The phenomenon of religion

SUMMARY

4.1 The influence of religious institutions on the family	92
4.2 Religious traditions, values and norms	96
4.3 Prohibitions and taboos	100
Culture and society	104
Here and elsewhere	106
Synthesis	108

CHAPTER 4

Influences on values and norms

How can religious values influence our behaviour where family, love, economics and ecology are concerned? How do we experience the norms and values of cultural heritage?

CONNECTIONS

■ ETHICS

- The values and norms of groups, institutions and organizations

- Transformation of values and norms

- Individuals and groups

- Rights and obligations: tenets, rules of conduct, laws

■ DIALOGUE

- Forms of dialogue: panel

- Means for examining a point of view: types of judgments

- Conditions that foster dialogue

4.1 The influence of religious institutions on the family

Religion has a definite influence on our personal environment. What is the source of this influence and why does it persist?

Doc. 4.2 Some religious communities specialized in nursing care. Shown here is a hospital for abandoned children who were cared for by the Catholic congregation of the Sisters of Providence.

Doc. 4.1 As soon as they started school, Québec children were taken charge of by nuns or by laypeople. Pictured are students who were part of the Sainte-Marie Convent Choir in the 1950s. A nun is leading the choir.

A 400-YEAR PRESENCE

The family, a person's first social circle, is especially influenced by religious traditions. In fact, family values and traditions were forged over the centuries by those who came before us.

A major force in society

The history of the Québec family has been marked by very close ties to religion. When New France first came into being, religion was a very large part of the lives of its inhabitants, both for Catholics and, for Protestants, at the beginning in the late 18th century. The Catholic Church shaped beliefs as well as attitudes and value of individuals and the community alike. The reason for this enormous influence was in part due to the omnipresence of the Church in education, healthcare, and care of the poor, the elderly and orphans.

The Catholic Church and its clergy were also invested in other major spheres of society. During the 19th century and the entire first half of the 20th century, the Catholic Church had a major influence on trade unions, journalism, the social economy and politics.

Did you know that the clergy even played a part in the creation of the Caisses populaires? The Catholic Church was an integral part of life in Québec society.

Doc. 4.3 In 1955, dignitaries of the Catholic clergy, including Paul-Émile, Cardinal Léger, attended a celebration in the company of Montréal Mayor Jean Drapeau (left), and Québec Premier Maurice Duplessis (right).

The omnipresence of parish priests

Parish priests were not simply spiritual leaders; they were important figures in parish life and often the most educated individuals in the village. They also had a great deal of authority where their parishioners were concerned.

The parish priest heard the faithful **confess** their **sins**. At different times, he was a referee, a teacher, a notary and an administrator. He regularly collected the **tithe**. He also made sure the faithful practised their religion, attended **Mass** and celebrated Catholic feast days. In some parishes, the parish priest even helped with family life, especially regarding a couple's duty to have many children. In fact, this aspect of the parish priest's life is often depicted in films and television series about that era.

Individual Collection

Doc. 4.4 During the second half of the 19th century, schools were no longer administered solely by religious congregations. Lay teachers replaced the nuns and priests. Now, in Québec, all public schools are run by laypeople.

For a long time, French-Canadian values were dictated by the Catholic Church. Following the conquest of Québec in 1760, in a society that would henceforth be dominated by a Protestant and Anglophone bourgeoisie, the clergy tried to find a way to protect Catholicism. Their solution was to safeguard and promote traditionalism, the French language, agriculture, morals and conservative customs.

The end of an era

Midway through the 20th century, an era marked by the **Quiet Revolution** and the **secularization** of institutions, Catholic and Protestant churches lost their power over society and its institutions. Their numbers dwindled. Judaism, which at that time was the third largest religious group in Québec, was not spared. Like many Christian churches, many synagogues were emptied.

Today, in spite of everything, Christian churches still play an evangelical role. All churches preside over the celebration of their respective religious rites. They are active in many private institutions, where they teach and do charitable work.

(to) Confess: in Catholicism, the confession of one's sins to a priest to obtain forgiveness.

Sin: a transgression of a divine law.

Tithe: an amount of money or a portion of the harvest collected by the Catholic Church. This contribution to the Church served to support the Church's clergy and help the poor.

Mass: a ritual ceremony of the Catholic religion, celebrated by a priest who offers God some bread and wine that, through consecration, becomes the body and blood of Christ.

Secularization: the action of secularizing, of making secular, of removing the religious aspect. A secular person (or layperson) is someone who is not part of the clergy.

Some history

The **Quiet Revolution** refers to the historical period that began in June 1960 when the Québec Liberal Party and its leader, Jean Lesage, took power. It marked the end of the "Great Darkness." These were the years when Maurice Duplessis, Leader of Union Nationale Party and Premier for nearly 20 years, was in power. At the time, the Union Nationale (now defunct) had very close ties to the Catholic Church whose traditional values it shared. With the election of the Liberal Party, these ties to the clergy were cut. The government became more involved in the affairs of the State and Québec opened its doors to the modern world. This period was a very important one politically, economically, socially and culturally.

Doc. 4.6 A June 24 *Fête Nationale* parade in Montréal.

TO KNOW MORE +

The Festival of Lights, or **Hanukkah,** is a Jewish holiday that is celebrated in December. This festival commemorates the return of the Jews to the Holy Temple of Jerusalem in the year 165 BCE. During this celebration, the Jewish community observes a variety of traditions. Families gather every evening for eight days to light one of the Hanukkah candles on the Menorah, an eight-branched candelabra. They begin by lighting the middle candle called the "shamash," which is then used to light the others. Hymns are sung. Children play with little tops called dreidels. Eating sweet doughnuts is another tradition.

Faith: a belief or conviction.

Doc. 4.5 Children lighting a Hanukkah candle during the Festival of Lights. On the table, the small tops (dreidels) can be seen.

FROM RELIGIOUS TRADITION TO FAMILY TRADITION

Family customs are sometimes influenced by religious traditions. Though you may not realize it, some of your family traditions originally come from religious practices.

The rituals involved in the practice of a given **faith** are often part of family life even though many religions consider faith to be a very personal matter. For some, these practices have an important religious meaning while for others, they have become family celebrations with no religious connotation. They have become customs that families carry on and pass down from one generation to another. This is true of well-known religious feasts such as Easter and Christmas for Christians and Protestants or **Hanukkah** for Jews.

Other celebrations and cultural traditions also stem from religious rites. For example, Québec's *Fête Nationale*, previously known as the feast of **St. John the Baptist**, as well as St. Patrick's Day, the patron saint of the Irish celebrated on March 17, or the Acadians' National Day celebrated on August 15, the day of the Assumption.

Some history

Over 2000 years ago, the summer solstice was marked by a pagan feast. With the arrival of Christianity, this feast was assimilated by the feast of St. John the Baptist, which was also celebrated at that time. This feast day was very popular in France where the king lit the St. John bonfire himself. The settlers of New France kept this custom alive.

On June 24, 1834, in an effort to make the feast day of St. John the Baptist a national holiday, patriot Ludger Duvernay organized a banquet in Montréal. This celebration was held yearly, but it was only in 1925 that June 24 became a statutory holiday. Then in 1977, the feast day of St. John the Baptist officially became known as *Fête Nationale*. Although this holiday has lost its Christian character, Mass is still celebrated in many towns and villages on June 24.

A day of rest and prayer

Many families have the habit of gathering around the dinner table for a good **Sunday** meal. These **weekly** gatherings, which take place on Saturday in Jewish families, also have religious roots.

In Christian families

Over time, Sunday, a day of worship and rest for Christians, has taken on a special significance for many families. For Catholics, Protestants and Orthodox Christians, Sunday is the day on which **services** take place in many churches and places of worship. In the past, working on Sunday was forbidden, but this is no longer true today.

In Jewish families

Saturday, which is known as the Sabbath, is a weekly day of worship for Jews. The Sabbath is the day on which all work stops from sunset on Friday to sunset on Saturday. It is a day for prayer and also for celebrating and rejoicing. Jews worship in synagogues.

In Muslim families

Friday is the day on which Muslims gather to pray. Their collective prayer takes place in a mosque, in the middle of the day. The men are obliged to attend. It is not forbidden to work before or after prayer. Although Friday is a special day, the Muslim Friday cannot be compared to the Jewish Sabbath or the Christian Sunday.

Keeping pace with religious traditions

The celebration of certain religious rites, such as the ceremonies that mark the arrival of a newborn, a marriage or a funeral, are all rites of passage that are part of family traditions. For some, the religious nature of the rite is important, and these rituals are also an occasion for families to get together. For others, the religious aspect is less important, and these rituals become occasions to share precious moments with loved ones. Even with the feasts and customs that have changed over time, we can still see religious traditions keeping pace with family and social life today.

Doc. 4.8 A Catholic priest celebrates mass.

Sunday: from Latin, *dies solis*, which means "day of the sun."
Weekly: takes place every week.
Service: a ceremony of worship in a given religion.

Doc. 4.7 Sunday prayer in a Christian Orthodox church.

4.2 Religious traditions, values and norms

Is the influence that religious traditions have on values and behaviour as great as the influence they have on the family? Why?

Judeo-Christian: that which falls within both Jewish and Christian spiritual values. Catholic, Protestant and Orthodox churches are all Christian churches.

Principle: a rule of conduct that is based on values that influence a person's or a group's behaviour.

Tenet (precept): a statement that expresses a teaching, a rule or a way of doing things.

SOCIAL RULES, RELIGIOUS VALUES

When we think about it, we realize that the values and norms of present-day society have **Judeo-Christian** attributes. The values and **principles** of Christianity are at the very core of our moral codes, those collections of rules that guide us both as individuals and as members of a community. Wouldn't you say that the following describe a responsible person: sharing, helping a neighbour, respecting others, forgiveness, being honest, and giving to the less fortunate? At one time, we would have said all of this makes a good Christian since the norms of the Catholic Church were at the very heart of the workings of society.

Many social rules are based on values conveyed through religious traditions. Surely, this is true for some of the regulations in your school's code of conduct or in the youth centres you attend. Codes of conduct generally include politeness and respect for others, but also include respect for physical premises and everything inside them.

Just think about the laws imposed by our legal system. Obviously, the purpose of these laws is to maintain social order but many of them are reminiscent of the great Judeo-Christian **tenets**, especially those contained in the **Ten Commandments:** Thou shalt not kill, Thou shalt not steal, etc. These tenets are universal in that they can be found in other religions.

TO KNOW MORE +

According to the Christian and Jewish religions, the Ten Commandments are the rules that God gave to Moses on Mount Sinai. Below is the ancient Biblical version:

20.3 Thou shalt have no other gods before Me.

20.7 Thou shalt not take the name of the Lord, thy God, in vain, for the Lord shall not hold him guiltless that taketh His Name in vain.

20.8 Remember the Sabbath day and keep it holy.

20.9 Six days shall thou labour, and do all thy work. But the seventh day is the Sabbath of the Lord. In it you shall not do any work, you, nor your son, nor your daughter, nor your manservant, nor your maidservant, nor your cattle, nor the stranger that is within your gates.

20.11 For in six days the Lord made Heaven and Earth, the sea, and all that in them is, and rested the seventh day: wherefore the Lord blessed the Sabbath day, and hallowed it.

20.12 Honour thy father and thy mother that thy days may be long upon the land which the Lord, thy God, giveth thee.

20.13 Thou shalt not kill.

20.14 Thou shalt not commit adultery.

20.15 Thou shalt not steal.

20.16 Thou shalt not bear false witness against thy neighbour.

20.17 Thou shalt not covet thy neighbour's house; thou shalt not covet thy neighbour's wife nor his manservant, nor his maidservant, nor his ox, nor his ass, nor any thing that is thy neighbour's.

Exodus 20: 3-17

Doc. 4.9 Norms that concern the family are constantly changing.

Moral codes and rules of conduct

There is an undeniable difference between our moral codes and the rules we've established to ensure the proper functioning of our society. This difference is in the consequences that must be faced for disobeying these rules. A thief found guilty must pay a fine, do some community work or go to prison.

People who disrespect others or who don't help those in need are not always punished, except perhaps through the guilt or shame they may feel afterwards.

Values for their time

Of course, some values and norms are still faithful to those taught in Christian churches. However, nowadays many religious tenets are being questioned.

Whether or not they are of religious origin, values change as times and **ideologies** change. Some norms based on religious tradition have disappeared over time. Take divorce, for example, which many religions condemn. For a long time, it was forbidden under Canadian law. Nowadays, not everyone agrees with this norm, and divorcees are no longer considered marginal in society. In 1969, for every 100 marriages there were 8.8 divorces. Thirty-five years later, the number was 53.5*.

Norms that were acceptable at one time may now seem a little strange to us. For example, did you know that at one time the Catholic Church compiled a list of literary and scientific works that Catholics were forbidden to read? This list, called the *Index*, existed between 1559 and 1966. The Catholic Church also condemned certain types of music like rock 'n' roll even though it was all the rage for your grandparents.

*Source: Statistics Canada

Doc. 4.10 Our behaviour is governed not only by moral codes, but also by the law of the land.

Ideology: a collection of philosophical, social, political, moral, religious and other ideas that are specific to a given period or social group.

© Veronika Vasilyuk/Shutterstock

Doc. 4.11 Christianity has always associated the sky with heaven, God and good. Following are some Quebécois expressions to that effect: "earning a place in heaven," "a gift from heaven," "go to heaven," "pray to heaven," etc.

Piety: a feeling of devotion and respect for God and all things religious.

Hell: in Christian tradition, a place of pain and turmoil for the damned.

"Earning a place in heaven"

The importance granted to Christian piety, especially that of Catholics, has long been at the core of Québec society's norms. The Catholic Church has always wanted that children were taught the tenets of Catholicism.

In the past, taking part in the religious life of the parish was compulsory for all Catholics. The clergy ensured that the faithful attended Mass, prayed, went to confession, paid tithes, celebrated religious feast days, and behaved in accordance with the teachings of the Church. This reflected the rules of conduct observed by Catholics, who made up most of the population. It was the only way for people to "earn their place in heaven," that is, after their death, to be able to go to heaven and stay there forever, rather than go to hell.

Different times, different morals

Many Christians still practise their religion. Although, sometimes, the way they celebrate their faith has changed with the values and norms of society. Living one's faith has become a far more personal act. There are many ways of living one's spirituality.

Québec's opening up to the world and the arrival of a large number of immigrants have allowed people to discover other religions and other forms of spirituality. These changes have also contributed to the transformation of values and norms.

TO KNOW MORE +

Catechisms are doctrinal manuals written by the Christian churches. They teach the faithful what they must believe and do to lead a Christian life. They include the Ten Commandments. In the past, the *Small Children's Catechism* introduced the teachings of the Catholic Church in the form of questions and answers that children had to memorize.

CHAPTER 4

DIFFERENT VALUES AND COMMON VALUES

The values underscoring religious beliefs bear witness in part to the culture from which they come. Some values and norms vary from one religion to another. What is insignificant for the believers of one religion may be very important for those of another. There are also values which are similar in many religions.

Native Spirituality

Native Spirituality is a good example of a vision that is different from those of other religious cultures. The spiritual traditions of Amerindians and Inuit are passed down by word of mouth from generation to generation. For most Aboriginals, the Earth is the mother of all life. Plants and animals have a spirit that must be respected, honoured and cared for. Amerindian and Inuit beliefs are indicative of the tremendous consideration they have for nature and all things in it. This respect for the Earth dictates their rules of conduct and guides their behaviour.

For example, since it is nature that feeds, clothes, shelters and heals humankind, there is **interdependence** between humans and nature. Exploiting or disrespecting these resources too much would lead to their disappearance and, as a result, the disappearance of mankind.

For Aboriginals, all living things have their own spirit and personality. The fruits of the Earth grow, live, die and return to Earth. This idea is what makes Aboriginals comply with the laws of nature and its cycle of renewal.

Animals are very important to Aboriginals. They are valuable for their meat, their skin, their fur and their great symbolic value. Animals are a source of inspiration. Depending on the nation, individuals are associated with a certain animal totem. This animal totem protects, guides and gives courage to the individual who bears its name. Individuals share the characteristic attributes of their animal totem.

The preaching of the gospel by Catholic and Protestant missionaries explains why nowadays, many Amerindian and Inuit communities are Christian. However, traditional spirituality is still present; in fact, it is seeing a resurgence in many communities.

Native: said of a people that have always lived in a given country. The Amerindians and the Inuit are Canada's Aboriginal Peoples.

Interdependence: dependence on each other.

© Scott Kapich/Shutterstock

■ **Doc. 4.12** The bear is symbolic of primal power, introspection and inner strength.

© James R. Hearn/Shutterstock

■ **Doc. 4.13** The wolf represents loyalty and fidelity.

4.3 Prohibitions and taboos

The influence of religion is felt in prohibitions, taboos and even social constraints. Is this the same everywhere? Why?

Blasphemous: that which bears outrage upon the divine, the sacred or religion. Blasphemy can also be an insult toward someone who is respectable.

Swear word: a blasphemous or rude expression.

Consecrate: to make sacred.

Doc. 4.14 The chalice (*le calice*) is a cup that contains the **consecrated** wine during mass.

BELIEFS AND CONSTRAINTS

The influence of religion on behaviour is not limited to traditions and values. It also affects prohibitions, taboos and social constraints. Some prohibitions are common to more than one religion. Whether or not they are respected depends on the community, the environment, the family and the individual.

Dictated by our beliefs, prohibitions influence the way we think, behave and express ourselves to a greater or less degree. Depending on the religious belief, clothing, food and medical treatment are also affected by prohibitions.

CURSING, IS IT SACRED?

The vocabulary of French-speaking Quebeckers includes words that have long been condemned by the Catholic Church under pain of punishment. These curses, **blasphemous** words, were first heard in Québec during the 19th century. These words refer to the Church's religious artefacts: the chalice, the tabernacle, the ciborium, the host or other words that are part of the religious vocabulary, such as baptism or sacrament. For many Catholics, these **swear words** break one of the Ten Commandments that states that the Lord's name must not be taken in vain.

You have surely heard these Québecois curses. Did you know from where these words originated? You will find some examples on these two pages.

Doc. 4.16 Christ is one of the titles given to Jesus. The word Christ signifies the "anointed", he who received anointment.

Doc. 4.15 The Calvary (*le calvaire*) is a representation of the crucifixion of Jesus. Such representations are usually found in cemeteries or at the intersection of two roads. Since it is the place where Jesus was put to death, a Calvary represents His crucifixion.

"Diluted" swear words

Pressured by the Catholic clergy who prohibited the use of these blasphemous swear words, people changed them in an attempt to make them less offensive: "tabarnouche" replaced tabernacle, "batèche" replaced baptism, "clisse" replaced Christ, etc.

Although many swear words typically used in Québec are still around, they have lost much of their blasphemous character. They are now used by people of different religions. Even though these curse words have lost their sacred symbolism for most people, their use is still considered inappropriate and generally in poor taste.

All religions have prohibitions

Bans on words with a religious connotation are not unique to Québec society. They existed in France before New France came into being and still exist today in most cultures and religions.

For example, Judaism forbids uttering or writing down the name of the Creator. It is also forbidden to represent the Creator in images, icons or statues. Islam also forbids any representation of God. According to a great number of schools that interpret Islamic law, it is also forbidden to represent the Prophet Muhammad. Failure to obey this rule can be considered blasphemous.

Doc. 4.18 The **ciborium** (*le ciboire*) is a covered vessel in which the consecrated bread is kept.

Doc. 4.19 A **host** (*une hostie*) is a round piece of unleavened bread that, once it has been consecrated, is essentially consumed by Catholics during **communion**.

Communion: the part of the Catholic and Orthodox mass or Protestant service during which the faithful receive consecrated bread.

Doc. 4.17 The **tabernacle** (*le tabernacle*) is a small cupboard that houses the ciborium.

Influences on values and norms

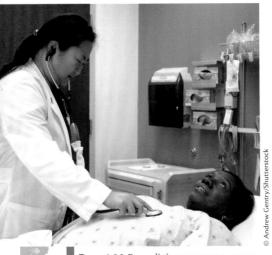

Doc. 4.20 For religious reasons, some patients prefer to be cared for by someone of the same sex.

BELIEFS AND PROHIBITIONS

Most religious traditions include various prohibitions that affect, among other things, food, clothing or medical treatment. These prohibitions are generally found in religious texts or are rooted in people's beliefs and customs. Many Québec institutions have adapted these practices in an effort to respect individual rights. This is called reasonable accommodation. The purpose here is to avoid having someone discriminated against because, among other things, of their sex or their religious convictions. This is stipulated in the Canadian and Québec Charters of Human Rights and Freedoms.

Healthcare respecting various religions

There are many prohibitions affecting medical treatment. For example, many religions or branches within the same religion do not allow abortion, organ transplantation or organ donation. Faced with all these prohibitions, Québec hospitals have adjusted their approach as much as possible, while remaining socially responsible to human life.

Religion in prison

Prisoners have the right to practise their religion provided security rules are obeyed. Space and multi-denominational religious services are provided on the premises. Correctional Services ensures that the diets established by some religions are available. They also make sure that detainees have everything they need to carry out their religious or spiritual rites. Native Spirituality is recognized in the same way as other religions. Amerindian prisoners are provided the services of a spiritual leader or an Amerindian elder just as detainees of other religious denominations might receive the services of a priest, a rabbi or an imam.

An accommodating work environment

For many years now, religious diversity has been recognized in both the public and private sectors. To facilitate the practice of religious rites in the workplace, personal or collective agreements regarding prayer, fasting, statutory holidays and dress codes have been reached. Since March 1990, for example, **Sikh** members of the Canadian Royal Mounted Police can wear their turban instead of the traditional felt hat.

TO KNOW MORE +

The Montreal Children's Hospital (MCH) was Canada's first pediatric hospital to implement measures to accommodate the diverse religious beliefs of patients from different backgrounds. To ensure respect and understanding for these patients, the hospital provides translation services in 60 languages for their staff and clientele. This service helps prevent misunderstandings regarding religious beliefs.

This spirit of openness is also seen in the cafeteria. For example, Muslims can find halal foods there. As well, there is a refrigerator reserved solely for Kosher foods for Jewish people.

The MCH also provides meeting rooms that are adapted to all denominations. Patients can avail themselves of the services of a priest for Christians, a rabbi for Jews, or an imam for Muslims.

Sikh: someone who practises Sikhism, a religion that originated in India. Among other things, Sikh men must wear a turban.

WOMEN AND PROHIBITIONS

In more than one religion, the role of women is not the same as that of men. Women's rights and behaviour are governed by a large number of rules and prohibitions which vary from one religion to another.

Some religious groups require that men be separate from women in their place of worship, especially during prayers.

Though not entirely unheard of, the presence of women in the various clergies is rare or is generally confined to areas of secondary importance, such as religious communities.

Women as spiritual "leaders"

The title of spiritual leader is no longer reserved only for men. In some Protestant churches, the term pastor also refers to female representatives. In fact, for several decades now, women can become pastors or religious ministers within the various ecclesiastic ministries. For example, the United Church of Canada has been **ordaining** women since 1936.

In Judaism, a woman can become a rabbi, that is, the spiritual leader of a Jewish community. However, this is not the case is all branches of Judaism.

Aboriginals do not have an organized clergy for their spiritual practices. However, certain people such as elders and shamans play an especially important role in their traditions. Shamans are both spiritual and physical healers and also preside over ceremonies. They have knowledge of the medicines and herbs that heal both the body and the soul. Shamans and elders may be men or women.

Ordain: to grant someone the sacred order of a particular church, that is, responsibility for a ministry.

Doc. 4.21 In some Protestant churches, women assume the role of pastor or religious minister.

Some history

Lydia Gruchy (1894-1992)

was the first woman to be ordained a pastor of the United Church of Canada.

The holder of a Doctorate in Theology from St. Andrew's College in Saskatchewan, Lydia Gruchy worked hard to become a religious minister. As soon as the United Church of Canada was created in 1926, Mrs. Gruchy put in her request to be ordained. She had to repeat her request many times because, at the time, the rules of the United Church banned women from holding this office. She was finally ordained on November 4, 1936, the same year the United Church of Canada permitted women to hold this position.

Lydia Gruchy became the first Canadian woman to receive the "Doctor of Divinity" degree from St. Andrew's College which gave this pioneering woman's name to its Chair of Pastoral Theology.

The influence of the Catholic religion on the values and norms of Québec society is brilliantly illustrated in Louis Hémon's novel, Maria Chapdelaine. *The story takes place in the early 20th century and provides insight into the society of that period.*

Doc. 4.22 *Leaving Sunday Mass at the Church of Péribonka.* This charcoal drawing is the work of Marc-Aurèle de Foy Suzor-Côté for the first edition of *Maria Chapdelaine,* published in 1916.

© Musée du Québec 34.76D

The novel depicts the way of life of the pioneers who lived north of Lac Saint-Jean in the early 20th century. It describes their habits and customs, their beliefs and superstitions, as well as the social structure of the period with the parish priest at the apex. The author describes how religion greatly influenced people's everyday lives.

The family is at the core of the story. In the novel, after the death of her mother, Maria Chapdelaine chooses to marry Euthrope Gagnon, although she loves someone else, so she can continue to care for her father, her brothers and her sisters, who need her. The major Judeo-Christian values of love, sharing, brotherhood, **self-denial**, and helping one another are dominant in the story of Maria Chapdelaine. Below is an excerpt.

Self-denial: devotion and voluntary self-sacrifice.

Since the coming of winter, they had often talked at the Chapdelaines about the holidays, and now they were drawing near.

"I am wondering whether we shall have any callers on New Year's Day," said Madame Chapdelaine one evening.

…

A sigh disclosed that she still was dreaming of the coming and going in the old parishes at the time of the New Year, the family dinners, the unlooked-for visits of kindred arriving by sleigh from the next village, buried under rugs and furs, behind a horse whose coat was white with frost.

Doc. 4.23 Three days before Christmas, the northwest winds arose and destroyed the roads.

Maria's thoughts were turning in another direction.

"If the roads are as bad as they were last year," said she, "we shall not be able to attend the midnight mass. And yet I should so much have liked it this time, and father promised."

…

Through the little window they looked on the gray sky, and found little to cheer them. To go to midnight mass is the natural and strong desire of every French-Canadian peasant, even of those living farthest from the settlements. What do they not face to accomplish it: Arctic cold, the woods at night, obliterated roads, great distances do but add to the impressiveness and the mystery. This anniversary of the birth of Jesus is more to them than a mere fixture in the calendar with rites appropriate; it signifies the renewed promise of salvation, an occasion of deep rejoicing, and those gathered in the wooden church are imbued with sincerest fervour, are pervaded with a deep sense of the supernatural. This year, more than ever, Maria yearned to attend the midnight mass after many weeks of remoteness from houses and from churches; the favours she would fain demand seemed more likely to be granted were she able to prefer them before the altar, aided in heavenward flight by the wings of music.

But toward the middle of December much snow fell, dry and fine as dust, and three days before Christmas the northwest wind arose and made an end of the roads.

…

The disappointment must be borne; Maria sighed, but the idea came to her that there might be other means of attaining the divine goodwill.

"Is it true, mother," she asked as evening was falling, "that if you repeat a thousand Aves on the day before Christmas you are always granted the thing you seek?"

"Quite true," her mother reverently answered. "One desiring a favour who says her thousand Aves properly before midnight on Christmas Eve, very seldom fails to receive what she asks." …

Long before daylight, Maria began to recite her Aves.

Louis Hémon, *Maria Chapdelaine*, Les Éditions CEC inc., 1997, pp. 128-130, from the original manuscript archived at the Université de Montréal, Fonds Louis-Hémon (p.106)

Doc. 4.24 *"Long before the actual day, Maria began to recite her Ave Marias."* Charcoal drawing by Marc-Aurèle de Foy Suzor-Côté for the first edition of *Maria Chapdelaine*, published in 1916.

Influences on values and norms

Here and elsewhere
Values and norms at the heart of our daily lives

In many countries, actions, behaviour, habits and customs reveal, among other things, the influence of religion on peoples' daily lives. Religious traditions also have an impact on values and norms.

The influence of religion on values and norms is very noticeable in India, where over 80% of the people are Hindu and religion permeates the actions common to everyday life. While travelling through the country, it is difficult not to notice that cows enjoy a special status in Hinduism. They are venerated by many Hindus because symbolic representations of the cow represent values they hold dear.

AUSPICIOUS COWS

This special status given to cows in India stems from an economy founded on cattle farming and agriculture. Cows represent life and fertility. The slaughter of cows is traditionally considered reprehensible. Hindus promote a diet based on milk and yogurt. According to tradition, only the lowest classes eat beef. Cows also symbolize wealth, abundance and a successful life.

Doc. 4.25 Cows symbolize wealth, abundance and a successful life, among other things.
Wikimedia

Doc. 4.26 Cows are part of the daily religious experience of Hindus.
Wikimedia

Doc. 4.27 Cows enjoy a special status in Hinduism.

We can therefore understand that cows have become a symbol of strength and **altruism**. These are very important values in Hinduism.

Cows are part of the daily religious experience of Hindus. They are even mentioned in the founding texts of Hinduism. Below is a short excerpt from the Rig-Veda devoted to the cow:

> She is the mother of the gods Rudra, the sister of the gods Vasu, source of **ambrosia**, sister of the gods Aditya. Before these critics, I declare, "Do not in any way harm this cow, that is without fault, that can be compared to the goddess Aditi."
>
> The cows have come and have brought us good fortune. In our stalls, contented, may they stay! May these multi-coloured cows bring forth calves for us, giving milk each day for the offering to the god Indra.
>
> O cows, you make the thin man sleek; to the unlovely you bring beauty. Rejoice in our homestead with pleasant lowing. In our assemblies we laud your vigour.
>
> Rig-Veda VIII, 90, 15; VI, 28, 1 and 6

Altruism: a tendency to love and a desire to help others.

Ambroisia: food for the gods.

Doc. 4.28 A cow participating in a celebration at Agra in India.

TO KNOW MORE +

Western newspapers enjoy showing so-called "sacred" cows strolling in the streets of large cities. This trend is becoming increasingly rare and such cows, that usually have an owner, are less "sacred" than starving. On rare occasions, some of these animals are freed by their owners as a sign of devotion. Regardless, the cow is a culturally important animal in India, and on holidays, it's not unusual for it to take part in celebrations. Sometimes, cows are decorated with colourful baubles and used to pull floats. The god Krishna spent his childhood in a forest north of India tending cows and at the same time, protecting the country's wealth. This is also why cows started being used in religious images.

Synthesis

- For over 400 years, the Catholic Church in Québec had a great deal of influence on its society's beliefs and values.

- 1760: The Catholic Church becomes a protector of traditions and the French language, morals and conservative attire, in a society governed by a Protestant, Anglophone bourgeoisie.

- During the 19th century and the first half of the 20th, the Catholic Church is omnipresent in education, healthcare and charity work, as well as in trade unions, journalism, the social economy and politics.

- The 1960s: The Quiet Revolution and the secularization of institutions. The Catholic and Protestant churches lose their hold on society and its institutions.

- The 1960s: Québec opens up to the world, large numbers of immigrants arrive bringing with them other religions and forms of spirituality that transform Québec's values and norms.

- Many family traditions stem from religious practices.

- In many religious traditions, one day a week is devoted to rest and worship.

- The values and norms of Québec society have a Judeo-Christian character: sharing, helping one's neighbour, respecting others, forgiveness, being honest, giving to the less fortunate, etc.

- Many laws are based on the main beliefs of Christianity.

- Certain values change with the passage of time and ideologies transform.

- Certain values characterize the beliefs and bear witness to the culture from which they came.

- The foundation of Amerindian and Inuit spiritual beliefs is respect for nature.

- All religious traditions include prohibitions and taboos.

- In many religions, the place held by women is not the same as that held by men. Depending on the religion, various rules and prohibitions dictate women's rights.

- Aboriginals, as well as the Jewish and Protestant churches, accept women as spiritual leaders.

1 In Québec, what religious denomination played a major role in trade unions, journalism, the social economy and politics?

2 Are the Ten Commandments unique to Christian traditions? Justify your answer.

3 What aspect of family life was influenced by the parish priest?

4 What is the Quiet Revolution and how did it impact on Québec society?

5 Name some holidays or family customs that have religious roots.

6 Does swearing exist in all religions? Give some examples.

7 On which day of the week do Christians rest and worship?

8 What do people generally do on the Lord's Day?

9 Give some examples of Judeo-Christian values found in the society's norms.

10 Explain why many norms and values are based on religious cultures.

11 What tenets of the Ten Commandments can be found in other religious cultures?

12 Explain what the expression "Earning a place in heaven" means.

13 Why can we say that there is a resurgence of Native Spirituality?

14 What was the importance of the *Small Children's Catechism*? Explain.

15 What was made possible by Québec's opening up to the world and the arrival of a large number of immigrants?

16 What does nature represent in Native Spirituality?

17 Why does the Catholic Church condemn swear words uttered by some Quebeckers?

18 What is a Calvary? Where is it generally found?

19 What is reasonable accommodation?

20 Which religions or church allow women to be spiritual leaders?

21 On which day of the week do Jews worship?

The phenomenon of religion

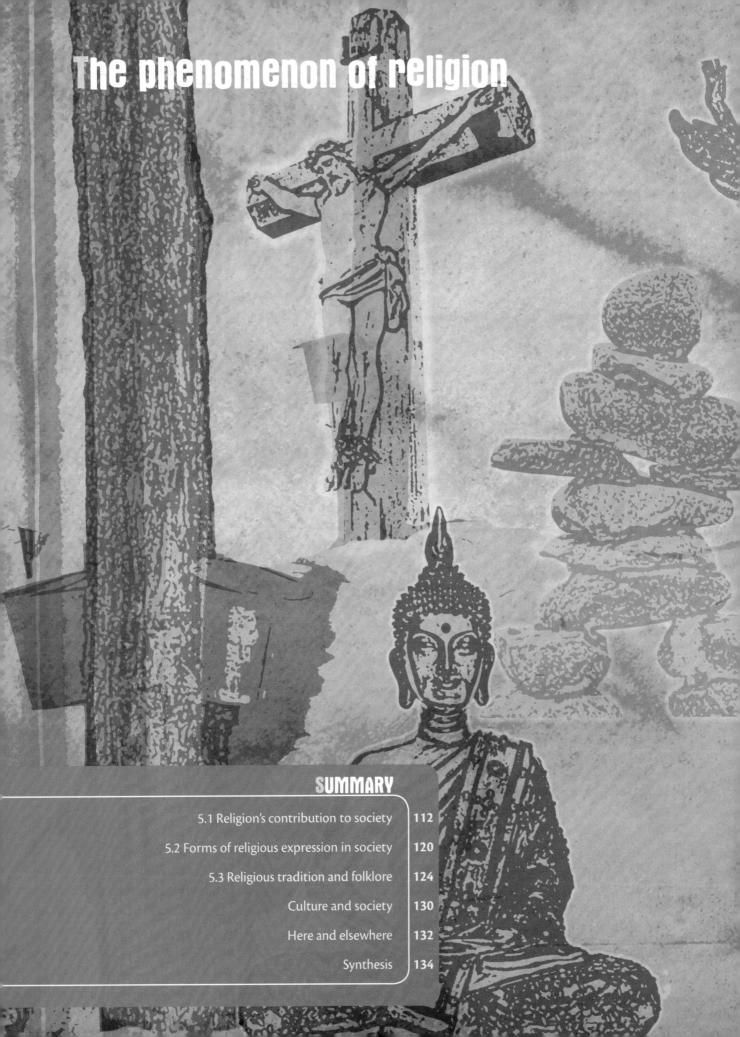

SUMMARY

5.1 Religion's contribution to society   **112**

5.2 Forms of religious expression in society   **120**

5.3 Religious tradition and folklore   **124**

Culture and society   **130**

Here and elsewhere   **132**

Synthesis   **134**

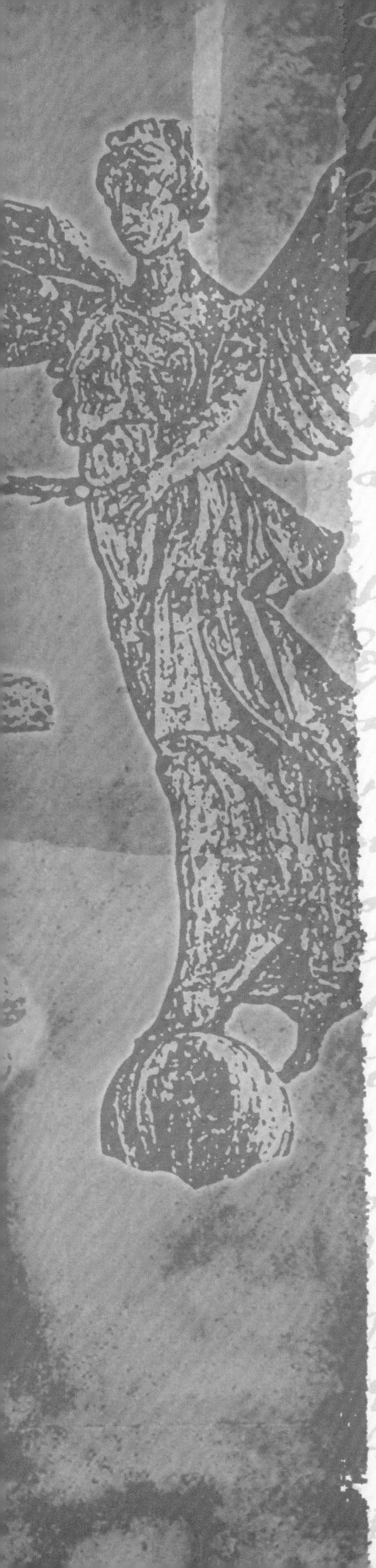

CHAPTER 5

The influence of religious traditions on society

How is society influenced by religious traditions?

How do religious traditions affect society?

What do the various religions bring to Québec society?

CONNECTIONS

- ETHICS
  - Limits to freedom
  - Individuals and groups
  - Transformation of values and norms

- DIALOGUE
  - Forms of dialogue: narration
  - Means for developing a point of view: description
  - Means for examining a point of view: types of judgments

5.1 Religion's contribution to society

*The rich legacy left by those who contributed to making Québec what it is today consists of the great achievements of our forefathers, that is, our **heritage**. Do you realize that our heritage also includes the values and norms that influenced and guided these great builders? Would you be able to recognize the influences left by these pioneers on Québec's modern society?*

Doc. 5.1 Churches and their steeples are part of Montréal's heritage buildings.

Heritage : art work (paintings, sculptures, stained glass windows, monuments, buildings, etc.) that is part of our past.

Foundation : a gift of money to be used as the donor sees fit.

Cooperative : an enterprise whose partners share equally in the work, in its management and in its profits.

The religious contribution to Québec's society is quite significant in many fields. The most visible sign of this contribution is, of course, the religious heritage buildings and monuments we find all around us. The values and norms rooted in various religious traditions are also part of Québec's religious heritage.

These are the values that influenced and guided the many important people, both religious and secular, who built our hospitals, schools, **foundations** and **cooperatives,** in addition to others. These builders put into practice the values and norms of their respective religions, whether they worked in healthcare, education, social or community endeavours, or even business and commerce. Whether Catholic, Protestant or Jewish, members of a religious community or laypeople, these men and women all shared common values that encouraged them to improve the living conditions of human beings.

RELIGION AND HEALTHCARE

From the establishment of New France, and even today in Québec, numerous healthcare establishments and charitable organizations owe their existence to the work carried out by religious and lay communities. Catholics, Protestants and Jews, among others, each contributed in their own way to improving the living conditions of the sick and the poor.

Some of the hospitals founded by Catholics during the era of New France still exist today; these include Montréal's Hôtel-Dieu and Québec City's Hôtel-Dieu.

Doc. 5.2 Hôtel-Dieu, founded in Québec City in 1639, is today a large teaching hospital.

Remember that at the time, there was no Medicare (medical insurance) and most people who were sick did not have the means to get care. The first hospitals in New France took in French colonists, Amerindians and when battles raged, even enemy soldiers. The religious communities that assumed this responsibility therefore played a very important role.

Nearly all Francophone hospitals in Québec were founded by Catholics during the 19th century and the first half of the 20th century. Between 1639 and 1955, the Augustinians founded 12 of these hospitals including Lévis, Roberval, Gaspé, Montmagny, Chicoutimi and Jonquière. Later, these institutions were integrated into the public health care system. In Montréal, Notre-Dame Hospital was founded in 1880 by Dr. Emmanuel Persillier-Lachapelle, secretary of the Faculty of Medicine at the Montréal campus of Laval University; Julie Hainault-Deschamps, of the Grey Nuns congregation; and Victor Rousselot, of the Society (of Priests) of Saint-Sulpice and parish priest of Notre-Dame Parish.

Other Montréal hospitals were founded by Protestant laypeople. For example, the Montréal General Hospital opened its doors in 1819 following financial campaigns launched by the Female Benevolent Society of Montréal, a charitable organization. The Royal Victoria Hospital was inaugurated in 1894 thanks to donations made by some influential Anglophone businessmen, among them, Lord Strathcona and Lord Mount Stephen. At the time, members of the Protestant bourgeoisie took it upon themselves to financially support social causes and charitable organizations.

Doc. 5.3 Hôtel-Dieu in Lévis, founded in 1892.

Doc. 5.4 The Royal Victoria Hospital, founded in 1894.

The influence of religious traditions on society

Doc. 5.5 The Laval University campus in Québec City.

The Montréal Jewish General Hospital opened its doors in 1934. Founded by Montréal's Jewish community, it is a non-denominational establishment that respects the principles of the city's various religions, cultures and ethnic communities. However, within its walls, the hospital practises the values advocated by the Jewish religion.

RELIGION AND EDUCATION

Charter: a law established by a monarch or a pope.

In the field of education, Québec's religious communities contributed not only to the establishment of schools, colleges, convents and seminaries, but also to that of universities. Laval University was set up in Québec City in 1852 when Queen Victoria granted it a royal **charter**; it was run by Catholics. In reality, the university was under the direction of the Seminary of Québec, which had been founded in 1663 by Monsignor Laval. In 1878, Pope Pius IX issued a charter authorizing the opening of an annexe to Laval University's Montréal campus. In 1920, this campus officially became known as the Université de Montréal.

McGill University was founded in 1821, thanks to the generosity of James McGill. This Protestant immigrant of Scottish descent arrived in Canada in 1766. Upon his death, he willed a plot of land and a large amount of money that was used to found the Montréal university that bears his name. Many benefactors of the period, namely Lord Strathcona, Sir William Macdonald, William Molson, and Peter Redpath have also contributed to McGill University's reputation and excellence.

Doc. 5.6 The McGill University campus in Montréal.

In 1846, the Protestant Institute in Pointe-aux-Trembles was created through the merger of a Protestant school in Mirabel, founded by Anne Cruchet-Amaron and a girls' school in Montréal, founded by Olympe Hoerner-Tanner (1807-1854), a Protestant missionary and teacher. Evangelical principles have always been at the core of this college's educational approach. Its excellent reputation was widespread and both Protestant and Catholic students were educated there in French until 1971.

RELIGION AND VALUES

You must know that in most religions, helping your neighbour is a fundamental value. There are many ways to do this. Following are a few examples.

Helping your neighbour

Religious communities and laypeople of all denominations have always come to the aid of orphans, the aged, the poor and the handicapped. Following secularization in the 1960s, the state gradually took charge of most of the people in need. Yet, many organizations continued to care for the less fortunate. In addition, many new charitable organizations were founded. Together, they are a major part of our contemporary social heritage. Following are a few examples.

Accueil Bonneau was founded in Montréal in 1877 by **philanthropist** Joseph Vincent, with the help of René Rousseau, a Sulpician monk and the chaplain of the Society of Saint-Vincent-de-Paul. The two men joined the Grey Nuns in providing a refuge for Montréal's homeless. Today, the Society of Saint-Vincent-de-Paul, the Sulpicians and the Grey Nuns still run Accueil Bonneau's kitchen and residences.

The Salvation Army, founded in London in 1865 and in Canada in 1882, was both a Protestant Church and a social service organization. Its mission consists of spreading the Christian doctrine and helping the needy, regardless of race, colour, creed, sex or age.

TO KNOW MORE +

Do you know what the *guignolée* is? In many Québec municipalities, early December is the time when food and donations are collected for the less fortunate. Early on, the guignolée was a Celtic year-end feast. During the celebration, the Druids gave mistletoe ("gui" in French), which they regarded as a sacred plant and gave as comfort to the sick, the poor and the soldiers. While doing this, they shouted *"Au gui l'an neuf,"* an expression from which the term "guignolée" originates. In Québec, the Society of Saint-Vincent-de-Paul, a Catholic charitable organization, established this custom during the second half of the 19th century.

Philanthropist: a person who contributes through personal deeds, through donations of money, through the founding of organizations, to help improve the plight of the less fortunate.

Doc. 5.7 There are homeless people living on the streets every day of the year. Shelters like Accueil Bonneau, provide meals and a bed for the night.

The influence of religious traditions on society

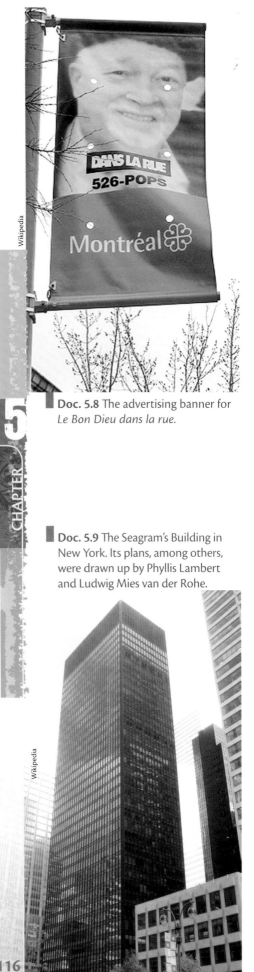

Doc. 5.8 The advertising banner for *Le Bon Dieu dans la rue*.

Doc. 5.9 The Seagram's Building in New York. Its plans, among others, were drawn up by Phyllis Lambert and Ludwig Mies van der Rohe.

Father Emmett Johns is the person behind *Le Bon Dieu dans la rue*. Commonly called Pops, this Catholic priest became famous because of his van. In Montréal in 1988, he began giving food, clothing, staples and above all, comfort to the city's homeless and runaway youth. *Le Bon Dieu dans la rue* has since diversified its services and still helps thousands of teens and young adults every year.

Although they are of different religious persuasions, all these people have come to the aid of their neighbour by providing services or helping to open hospitals, educational institutions and shelters, these people all share common values. These values are still an integral part of Québec society.

Philanthropy

Improving the living conditions of human beings is a fundamental value in many religious traditions. The following are a few philanthropists, notably those of the Jewish faith who understood and helped put this value into practice.

Maurice Pollack (1885-1968) was a Jewish immigrant born in the Ukraine. He immigrated to Canada in 1902 and distinguished himself in Québec City where he opened a large department store. Pollack was not only a prosperous merchant but also a generous philanthropist. He set up a foundation whose mission was to provide financial aid to various organizations. Laval University, McGill University and the symphony orchestras of Québec City and Montréal all benefitted from the help his foundation provided. A contribution from the Maurice Pollack Foundation allowed McGill University to avail itself of a professional concert hall, aptly named Pollack Hall. A Laval University pavilion also bears the name of this major donor.

Samuel Bronfman (1889-1971) built the largest distillery in the world. In addition to presiding over the Canadian Jewish Congress from 1939 to 1962, this businessman was a major philanthropist. His immense fortune allowed him and his wife, Saidye, to set up a foundation to support social, cultural and educational causes. In fact, the Bronfmans were convinced that society could not move forward unless the community was involved.

Samuel and Saidye Bronfman's children also contributed to Québec society, notably their daughter Phyllis Lambert, who was born in 1927. A very well-known architect, she designed and oversaw the construction of the Saidye Bronfman Centre for the Arts in Montréal. She is also credited for the Canadian Centre for Architecture (CCA), an international research centre and museum, which she built in this city with the conviction that architecture was of public interest.

Phyllis Lambert spent much of her life and fortune promoting architecture and the conservation of our cultural and religious heritage. She helped set up Heritage Montréal, a non-profit organization that works to promote and protect Montréal's heritage. During the 1990s, she took on a project to restore the 1000-year old Ben Ezra Synagogue in Cairo, Egypt, and to open an interreligious centre there. Political strife in the area prevented her from doing so (*New York Times*, September 10, 1995).

RELIGION AND ECONOMIC LIFE

The values rooted in religious traditions which have pushed people to improve the living conditions of their neighbours can also be found in economic life. The Catholic Church encouraged entrepreneurs to contribute to social work. Companies founded during difficult times in history made it possible for thousands of people to improve their lot in life. Following are two examples.

Nazaire Dupuis (1844-1876) was of Acadian descent. In 1868, this fervent Catholic started a small business that would quickly become one of the largest department stores in Montréal. The success of Dupuis Frères was based on three ideological pillars: the Catholic religion, family and nationalism. Dupuis Frères was the business marketplace of the city's Francophone population. During the 1950s, it employed some 1500 people, mainly women. The store closed its doors in 1978.

BANQ

■ **Doc. 5.10** The Dupuis Frères department store in 1877, St. Catherine Street, Montréal.

Alphonse Desjardins (1854-1920) was born in Lévis to a Catholic family of 15 children. He held various positions, including those of journalist, secretary-treasurer of the Board of Trade of Lévis, and French **stenographer** at the House of Commons. Following a series of poor harvests at the end of the 19th century, many farmers went bankrupt. Realizing the gravity of the situation, Alphonse Desjardins decided to found a savings and loan co-operative that would make it possible for workers and farmers to borrow and to save money. So in 1900, the first Caisse populaire opened its doors in Lévis. The founder of the new co-op was successful in garnering the support of the Catholic Church, which inspired trust among the people. In 1913, Desjardins was honoured by the Pope for his contribution to Catholic social action.

These examples illustrate well how, over the centuries, builders from different religions participated in transforming Québec society in their own way. Thanks to their accomplishments and generosity, they contributed to improving the quality of life for a great many people.

Wikipedia

■ **Doc. 5.11** Alphonse Desjardins in 1915.

The influence of religious traditions on society

117

Some history

Joseph Casavant (1807-1874)

Joseph Casavant left his trade as a blacksmith at the age of 27 and went to study Latin at the College in St. Thérèse where he was put to work repairing the college's organ. News that this young man had been able to restore the broken instrument spread quickly. Churches commissioned Joseph Casavant to fix their organs and he soon became the first Canadian-born **organ builder** of importance. When he retired in 1866, Casavant had built some 17 instruments, including those in the Catholic cathedrals in Bytown (Ottawa) and Kingston, Ontario. Once his two sons, Claver and Samuel, had mastered their craft in Europe, they continued in their father's footsteps. Casavant Frères of St. Hyacinthe has earned a worldwide reputation for its quality instruments. Since the company was first founded, some 4000 organs have been built and sold throughout the world. To acknowledge this pioneer, avenues in St. Hyacinthe, Québec City, Montréal and Gatineau bear his name.

Organ builder: someone who makes or builds musical instruments.

TO KNOW MORE+

Guido Nincheri, artist, (1885-1973) probably produced more religious works than anyone else in Canada during the 20th century. Originally from Italy, Nincheri set up his stained glass shop in Montréal in 1913. Undoubtedly the Church of St. Leon in Westmount, on which he worked from 1928 to 1944, is his best work. In 1933, Pope Pius XI appointed him Knight-Commander of the Order of Saint Sylvester, thereby proclaiming his exceptional contribution to our Catholic heritage.

RELIGION AND HERITAGE WORKS

Over the centuries, various religious traditions in Québec have substantially enriched our religious heritage. Christians, who began settling in Québec more than 400 years ago, left us masterpieces in various media: architecture, sculpture, stained glass and paintings. The Jews, whose religion does not allow representations of the divine, built magnificent synagogues. More recently, immigrants of Buddhist, Hindu and Sikh religious traditions built temples whose architecture is often nothing less than spectacular. The legacy left by most of these religions is still very much alive. This is true of the Christian religious heritage and also of Native Spirituality which we will be covering later in this section.

The Christian religious heritage

The Catholics, Anglicans, Orthodox and Protestants left a very rich legacy. The following are some of the artists and masterpieces that contributed to it.

Ozias Leduc (1864-1955), one of Québec's greatest painters, has contributed substantially to Québec's religious heritage. He decorated more than 30 churches and chapels in Québec, Nova Scotia and the Eastern United States.

Doc. 5.12 The interior decoration of the Mont-Saint-Hilaire Catholic Church, in the Montérégie, created between 1896 and 1900, is one of the most remarkable works of Ozias Leduc, a native of the area. Leduc spent most of his career decorating churches and chapels.
Wikipedia

Doc. 5.13 Religious heritage is found not only in churches. Raoul Hunter's bronze statue of Mother Émilie Gamelin (1800-1851), founder of the Sisters of Providence, can be found at the Berri-UQAM Métro Station in Montréal. This work of art represents a nun carrying a basket full of provisions and extending her hand to the less fortunate.
Wikipedia

Doc. 5.14 The Protestants also left many heritage works. This photograph shows a magnificent stained glass window from Québec City's St. Andrew's Presbyterian Church, built in 1810. The church also houses a Casavant organ. It is Canada's oldest English-speaking congregation of Scottish origin.
© Conseil du patrimoine religieux du Québec, 2003

Aboriginal heritage art

Heritage works of art associated with Native Spirituality are rich and diverse. Natural sites are considered heritage landmarks and form part of what is known as a living legacy because even today, they are the very heart of Aboriginal traditions and are closely related to spirituality and to the spirits.

Aboriginals pass down a substantial collection of narratives, songs, know-how and stories from generation to generation by oral tradition. For instance, some of these legends explain how the spirits created the wind, or natural contours in the land, such as valleys and mountains.

Aboriginals also produced numerous artefacts related to their spirituality. Some of these ritual objects, considered taboo, are destroyed after being used; they must not be photographed or kept. Others can be shown to the public like the drum pictured below, which, according to the spirituality of the Ilnuatsh of Lac-Saint-Jean, makes it possible to contact the world of the invisible.

For some Aboriginal communities in Canada, heritage related to buildings is also an important element of their spirituality. For example, the Kahnawake Mohawks and the Huron-Wendat of Wendake hold their religious ceremonies in traditional longhouses.

Doc. 5.15 Ilnu drums are made of stretched caribou hide that is laced onto a wooden frame with babiche (rough, hand-cut leather strands).
© The Mashteuiatsh Amerindian Museum, Photo Louise Leblanc, Québec

Forms of religious expression in society

In a multi-ethnic society like that in Québec, forms of religious expression are plentiful and diverse. Do you know what these forms of religious expression signify? Where they come from? What role they play?

A DIVERSE RELIGIOUS LANDSCAPE

Forms of religious expression are elements that are specific to a religion, such as writings, symbols, practices, monuments, buildings and objects. In Québec, the most visible and most numerous forms of religious expression are mainly from Judeo-Christian traditions. The Québec landscape is dotted with churches, roadside crosses and statues reminiscent of the Catholic practices of the early pioneers. However, over the years, these representations have become more and more diversified. Nowadays, we can admire works of art, sculptures and buildings that do not originate from Christian or Jewish religious traditions. Have you ever seen any? Can you recognize them?

PLACES OF WORSHIP OF EVERY DENOMINATION

From the most majestic to the most discreet, religious buildings arose curiosity and interest, whether through their beauty, their meaning, or their use. Beyond the obvious differences, churches, temples, synagogues, pagodas and mosques are, first and foremost, places where religious rites are practised on a regular basis.

Sometimes, the architecture, shape and construction materials of religious buildings provide clues that help to associate them with one denomination or another. For example, the domes and steeples of Catholic, Orthodox and Protestant churches make them easy to recognize.

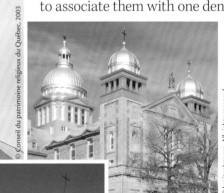

Doc. 5.16 Whether Catholic, Orthodox or Protestant, large or small, Christian churches almost always have a steeple topped with a cross.

However, the architecture of temples, synagogues and mosques, especially those in the Montréal area, is usually much more discreet. Although some synagogues are rather imposing, more often they are buildings that do not really stand out from neighbouring houses. Many mosques are set up in buildings that may have previously been used for quite a different purpose. On the other hand, some Buddhist or Sikh congregations have erected temples with a strikingly unique architecture.

Doc. 5.17 A Montréal house that has been turned into a Buddhist pagoda.
Photo Patrick Fuyet

Doc. 5.18 The Shaare Zion synagogue.
© Conseil du patrimoine religieux du Québec, 2003

Doc. 5.19 Montréal's most imposing Sikh temple.
Photo Patrick Fuyet

A DECOR THAT IS AN EXPRESSION OF THE DIVINE

Entering a religious building brings us into contact with the abundant richness of the forms of religious expression it contains. Whether this richness is architectural, decorative or utilitarian, the diversity of forms of religious expression is specific to each religion and varies from one place to another. We must remember that some religions, such as Judaism and Islam, forbid any representations of the divine.

Photo Patrick Fuyet

Doc. 5.20 The large building of the mosque in Ville St. Laurent.

The degree of importance given to the decor and the architecture of places of worship is largely dependant on traditions. In most synagogues, mosques, and Protestant Churches, the decor can be quite bare with very little ornamentation. Catholic Churches, on the other hand, are often lavishly decorated.

© Matt Apps/Shutterstock

Doc. 5.21 The interior of this Lutheran Church is very simple.

© Conseil du patrimoine religieux du Québec, 2003

Doc. 5.22 The decor in most synagogues is very plain.

The influence of religious traditions on society

Doc. 5.23 The Crucifixion, Notre-Dame Basilica.

Doc. 5.24 A large bare cross in a Protestant church.

Doc. 5.25 An Orthodox cross on the dome of a church.

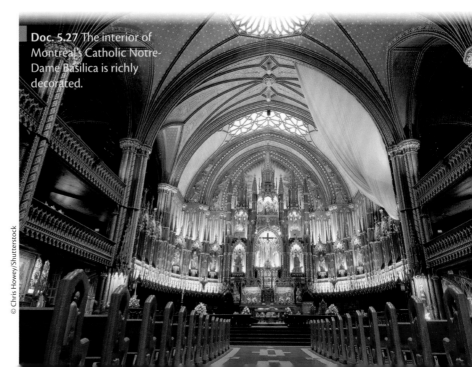

Doc. 5.26 Crosses on graves in a cemetery in the Gaspé.

The layout of holy places includes objects of worship and spaces reserved for religious rites. At the entrance of temples of many religions, there is a special place for the mandatory **ablutions** that must be performed before entering the building. In some synagogues, mosques and Hindu temples, for example, a source of water is made available to the faithful for ritual washing before going inside to pray. The faithful wash certain parts of their body, and, symbolically, purify themselves. In Catholic Churches, small basins, called Aspertion Fonts, are located at the entrance of the church so the faithful can dip their fingers in water called Holy Water before making the Sign of the Cross.

Crosses

Anyone who tours Québec will come upon all sorts of crosses. Near religious buildings, on top of steeples, on roadsides and in cemeteries, these religious expressions linked to Christian denominations are both numerous and diverse.

For Christians, the Cross symbolizes the death of Jesus, but it also reminds them of the meaning of His death. Therefore, Christianity looks upon the Cross as a major symbol of God's love. The shape of the Cross may vary. Protestant crosses are usually bare, without any representation of the crucified Christ. When worn as jewellery, they are often accompanied by a dove. Unlike Catholic and Protestant crosses that have only one horizontal beam, Orthodox crosses have three: the upper beam symbolizes the sign that was nailed to the Cross stating the motive for his conviction, "King of the Jews" and the lower, slanted beam symbolizes the Cross's footrest. Catholic and Orthodox crosses usually carry an image of Christ and are called crucifixes.

Ablution: the act of washing to purify oneself.

Doc. 5.27 The interior of Montréal's Catholic Notre-Dame Basilica is richly decorated.

Doc. 5.28 A roadside cross and inuksuk are sacred reference points.

Doc. 5.29 Statues representing St. Joseph and the Infant Jesus.

Sacred reference points

Roadside crosses are part of a very old tradition that originated in Europe, especially in Brittany. These are, above all, religious symbols, but they are also reference points. On the back roads of Québec, crosses that are five or six metres high can still be found. They are made of wood, wrought iron or some other material. Roadside crosses have long been places to stop and pray, especially at a time when churches were few and far between. Many of them are considered historical treasures and are part of Québec's religious heritage. The Inuit stack rocks to form human-shaped reference points, called inuksuks. Inuksuks are also used to mark sacred sites or warn of impending danger. Inuit tradition forbids their destruction.

Statues

Statues play a major role in those religions that allow representations of the divine. Catholics very often represent Jesus, the Blessed Virgin, the saints and the angels in the form of statues. They place them inside or outside churches, in cemeteries and in gardens. Hindus also have a very large number of statues of their divinities; they use these statues to decorate their temples. The Buddhists, for their part, have representations of the Buddha.

Doc. 5.30 The façade of the Church of Saint-Pierre on Île d'Orléans is adorned with statues.

Doc. 5.31 A statue of the Blessed Virgin in Notre-Dame-de-Bonsecours Chapel in Montréal.

Doc. 5.32 Statues of three divinities above the entrance of a Hindu temple.

Doc. 5.33 One of the many representations of Buddha in a meditative position.

Doc. 5.34 A statue of the bodhisattva Guanyin in front of a Buddhist pagoda in Montréal.

Doc. 5.35 An angel with open wings in Mount Royal Park.

The influence of religious traditions on society

123

5.3 Religious tradition and folklore

Up to this point in the chapter, we've seen that various religions have made numerous contributions to society. Did you know that religious influence goes back so far as to be part of the tales and legends of Québec folklore?

Doc. 5.36 This 15th century painting depicts the Devil trying to tempt St. Augustine (354-430), one of the great figures of the Catholic denomination, by showing him The Great Book of Vices.

LEGENDS AND BELIEFS

Certain components of religions influence a society's customs, its cultural expressions and its beliefs. Among these are sacred stories. All religious traditions have their own specific sacred stories that make up some of their basic elements. They influence the way the faithful see themselves, the way they view history, their beliefs and fears, their heroes and enemies, good and evil, the divine and the supernatural.

Therefore, it's not surprising that traditional legends and tales are often adaptations of stories specific to a religious tradition where representations of the divine, as well as mythical and supernatural beings, are found.

In Amerindian communities, stories, in addition to rituals and rules, are very important. From one community to another, legends abound and fulfil a variety of functions. For example, they tell of the origin of the world, the origin of a stream, or they portray actions that can serve as models for human behaviour.

Over time, many of the Amerindian legends were modified by the Catholic and Protestant missionaries who taught the Aboriginals about God and the Bible. This is why, in these stories, spirits, chamans or humans transformed into animals are sometimes mixed in with figures or expressions from Christian religions, like a priest or a chapel.

Although many of these stories are now in written form, for the most part they were passed down from generation to generation by word of mouth. Even today, throughout the world, this oral tradition is closely linked to the art of storytelling in many societies.

TO KNOW MORE +

An Atikamekw legend

A very long time ago, when the world was first created, the Elders held a Grand Council. One of the Elders said, "I want to become a silver birch tree to help the humans. I am rich, so I'll tell them to take my bark to make the things they need: canoes, houses, baskets….Through me, they will understand the importance of communicating with nature."

FORMS OF RELIGIOUS EXPRESSION IN FOLKTALES

Folktales are often based on superstition and belief. They are tales of fantasy and the supernatural in which a **transgression**, prompts the apparition of the Devil and his impish accomplices, or mysterious beasts such as werewolves, and "long-tailed" beasts. Others might present the Devil transformed into a local monster, spirit or natural element, like fire or a volcano.

The inclusion of the Devil, in any of his many forms, helps to symbolize evil. This is why he is generally seen in opposition to a popular hero, or a divine or religious figure that always represents the victory of good over evil.

Québec tales and legends

In Québec's 19th century religious context, good was almost always represented by the parish priest. He would become a hero by saving his parishioners from the fires of hell. This line of reasoning shows us just how important the role of the parish priest was in the parishes of the time.

Rose Latulippe

The legend of Rose Latulippe is a good example of this type of folktale. On **Mardi Gras** night, a young woman called Rose Latulippe let herself be seduced by the Devil who had transformed himself into an attractive stranger for the occasion. Despite her father's warnings and the fact that it was forbidden to dance on **Ash Wednesday**, Rose continued her little caper with the Devil, even once midnight had come and gone. It was the parish priest who rose to the occasion and saved the young woman by forcing Satan to disappear, leaving behind the nauseating smell of **sulphur**.

Doc. 5.37 An illustration showing the Archbishop of Canterbury trying to chase away the Devil with a red-hot poker.

Transgression: the act of not obeying an order, law or rule.

Mardi Gras or Shrove Tuesday: a holiday related to the carnival that precedes Ash Wednesday.

Ash Wednesday: the first day of **Lent**.

Lent: in Catholic and Orthodox Churches, as well as in Anglican Churches, the 40-day period preceding Easter. During Lent, Christians are asked to pray more and to abstain from eating certain foods (meat and sweets).

Sulphur: a chemical element that smells like rotten eggs.

BANQ

Doc. 5.38 Rose Latulippe dancing with the attractive stranger.

The influence of religious traditions on society

Doc. 5.39 The large canoe was on the snow in a clearing, ready to fly over the mountains.

Doc. 5.40 Since the loggers did not keep their pact with the Devil, the canoe plummeted them into the void.

The Bewitched Canoe

In Québec legends and folktales, it's generally the Devil, the Christian's number one enemy, who, under various forms tries to lead the characters down the path of sin.

"The Bewitched Canoe" is one of Québec's most famous legends. It tells the story of some loggers who make a pact with the Devil to leave the logging site for one night to visit their women aboard a flying bark canoe. In exchange, the Devil warned them not to touch any crosses atop church steeples and not to utter the name of God during the voyage; otherwise, their canoe would come tumbling down. The following is an excerpt:

"… The large canoe was on the snow in a clearing. We kept saying: Satan! King of Hell, we promise to deliver our souls to you if within the next six hours we pronounce the name of God, your Master and ours or if we touch a cross during the voyage. In return for this, you will transport us through the air, to the place we want to go, and you will bring us back to the logging site in the same way!"

"The Bewitched Canoe", Canadian legend, Honoré Beaugrand, Montréal, 1900.

© Clara Natoli/Shutterstock

Doc. 5.41 Christ chasing away the Devil.

TO KNOW MORE +

Some popular expressions and their meaning

To be more Catholic than the Pope
Said of someone who is too honest.

Leave it in God's hands
Put one's trust in another

Have a devil of a time
To have difficulty making ends meet.

Like the Devil and holy water
To spend enormous energy to get out of a bad situation. For Catholics, holy water has the power to expel Satan.

Go to Hell
To send someone away as far as possible, to where the Devil lives, to get rid of someone.

Poor as a church mouse
Said of a very poor person.

Try the patience of a saint
To exasperate someone, be impatient.

The devil's in the details
It's often the small details that make something difficult or challenging.

Have the face of an angel
Portray innocence.

FAR-REACHING RELIGIOUS EXPRESSIONS

The preceding chapter taught us that even our vocabulary is influenced by religious traditions. This contribution to our culture is found in many popular expressions. Did anyone ever tell you that you were such a blessing or a real angel?

Many Québécois expressions refer to God, to religious or biblical figures, to various representations of the divine, and to angels or the Devil. As in folktales, such references to God, or religious figures or the divine usually represent good or perfection. The Devil generally represents evil.

God and the Devil are often found in the same expression but not always to oppose good and evil. For example, we say: "God knows and the Devil doubts" to express a fact, or "Fear not God, nor the Devil" to speak of someone who has no faith.

Unlike swearing, expressions that use religious terms are not transgressions. Rather, they are a manifestation of a way of life focused on religious practices. Certain expressions have been forgotten over time. Others have survived down through the generations and still add a little colour to today's popular language.

Divination: attempting to foretell the future by interpreting signs or omens.

Purgatory: for Catholics, a place or state for temporary suffering where souls finish atoning for their sins before going to heaven.

Ward off: to get rid of an evil power..

Doc. 5.42 Objects in the form of a cross are sources of superstition for some people.

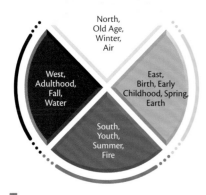

Doc. 5.43 The Amerindian Circle of Life

SUPERSTITIONS

A society's superstitions are closely linked to its beliefs and its culture. As such, they are often influenced by religion. Nevertheless, many of them are not religious in origin.

Like its folktales and expressions, many Québec superstitions have been influenced by Christianity. For a long time, the Catholic clergy had a rather dim view of these superstitions since it considered them a "moral menace," a form of sorcery and divination.

Yet, one might suppose that some superstitions have contributed to keeping a few Christians in line. It used to be said that cursing excessively could conjure up the Devil. Or that failure to pay the tithe would anger the souls in purgatory which would then bring about some tragic event.

Objects, numbers and superstitions

One superstition related to objects is that of arranging table utensils in the form of a cross; it is said to bring bad luck. Objects arranged in the form of a cross have long had various symbolic meanings, both positive and negative, depending on their nature and context. On the other hand, the Sign of the Cross is still used to encourage bread to rise, make the day a good one or to ward off evil. For example, sports figures sometimes make the Sign of the Cross before a hockey game or a tennis match. Along the same lines, holy water and consecrated bread are seen as good omens.

In some religious traditions, certain numbers have a specific significance. One must point out that numbers do not exist independently but are more often part of an enumeration or list specific to each religious tradition, and must be considered within their own context. There are a great many references to these. For example, Amerindians consider the number 4 as significant. The Circle of Life, a fundamental symbol of Native Spirituality, is divided into four parts. Each of these parts is associated with one of the four elements (wind, earth, fire and water), the four stages of life (infancy, adolescence, adulthood and old age), the four cardinal points (north, east, south and west) and the four seasons (spring, summer, autumn and winter).

The number 13

The fear some Christians have of the number 13 seems to date back to The Last Supper, that is, the last meal Jesus shared with His **apostles**. The 13th guest was Judas, who handed Jesus over to His executioners in exchange for money. So, this number was a sign of evil. As for Friday the 13th, this date seems to represent the height of bad luck since Christ died on a Friday. But not everyone shares this explanation. There are people who say the number 13 refers to one of the best known Tarot cards, that is, the Death card.

In Judaism, however, the number 13 is seen as a rather auspicious number. In fact, the bar mitzvah initiation rite is celebrated when a young man reaches his 13th birthday. It acknowledges the attainment of his religious manhood. The young man may then wear phylacteries and recite Torah blessings during religious services. When a girl is 12 years old, her religious womanhood is celebrated with the bat mitzvah. This latter ceremony has only been in existence since the 19th century.

Whether or not it is a religious viewpoint, fear of the number 13 is nevertheless widespread. This is so widespread that many buildings don't have a 13th floor, hotels don't have a Room 13, or a 13th Floor. Some airplanes don't have a Row 13 and none of the Formula 1 sports cars carry the number 13.

As we can see, superstitions are not always associated with religious expressions. For example, there's the fear of walking under a ladder, breaking a mirror, which brings seven years of bad luck, or crossing in front of a black cat. As well, there are formulas and gestures to ward off bad luck, like touching wood or throwing salt over one's shoulder. Each society has its own superstitions which like accents, vary from one region to another.

Doc. 5.44 Fear of the number 13 is called triskaidekaphobia

Doc. 5.45 A young man wearing a phylactery on his forehead carries the Torah scrolls during a bar mitzvah.

Apostle: each of Jesus' twelve companions and other disciples who preached His teachings.

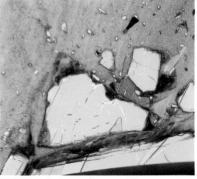

Culture and Society
The many representations of the world

As we've seen in this chapter, the influence of religious traditions affects many aspects of our society. What's more, spirituality is no longer limited to the major religions, and nowadays, our representations of the world take various forms. Many people have developed an interest in beliefs and practices that are non-religious and that, sometimes, are based on ancient traditions. Following are a few examples.

YOGA

It is rare to find people who don't know yoga by name. Yoga is a spiritual discipline that is based on personal ethics and consists of various concentration and meditation exercises in specific positions. More precisely, yoga is a technique whose goal is to free humans from the cycle of rebirths in a human, animal or divine body. It is practised in an effort to reach the ultimate level of enlightenment. People who are not Hindu but who practice yoga, use it to keep in shape, become more flexible, relax, and sometimes to meditate.

TAI-CHI

Many forms of meditation of Asian origin are now practiced here in the West. Tai-chi is one of them. This Chinese type of gymnastics consists of a combination of postures and gestures inspired by the martial arts and performed very slowly. Tai-chi's roots are in traditional Chinese medicine, that is, *qi gong*, which uses the mind to move vital energy *(qi)* within the body. In the West, tai-chi is especially well-liked because of its health benefits. In fact, it is recommended by the Public Health Agency of Canada especially for older people. It is said to improve mobility and flexibility and to reduce stress.

Doc. 5.46 One of the poses in classical yoga.
© GeoM/Shutterstock

Doc. 5.47 The practice of tai-chi is very popular in China.
© Thomas Barrat/Shutterstock

ASIAN MARTIAL ARTS

The Asian martial arts are a good example of the influence that religious traditions have on society. These fighting techniques: karate, judo, kendo, aikido, etc., derived from military training, have become increasingly popular internationally over the past few years. Even though they are mainly seen as sports activities (judo and tae kwon do are Olympic disciplines), Asian martial arts are closely related to spirituality. They focus not only on becoming master of one's body, but also of one's mind.

Doc. 5.48
A karate competition.
© Tito Wong/Shutterstock

Doc. 5.49
A judo competition.
© Goran Cakmazovic/Shutterstock

ASTROLOGY

People have been interested in the **divining** art of astrology for a very long time. Even in antiquity, people tried to interpret the stars in an attempt to predict the future. Whether their astrological sign is Leo or Gemini, a great many people believe that the sign under which they were born has great meaning. At the beginning of every year, bookstores are flooded with bestsellers containing predictions for the upcoming year, and horoscopes are very popular in many daily newspapers and magazines.

Doc. 5.50
The signs of the Zodiac.
© Maisei Raman/Shutterstock

FENG SHUI

Feng Shui is based on concepts that originate from Taoism, a religion that has existed in Asia since the 6th century before Christ. The term feng shui means wind and water. Feng shui, a philosophy of life based on the art of creating a harmonious living/working space, has existed in China for thousands of years. According to feng shui believers, this art helps to circulate vital energy and as a result, promotes well-being, health, success and happiness. An inharmonious arrangement brings about negative influences. The art of feng shui can be applied not only to living space but also to work space and garden space, for example.

Doc. 5.51 Feng shui believers are convinced that the layout of their living space improves their well-being.
© Natalia Bratslavsky/Shutterstock

Divining: as related to divination.

The influence of religious traditions on society

Here and elsewhere
Mythical beings called gargoyles

© Ernesto Lopez Albert/Shutterstock

© Ralph Herschbach/Shutterstock

© luminouslens/Shutterstock

© Pete Hoffman/Shutterstock

Do you know what gargoyles are? They are those strange stone statues that adorn large buildings. With their mysterious looks, these gargoyles are, in fact, water ducts that keep rain water away from building walls in an effort to preserve them. It's no coincidence that their name reminds us of the rumbling of our stomach just a few minutes before the lunch church bell rings. The term comes from the Latin *gargula*, which means the gullet or throat, and the English verb to gargle.

The earliest gargoyles date back to antiquity, but it was not until the Middle Ages, during the 12th century, that they actually began to appear. Later, they became widespread, especially in Europe during the 13th century.

DESCENDANTS OF THE DRAGON?

There is a legend that links the origin of gargoyles to Christian tradition. It tells the story of a dragon that lived a very long time ago. This dragon preyed upon the inhabitants of the French town of Rouen. An Italian priest took it upon himself to rid the townspeople of this beast provided they received the sacrament of baptism and built a church. The priest captured the dragon and burnt it at the stake. The creature's head and neck did not burn. It was then decided to hang it up for everyone to see. One version of this legend relates that the head of the dragon was hung on the new parish church and became the first gargoyle.

In addition to this legend, there are also many others that explain the significance of gargoyles and why they are present on many Christian churches.

Some people say that gargoyles served to keep evil away from the churches. It is also said that they kept Christians away from temptation and sin, and by their very representation, made Christians fear the torments of Hell. Other sources say that gargoyles represented sinners who had been turned into stone or that they were evil figures that urged the faithful to take refuge inside the church.

CHAPTER **5**

Not all gargoyles are horrific in appearance. In fact, they have 1001 faces. Sometimes monstrous, sometimes funny, their various forms can be inspired by the world of the supernatural and the mythical. As a matter of fact, some gargoyles are more or less realistic representations of humans. Many are in the form of an animal and are original: lions have wings, birds have horns, and dogs have flowing manes! Others seem to come from a fantasy world where fanged devils, dragons, sirens and winged creatures live.

GARGOYLES IN CANADA

Although gargoyles originated in Europe, they can be found everywhere, even in Canada. Below are a few examples.

Doc. 5.52 Gargoyles looking down from Montréal's Christ Church.

Doc. 5.53 Gargoyles atop the Peace Tower on Parliament Hill, in Ottawa.

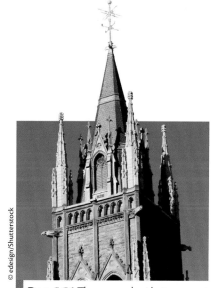

Doc. 5.54 The gargoyles that are part of Montréal's Anglican St. James United Church.

DISAPPEARING CREATURES

Although we do find gargoyles in America, it's in Europe that they are most numerous. Very few of the gargoyles of the Middle Ages remain. Some were ravaged by time and **inclement weather**, while others were destroyed when the buildings they adorned were themselves demolished. Some were restored as they aged, but the newer ones, which were never used to divert water, were built solely as ornaments.

Doc. 5.55 Gargoyles decorate the clock tower of Toronto's former City Hall.

Inclement weather: bad weather.

Synthesis

- The different religions in Québec society have substantially contributed to health and education, as well as social, community, business and commercial organizations.

- People of various origins and of various religious groups have contributed to Québec society's economic life and to the advancement of its norms and values.

- Since New France came into being, many Québec health establishments and charitable organizations have come into being due to the initiative of religious communities and laypeople. Helping one's neighbour is a fundamental value in most religions.

- Many religious congregations and community lay groups of all denominations have helped orphans, the aged, the poor and the handicapped by creating organizations such as Accueil Bonneau, the Salvation Army, Le Bon Dieu dans la rue and others.

- Forms of religious expression and religious elements are specific to a religion; these include its writings, symbols, practices, monuments, buildings or objects. In Québec, the most prevalent and numerous forms of religious expression come predominantly from the Judeo-Christian tradition.

- Christian churches are recognizable by their domes and steeples. Temples, synagogues and mosques, are found mostly in the Montréal area, and are often more discreet.

- All kinds of crosses can be found throughout Québec. For Christians, the Cross is symbolic of the Crucifixion of Jesus, but also of the gift of His life to renew His covenant with God.

- Wayside crosses have been places of prayer and reference points. In Inuit culture, inuksuks serve as reference points and mark holy places.

- Statues have an important place in religions where the divine is represented.

- The influence of religion can be found in folktales and legends.

- For the Amerindians, stories, like rules and rituals, serve very important functions. From one community to another, legends abound and serve a variety of functions.

- Many Québécois expressions refer to God, to religious or biblical figures and to various representations of the divine.

- Like the stories and expressions, many of Québec's superstitions are influenced by Christianity.

1 What is Québec's most visible form of religious expression?

2 What famous person was decorated by the Pope in recognition of his contribution to Catholic social action?

3 On what three ideological pillars was the success of Dupuis Frères based?

4 What was the religion of philanthropist Maurice Pollack?

5 What does it mean to be a philanthropist?

6 Why was the role of religious communities so important in healthcare from the time of New France until the first half of the 20th century?

7 Which creation of community is responsible for the Francophone hospitals in various regions of Québec, such as Lévis, Roberval, the Gaspé, Montmagny, Chicoutimi and Jonquière?

8 Explain the relationship between the *Female Benevolent Society of Montréal* and the Montréal General Hospital.

9 What was the role of Pope Pius IX in the creation of the Université de Montréal?

10 What is Accueil Bonneau? What role does it play?

11 What is the relationship between the *guignolée* and the Saint-Vincent-de-Paul Society?

12 Why are the most prevalent and numerous forms of religious expression in Québec essentially from the Judeo-Christian tradition?

13 Why are some places of worship devoid of decoration and pictorial art?

14 What is an ablution and what does it symbolize?

15 Is the shape of the Cross the same for all Christians?

16 What ritual customs are associated with roadside crosses?

17 Why are Christian figures or Christian elements found in many Amerindian stories?

18 Why does the Devil play such an important role in legends?

19 Why is it forbidden to dance on Ash Wednesday, according the legend of Rose Latulippe?

20 What does the expression "Like the Devil and holy water" mean?

21 In folktales, why is the Devil put in opposition to a popular hero, or a religious or divine figure?

22 What is triskaidekaphobia?

23 What is the purpose of throwing salt over one's shoulder?

24 In which areas have norms and values evolved because of the contribution of various religions?

The phenomenon of religion

Summary

6.1 The diversity of representations of the divine in the media   **138**

6.2 The diversity of mythical and supernatural beings in literature and the media   **144**

6.3 The fundamental elements of religious traditions in literature and the media   **149**

Culture and society   **152**

Here and elsewhere   **154**

Synthesis   **158**

CHAPTER 6

The diversity of forms of religious expression in literature and the media

Religious traditions are very important. They affect individuals, family, society, institutions, organizations, language and folklore. But did you know that the presence of religious traditions can be felt mostly in literature and the media?

Connections

- ■ ETHICS
  - Reflections on freedom: physical and social constraints
  - Individual and collective forms of expression
  - The role of the media in the transformation of values and norms

- ■ DIALOGUE
  - Forms of dialogue: interview
  - Means for developing a point of view: synthesis
  - Means for examining a point of view: reality and judgments of value

6.1 The diversity of representations of the divine in the media

References to religious traditions are plentiful and diverse.
Can you recognize representations of the divine or symbols
related to the divine in the media?

Doc. 6.1 A statue of Buddha preaching his message watches over a temple in Vienna, Austria.

Wikimedia

REPRESENTATIONS OF THE DIVINE

What is a representation of the divine? As a noun, the term divine means everything that comes from God or gods. The list of different types of representations is endless. Some are in the form of images while others consist of giving the divine names or attributes, like feelings, physical characteristics, proper names and labels. Symbols are also associated with the divine, like colours, forms, elements and plants.

Names and attributes given to the divine

Some religious traditions, such as Christianity, give the divine human physical attributes. Others, like Hinduism, do not always represent the divine as such. Rather, the divine may take on a human form or an animal form or perhaps a mixture of the two when coming into contact with the world of humans. Religions like Judaism or Islam and denominations such as Protestantism, forbid representing God in images.

The divine is given any number of proper names, labels or feelings. Following are some examples: God, Lord, Jesus, Christ, God the Father, God the Son, God the Holy Spirit, A-do-naï, Great Spirit, Wakan-Tanka, Brahma, Vishnu, Shiva, El Shaddai, the Awakened One, Consoler, the Enlightened One, Creator, Truth, Most Merciful, Infinite Holiness, Manitou, All Powerful, Omnipresent, Eloquim, Fairness, Magnificent, Most Holy, Infinitely Great, Light, Eternal, Protector, Purity, Infinitely Just, Infinitely Good, and Infinitely Perfect.

Symbols associated with the divine

All religious traditions have symbols that are associated with the divine. For example, colours and the elements of nature, fire, wind, water and earth, the stars, shapes and plants, are all symbols with which they are associated.

Colours

In all cultures, religious people speak of the divine in terms of the reality that surrounds them (colours, forms, elements of the body or of nature, etc.). For Christians, white is the colour associated with Jesus' garments during His Transfiguration. According to the gospel, for a short time during His life on Earth, Christ underwent a transformation in His corporal appearance, a transfiguration that revealed His infinite closeness to God. White is also the colour of the clothing worn by the Pope, who for all Catholics, is the successor of Peter the Apostle.

Elements and stars

Of all nature's elements, there is no doubt that fire is the most often associated with divine power. For example, for Christians, the flame symbolizes the Holy Spirit. The flame in the sanctuary lamp of Catholic churches symbolizes God's presence. For Jews, the flame of the menorah indicates the presence of God. Hindus burn offerings to render homage to their divinities. For many religions and spiritualities, the Sun, light and the stars are also symbolic of the divine.

Forms

The circle is a symbol that is associated with the divine. It represents the Divine Breath, without beginning and without end. Three intertwined circles evoke the Christian Holy Trinity, one God in three persons: the Father, the Son and the Holy Spirit. For Catholics, Jesus, His Mother, the Virgin Mary, and the saints are often represented crowned with an aureole or **halo**. This is a symbol of holiness. The term aureole comes from Latin and means crowned in gold. This ring also refers to the Sun and the Divine Light, particularly because of its round form and its luminosity. Most Native traditions see the circle as the gateway to spirituality.

Doc. 6.2 Three intertwined circles evoke the Holy Trinity.

Halo: a ring of light or a coloured circled that surrounds the head of holy figures in Christian pictorial art.

TO KNOW MORE +

Doc. 6.3 In Christian Orthodox churches, icons can be found on the iconostasis, a wall that separates the central part of the church where the faithful congregate, from the sanctuary where the altar is located. On Orthodox icons, the halo is omnipresent. It takes the form of a golden circle around the head of a saint. For Orthodox Christians, these icons are objects of great veneration. They are said to be windows to the world of the divine.

© Alexey Goosev/Shutterstock

Representations of the divine

In religious traditions that allow representations of the divine, the positioning of the hands is very meaningful. In Christian religions, Jesus is often represented with His hands outstretched and His palms turned upward, toward Heaven, as a sign of welcome. We also see representations of Jesus with one hand raised in blessing, protection and forgiveness. These gestures are representative of the attributes conferred upon Him.

Doc. 6.4 A stained glass window represents Christ healing a sick person. The sick man is being blessed by Christ. Both have halos above their heads.
© Jurand/Shutterstock

Hand positions are also important in representations of Hindu divinities. Gods are often portrayed with their right hand raised to shoulder height as a sign of blessing and protection. Both gods and goddesses are also often portrayed holding a lotus flower in their hand. The lotus flower, which is a very strong symbol in Hinduism, represents life and fertility. It is said that the god Brahma appeared above a lotus flower that held all creatures, and that had grown in the navel of the god Vishnu while he was resting on the cosmic ocean.

Doc. 6.5 A stained glass window represents the baptism of Jesus by St. John the Baptist. Jesus is clothed in white, a symbol of purity. A dove surrounded by a golden circle symbolizes the Holy Spirit descending upon Him in a ray of light. St. John the Baptist and Christ each have a halo, a symbol of holiness.
© Keith McIntyre/Shutterstock

CHAPTER 6

Many Hindu traditions invoke Vishnu as a supreme divinity, a divinity who can take any form and who is venerated under a thousand different names. It is said that this great god generally uses the name Vishnu when he descends to Earth to restore order when the world is threatened.

In the picture on the right, Vishnu has four arms, indicating that he is all-powerful and omnipresent. This god intervened on the world's behalf as a warrior during the war of the Bharatas. This is why in his upper right hand he is holding a disc with which he slices off the heads of his adversaries, and in his lower right hand a club with which he crushes them. A more spiritual significance is often accorded to these weapons; it states that Vishnu is a god who rids the world of all forms of ignorance. The conch shell he is holding in his upper left hand is also part of his arsenal. By blowing into this shell, he produces a sound that frightens all his enemies. This sound is not too different from the sound of the Veda or the famous OM which is a shortened version of the Veda. At the same time, he reassures the faithful by making the sign for the absence of fear in his lower left hand.

Vishnu's specific function is to maintain world order when it is threatened. However, wearing a royal tiara and adorned with various jewels, this god is also the one who destroys all forms of opposition and recreates beings. Here, like Brahma, he appears on a base in the form of a lotus flower. He can also be represented with a lotus flower in one hand. In this picture, Vishnu wants to be seen as an extremely seductive supreme divinity for those who surrender themselves to him because he can do anything; he can create, protect and destroy at the same time.

Doc. 6.6
A statue of Vishnu, the Preserver and Protector in Hindu tradition.
© Dmitry Rukhlenko/Shutterstock

Some history

The origins of the divine character attributed to the colour white are ancient. Since the time of Ancient Egypt, the Egyptians wrapped the bodies of their dead in a piece of white cloth.

The Jews adopted the colour white for some of their holidays. On the Jewish New Year, Rosh Hashanah, the faithful are clothed in white. The Torah is also rolled in white fabric.

The Celts reserved white clothing for the Druids, who were considered to be intermediaries between gods and humans, as well as for divinities.

For Christians, white is associated with baptism and marriage, among other things.

Doc. 6.7 The Druids and the divinities were dressed in white.

THE PHENOMENON OF RELIGION AND THE MEDIA

As the 21st century begins, we are living more than ever before in a world where advertising is everywhere. We see it everywhere on television, in the print media, on the Internet, on roadside billboards, in the métro, on buses, and sometimes even in the sky on long banners pulled by airplanes. In this proliferation of advertising messages, there are familiar symbols and elements whether we live in Montréal, Los Angeles or Paris. Many of these symbols come from religious traditions. According to marketing experts, advertisers use elements of religious tradition because even without any words, everyone understands them.

"Divine" images

Advertising sometimes uses gods and goddesses directly to help sell various products. In India, gods are so numerous that they are often used in advertising everywhere. The god who is best suited for the qualities of the product to be sold is the one chosen. For example, Lakshmi, the goddess of beauty, luck and prosperity, is venerated in rural India. She appears on billboards that advertise a specific brand of tractor. A battery manufacturer boasts about the power of his product by associating it with Shakti, the goddess of power.

Doc. 6.8 The goddess Lakshmi surrounded by the goddesses Parvati and Saraswati.

Doc. 6.9 The terms "paradise" and "heavenly" are often used to describe vacation destinations.
© Petra Silhava/Shutterstock

"Divine" advertising terms

References to the divine in advertising don't consist simply of images but are also found in common advertising vocabulary.

Some of the descriptive terms associated with the divine refer to the all-powerful, to protection, to perfection, to the ideal and to happiness, so it is not surprising that advertisers use these terms to describe their products.

Products that help people to experience pleasure or find comfort often use terms like divine, paradise or heavenly, pure, Eden, etc. These terms are associated with foods, drinks, clothing, pillows and vacation destinations. We can buy divine chocolate, pure water, a taste of heaven and heavenly beaches.

Doc. 6.10 Advertising regularly promises that an all-powerful product will perform real miracles.
© Thomas M. Perkins/Shutterstock

Other terms associated with religious realities are used to describe such everyday items as appliances or cleaning products. For this type of product, ads use terms like miraculous, blessing, powerful, etc. These ads promise us that such a liquid will accomplish miracles in removing carpet stains or that an extraordinary vacuum cleaner will be a real blessing for today's busy 21st century families.

Regardless of how they are used, whether exaggerated or not, terms that are associated with the divine have the advantage of being full of imagery which is as good as gold since they convey a great deal in a very few words.

Doc. 6.11 White, the symbol of purity and cleanliness, is widely used in advertising.
© LeahAnn Thompson/Shutterstock

The diversity of forms of religious expression in literature and the media

6.2 The diversity of mythical and supernatural beings in literature and the media

Do we borrow certain references from religious traditions or mythology found in literature and the media?

Mythical: that which comes from the supernatural, the imaginary.

Doc. 6.12 A statue of the legendary Robin Hood in front of England's Nottingham Castle. Although Robin Hood is a fictitious character, Nottingham Castle does indeed exist.

MYTHICAL AND SUPERNATURAL BEINGS

But what do we mean by mythical and supernatural beings? Mythical beings, as the name implies, are related to myths. Myths are stories of the supernatural handed down through tradition. Through their exploits, the **mythical** beings in these stories (heroes, divinities, mythical animals, etc.) provide a tentative explanation for natural and human phenomena. The ancient Egyptian, Greek and Roman religions gave the world the gift of a very rich mythology.

Supernatural beings have powers that defy the laws of nature. Among them are angels, spirits, the Devil and his many incarnations, etc. The boundary that separates mythical beings from supernatural beings is a very fine line since some of them, like Medusa, are mythical beings that have supernatural powers.

GODS AND MYTHICAL HEROES

Long before movies, literature told us all about mythical Greek and Roman gods and heroes, like Aphrodite, Saturn, Ulysses and Hercules. There were also the adventures of heroes from the Breton mythology of the Middle Ages, such as the legend of King Arthur and his sword Excalibur, where the characters struggled against the forces of evil to find the Holy Grail or Holy Chalice. Among the legend's heroes were Sir Lancelot, the Lady of the Lake, and Merlin the Magician, and their adventures have been the subject of a great many novels and movies. Robin Hood, defender of the poor and oppressed, who fought for good over evil, was another legendary hero from the Middle Ages. His adventures have appeared repeatedly in novels, films and comic books.

© Mark William Richardson/Shutterstock

Modern heroes

Literature and movies have created amazing heroes. When we hear the word "hero," we immediately think of the superheroes whose powers promote good and protect people against the forces of evil. We admire them for their powers, but we also admire them for their strong image and allure.

Literature and movies have introduced us to many such superheroes. They all have supernatural powers: superhuman strength, the ability to fly, immortality, the gift of magic, the ability to make themselves invisible, etc. Superheroes are usually associated with mythical features, like wings or some item that has magical powers (a wand, a light sword or a magic potion). The adventures of some comic book heroes have been adapted for television or film.

The quest for good is also part of many modern video games, where superheroes are numerous. Here again, they generally have supernatural powers and mythical features.

Whether they are mythical characters of antiquity, the Middle Ages or modern times, both heroes and superheroes have always had a quest, an ultimate goal–to re-establish the order of things, protect humanity from the forces of evil, devote themselves to saving others or even die for them. In short, heroes are constantly struggling for good to triumph over evil. And this struggle of good versus evil is very present in the sacred texts of most religions.

© Christos Georghiou/Shutterstock

Doc. 6.13 A superhero flying over the city, as we often see in movies.

TO KNOW MORE +

Heroes of a different kind

Today, heroes are not always make-believe. Very often, the media make heroes out of political, film or sports stars. These heroes don't have supernatural powers or mythical features. But some, in their own way, use their talents, their achievements, their commitments to various causes, and their generosity to inspire others and better humanity.

In Québec, Maurice Richard was one of the greatest hockey players of all time. His exploits on the ice and his spectacular goals made him a national hero. He believed that passion and determination could move mountains and make dreams come true.

Doc. 6.14 In Gatineau, the Government of Canada erected a statue in memory of the legendary Maurice Richard.

Wikipedia

Doc. 6.15 A 17th century marble bust by Italian sculptor Bernini. It represents Medusa with her snakes for hair.

Wikimedia

Doc. 6.16 A mythical representation of the griffin.

© Margie Hurwich/Shutterstock

Videowokart/Shutterstock

Doc. 6.17 A protective dragon keeps watch on the roof of an Asian temple.

SOME MYTHICAL ANIMALS

Among the mythical beings of legends are many animals that have inspired works of art and been included in novels, movies and cartoons. Below are some examples. Do you recognize some of them?

The **unicorn** is a mythical animal, a type of horse with a long twisted horn on the front of its head. In the legends of the Middle Ages, the unicorn symbolized strength and purity. In the East, it is said to bring good luck.

The **siren** is a mythical being, who according to Greek mythology is half-woman, half-bird. She sings above the seas to attract sailors. In the mythology of the Middle Ages, the mermaid (siren), had the head and body of a woman and the tail of a fish. Her beautiful singing lured sailors to their death on nearby reefs.

Medusa, who had snakes for hair, the teeth of a wild boar and golden wings, is a legendary monster in Greek mythology. Anyone who looked at her would turn to stone.

Pegasus, a horse in Greek mythology, is said to have been born of the blood of Medusa. He was a mount for Zeus, the god of all gods, who transformed Pegasus into a constellation. He has always been a source of inspiration for poets, painters and writers alike.

In Greek and Celtic mythology, the **dragon** is a creature that is often associated with fire. Its body is covered with scales that resemble those of a reptile. In the West, along with the snake, it is a symbol of evil. In the East, however, it is venerated as a bearer of light and wisdom. Dragons protect the teachings of Buddha.

The **leviathan** is a sea monster that is mentioned in the Bible. Its name means "colossal monster." During the Middle Ages, its open mouth represented the gates of hell.

Among these mythical animals, we also find legendary beings that originated, in part, in ancient mythology, like the **griffin**, a mythical winged-beast, with the head of an eagle and the body of a lion.

SUPERNATURAL BEINGS

Angels, devils and spirits are supernatural beings that are generally associated with one or more pages in the history of a religious tradition. They sometimes represent an ideal to which humans aspire. On the other hand, they can also represent beings that we don't want to associate with because they symbolize evil. The role of a supernatural being is generally to make us aware of a moral lesson, a teaching or a rule of conduct.

Ways of incarnating supernatural beings vary from one religious tradition to another. Christians, for example, have angels with two wings. Such supernatural beings also exist in the Jewish and Muslim religions but, in general, they are not represented because these religions forbid any image representation of supernatural beings. In the above-mentioned three religions, angels usually play the role of messengers.

Supernatural beings are very present in literature and the media. Some are taken directly from religious narratives, for example, the angels, the spirits, and the Devil. Others have their origins in mythology, as is the case for gods and goddesses.

The colours of good and evil

White and black are the traditional colours of good and evil. As mentioned previously, white is linked to purity, sainthood and good. To further accentuate the symbolism of the colour white, it is usually contrasted with black, which represents evil.

Besides black, red or fire is also associated with evil. Fire represents hell where, according to several religious traditions, the Devil resides. Red also indicates shrewd or cunning characters that are associated with insects, repulsive-looking animals or animals that represent danger such as snakes, spiders, rats or hyenas.

Doc. 6.18 The Archangel Gabriel is part of the Jewish, Christian and Muslim traditions. His role was that of a messenger. For the Jews, he announced a prophecy in the Old Testament Book of Daniel. For Christians, the Archangel Gabriel announced to Mary that she would give birth to a son. For Muslims, Gabriel revealed the divine message of the Koran to the prophet Muhammad. Only Christians represent the Archangel Gabriel in image form.

© Massimiliano Pieraccini/Shutterstock

Wikipedia

Doc. 6.19 At a medieval festival in France, the Devil was completely dressed in red.

Wikipedia

Doc. 6.20 In this work of art from the Middle Ages, we see the Devil painted in black and trapped in hell.

The diversity of forms of religious expression in literature and the media

147

Doc. 6.22 As pretty as a picture.

© Noam Armonn/Shutterstock

ANGELS, DEVILS AND SPIRITS IN THE MEDIA

Supernatural beings are found not only in literature and in movies but oftentimes in advertising as well. Angels in particular, and all things associated with them, like the sky, wings, halos or heaven, help sell a variety of products.

For example, take the advertising campaign for a popular brand of cream cheese. The ad takes place in Heaven, where angels are savouring the white product. Besides asserting that the cheese is "divine," its lightness and whiteness are associated with angels and the clouds in the background.

In advertising, angels also symbolize serenity, gentleness and wisdom. A child is given wings and a halo in order to convey a pretty-as-a-picture image. The colour white is also commonly used. It is used to advertise all kinds of products especially face and body soap or laundry detergent. The reason for this is simple: white means pure, cleanliness, neutrality, etc.

Allusions to Paradise or Heaven are also numerous. As opposed to hell, Heaven symbolizes the very best place to find oneself in. Ads show that in Heaven, we eat better, sleep better, the whites are whiter, and we have everything our heart desires!

If representations of the divine are abundant in advertising, the Devil and hell also have a prominent place when it comes to selling products. For example, many ads use the Devil and hell as a negative illustration for cigarettes or an upset stomach. A devilish character is also used as a temptation to sin. In such cases, this character is represented as inoffensive, almost cute, in an effort to seduce people into enjoying a treat of some kind.

Every year, literature, particularly movies, introduces us to supernatural beings that are often inspired by religious stories. This is especially true in books and movies destined for youths.

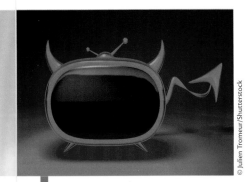

Doc. 6.23 A rather cute representation of the Devil.

© Julien Tromeur/Shutterstock

6.3 The fundamental elements of religious traditions in literature and the media

How can religious traditions influence literature and the media?

There are times when literature and the media help people know more about different religions. Books, movies, the Internet, advertising and information media all provide opportunities to explore the fundamental elements of a religion: its stories, rites and rules. To recognize these fundamental elements, the table below provides a general view of the origins, characteristics, functions and types of stories, rites and rules of religious traditions.

STORIES, RITES AND RULES

	ORIGINS	CHARACTERISTICS	FUNCTIONS	TYPES
STORIES	Stories emerge from a sacred founding experience, for example, the Ten Commandments being revealed to Moses, or the creation of the world.	The main characteristics of stories are that they: • are written in symbolic language • involve extraordinary characters • often tell of legendary exploits • portray an event taking place at some other time • ignore historical reality • convey inspirational values	Stories feed the senses and help to understand the sacred experience.	There are many types of stories: • founding stories • creation of the world • creation of human beings • creation of divinities • regenerative • etc.
RITES	Rites often originate from sacred stories.	Rites are symbolic sacred gestures or actions that help to communicate with the supernatural or the invisible.	The purpose of rites is: • to recapture the story from which they originate • retrace the origin of the story • rediscover the sacred experience • communicate with the divine	The main types of rites are: • initiation rites • funeral rites • sacrificial rites • rites of passage • liturgical rites • rites associated with religious practices • etc.
RULES	In general, rules emerge from sacred stories or their interpretation.	Rules prescribe various behaviours and set standards of conduct.	Rules make it possible to: • distinguish between good and evil • convey the values of a particular religion • indicate the path to follow in order to attain spiritual happiness	Among other things, rules may be related to behaviour in family situations and romantic relationships; they may also be related to practices related to food and **clothing** or social and religious duties.

The diversity of forms of religious expression in literature and the media

Doc. 6.24 A painting of the Last Supper where Jesus is depicted distributing the bread and wine to His Apostles.

STORIES REPRESENTED IN LITERATURE AND THE MEDIA

The ancient stories, told over and over, often originate from stories contained in the sacred texts of different religions. They are a source of inexhaustible inspiration for the fine arts, literature, and the media like movies, television, the Internet and advertising.

For example, artists have always been partial to the story of the Last Supper which was the last meal Jesus shared with His Apostles before He died on the Cross. There are frescoes, paintings, engravings and stained glass windows where Jesus is depicted distributing the bread and wine to His Apostles. Numerous films, some of which are masterpieces, and some advertisements, are inspired by the story of the first celebration of the Eucharist contained in Scripture. When you read the following text, you'll notice that there is a rite and a rule that stem directly from this story.

STORY	RITE	RULE
"He took bread, gave thanks and broke it and gave it to them saying, 'This is My body given for you; do this in remembrance of Me.' In the same way, after the supper He took the cup, saying, "This cup is the New Covenant of My blood which is poured out for you." Luke 22:19-20	For Christians, the celebration of the Lord's Supper or Communion. Holy Communion.	**"Do this in remembrance of me"** Jesus' commandment to repeat His gestures and His words is intended for the liturgical celebration by the Apostles and their successors, of the life, death and resurrection of Christ. Catechism of the Catholic Church Catechism of the Catholic Church

STORIES REVISITED IN ADVERTISING

Some ad creators have distorted some of the elements of religious traditions and have been heavily criticized for it. This was the case in European fashion ads that had altered Leonardo da Vinci's masterpiece, *The Last Supper*. The creators of the ads replaced Jesus and His Apostles by women; this drew the ire of the Catholic Church in France.

Doc. 6.25 Leonardo da Vinci's fresco *The Last Supper*, created between 1495 and 1497, is one of the many depictions of the last meal Christ shared with His Apostles. Ads have copied and reproduced this masterpiece countless times.
Wikimedia

Advertising uses biblical stories or the characters in these universally renowned stories. By doing this, advertisers ensure that even if they use only a few pictures, the public will recognize the characters, the story, and the main elements. The story of Creation has been a source of inspiration for many artists. Michelangelo's masterpiece, *The Creation of Adam*, comes from the Book of Genesis. Note that this story includes a rite and a rule.

Wikipedia

Doc. 6.26 One of the great masterpieces of religious art, *The Creation of Adam*, painted by Michelangelo in the 16th century on the ceiling of the Sistine chapel in Rome is often reproduced in ads.

STORY	RITE	RULE
. . . "The Lord God formed man from the dust of the ground and breathed into his nostrils the breath of life, and the man became a living being. Now the Lord God had planted a garden in the east, in Eden; and there he put the man he had formed. And the Lord God made all kinds of trees grow out of the ground–trees that were pleasing to the eye and good for food. In the middle of the garden were the tree of life and the tree of the knowledge of good and evil". Genesis 2:7-9 "So the Lord God caused the man to fall into a deep sleep, and while he was sleeping, he took one of the man's ribs and closed up the place with flesh. Then the Lord God made a woman from the rib he had taken out of the man, and he brought her to the man. The man said, 'This is now bone of my bones and flesh of my flesh; she shall be called woman, for she was taken out of man.' For this reason a man will leave his father and mother and be united to his wife, and they will become one flesh." Genesis 2:21-24	Marriage between a man and a woman	In the Catholic church, marriage is indissoluble. "That this means an indestructible union of their two lives, the Lord Himself points to it, reminding us of what the Creator's will was from the very beginning." Catechism of the Catholic Church

Michelangelo's masterpiece has often been used is ads. For example, one manufacturer of electronic devices used just one part of the painting. It reproduced the hands of both God and Adam with cellular phones. The picture of the hand of God giving life to Adam is also often used to illustrate the creative spirit, happiness and life.

Doc. 6.27 A photograph inspired by Michelangelo's masterpiece.

© James Steidl/Shutterstock

Culture and Society

Québec literature is full of imaginary stories that feature fantastic phenomena, mythical beings and mysterious beasts. Reworked by a contemporary Québec author, the following is the story of the long-tailed beast which is perceived to be the incarnation of the Devil.

Doc. 6.28 The long-tailed beast still roams in the great forests of the North.

THE LONG-TAILED BEAST

Long ago, you could catch a glimpse of the "long-tailed beast," especially around loggers' campsites in Northern Québec. And it was in 1912 that Pierriche Desrosiers saw it in broad daylight near the old Dautraye Manor, in Lanoraie. Although he couldn't accurately describe the beast, Desrosiers did say it had a hairy red tail that was an incredible two metres long.

Others who caught a glimpse of the beast claimed it was difficult to describe because, apparently, it was the last of its kind. The story goes on to say that with no father or mother, the beast came out of the murky depths, created for the sole purpose of tormenting the living. The long-tailed beast deliberately showed itself only every fifty years when the night was especially dark and a storm was ripping through the skies. In times past, people who made eye contact with the long-tailed beast disappeared in a flash, leaving no clue as to their whereabouts. Even today, it is said that the bold hunters who dare to follow it also vanish into the woods without any trace of what happened to them.

This one-of-a-kind beast, identifiable only by its tail, still roams the great forests of the North. It can easily hide in the woods because it blends in with its surroundings. Unfortunately, it is still a serious threat to anyone who ventures into the forest. Every summer, many careless campers disappear. Although the authorities are quick to deny that a long-tailed beast is involved in the disappearances, it is obvious to the members of various cryptozoology societies throughout the world that such a beast exists in Québec's large expanses.

Perhaps the long-tailed beast is the last of the "spirits of the Earth," commonly called "ogre snakes," that in the past inhabited the entire American West. In Sioux oral tradition, this creature, which is very sensitive to any degradation of its environment, is said to have migrated north at the beginning of American industrialization.

Bryan Perro and Alexandre Girard,
Créatures fantastiques du Québec, Éditions du Trécarré, 2007

Doc. 6.29 This is how some people imagined the long-tailed beast...

Doc. 6.31 The long-tailed beast deliberately showed itself only when the night was especially dark and a storm was ripping through the skies.

Doc. 6.30 Others believed it looked like this...

The diversity of forms of religious expression in literature and the media

Here and elsewhere

The beliefs of antiquity had characteristics all their own. This is obvious when we think about Greco-Roman mythology whose gods, goddesses, monsters, heroes and legends have greatly influenced the media and literature. Nearer to our time, during the Middle Ages, more legends, this time of Breton origin, inspired a great many authors and filmmakers.

CHAPTER 6

Wikipedia

Doc. 6.32 *The Birth of Venus,* painted by Sandro Botticelli around 1485.

GRECO-ROMAN MYTHOLOGY

The goddess of beauty and love is called **Aphrodite** (in Greek mythology) or **Venus** (in Roman mythology). It is said that she was born in the ocean. Some stories say that Venus' father is Uranus, god of the sky; others say that her father is Zeus, the god of gods, or Poseidon, the god of the sea. The beautiful painting, *The Birth of Venus* by Sandro Botticelli (1445-1510), depicts the birth of the goddess.

Aphrodite is the mother of many well-known gods, among them, Eros, the god of love.

Wikipedia

Aphrodite is known for her anger and the punishments that came with it. In fact, it is said that for her, love was a formidable weapon.

Heracles (or **Hercules** in Roman mythology) is that well-known mortal who successfully carried out his notorious 12 labours, allowing him to attain the title of god at the end of his life. Son of Zeus and Alcmene, a mortal woman, Hercules had his father's super-human strength which he used to conquer the most frightful monsters. This strength also made it possible for him to achieve, in ten years, twelve labours that were considered impossible to perform. Nowadays, we call these the Twelve Labours of Hercules. Because he was mistakenly suckled by Hera, Zeus's wife whose flowing stream of milk created the Milky Way, Hercules became immortal.

Doc. 6.33 A marble statue of Hercules by the sculptor Jean Cornu (1650-1710) in the gardens of the Château of Versailles in France.

Cronos (or **Saturn** for the Romans) was born of Uranus (the Sky) and Gaia (the Earth). Since Uranus did not like his children, Gaia pushed Cronos, the youngest of her sons born of that union, to kill his father.

When Cronos became a father himself, he was afraid his children would turn against him, so he decided to eat them as soon as they were born. His wife, Rhea, managed to save her youngest child, Zeus, by handing Cronos a stone wrapped in a blanket rather than the baby. This is how the life of Zeus, god of gods, was spared.

Athena (or **Minerva** for the Romans) is the goddess of wisdom and knowledge. She was born from the head of her father, Zeus. It seems this unusual birth is due to the fact that Zeus had eaten Metis, Athena's mother, when she was pregnant. Zeus likely did this because he was afraid of being dethroned by the child who was to be born of this union. It is to this goddess that the city of Athens owes its name. The inhabitants of this city have adopted this protective goddess because of the olive tree she gave them as a gift.

Ulysses is one of the heroes who is in fact mortal. Unlike Hercules, both his parents were mortals. He is known mainly for his trickery during the Trojan War. Hidden inside a wooden horse, his army of warriors succeeded in getting inside the enemy's fortress. This is how they seized the city of Troy.

Doc. 6.34 Detail from the fresco, *Allegory of Divine Providence*, by the painter Pietro da Cortona. Cronos is seen devouring one of his sons.

Doc. 6.35 The Parthenon atop the Acropolis in Athens, Greece.

Ulysses is a major figure in literature because he is at the very heart of the *Odyssey*, in which its author, Homer, tells of his many exploits. During his attempts to win back his country and find his wife Penelope after the Trojan War, Ulysses gouged out the eye of the Cyclops Polyphemus, son of Poseidon, who had imprisoned him. This confrontation is illustrated on a Greek goblet that dates back to 565-560 BCE. Ulysses was very fortunate in that he was able to count on the help of certain goddesses during this very difficult return journey.

Doc. 6.36 Ulysses gouging out the eye of the Cyclops Polyphemus. Wikipedia

The diversity of forms of religious expression in literature and the media

155

Here and elsewhere

Some history

The legend of King Arthur has inspired many a writer. In 12th century France, Chrétien de Troyes wrote five books about King Arthur's court: *Erec and Enide, Cliges, The Knight of the Cart* (Sir Lancelot), *The Knight of the Lion* (Yvain) and *The Story of the Holy Grail* (Perceval).

THE LEGEND OF KING ARTHUR

The Legend of King Arthur is a fictitious narrative from British mythology. It deals with the struggle between the Celts and the invading Anglo-Saxons in Great Britain during the 5th and 6th centuries. This very complicated legend explores various themes including power, chivalry, the supernatural and love. Below, you'll find an abridged version.

As a young man, Arthur succeeded in removing the sword Excalibur from the rock in which it was embedded. It was because of this exploit that he was crowned King of Brittany. Arthur set up his court in Camelot and married the beautiful Guinevere. With the advice of Merlin the Magician, Arthur created the Round Table, a group responsible for protecting the kingdom where all knights were considered equal. Among them was Sir Lancelot, a knight who had been brought up by the Lady of the Lake, a fairy. Sir Lancelot, the King's greatest knight, later had a romance with Queen Guinevere.

The Knights of the Round Table went looking for the Holy Grail, the chalice from which Christ drank during His last supper with His Apostles. Several knights including Sir Lancelot set out on the quest for the Holy Grail and failed. Finally, it was Sir Galahad the Pure, son of Sir Lancelot and Elaine, who succeeded in finding the Holy Grail with the help of two knights, Perceval and Bohort.

One day, the King learned of the affair between Sir Lancelot and Guinevere and condemned the Queen to be burned at the stake. Sir Lancelot rescued her and the lovers fled. The King went after them, leaving his kingdom in the hands of his illegitimate son Mordred, but Mordred rebelled against him. Arthur confronted Mordred's troops in an effort to win back his kingdom but he lost his life during the Battle of Salisbury.

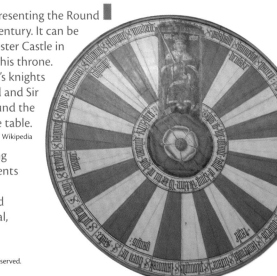

Doc. 6.37 This work of art representing the Round Table dates back to the 14th century. It can be found in the Great Hall of Winchester Castle in England. It depicts King Arthur on his throne. The names of 24 of the King's knights including Sir Lancelot, Sir Galahad and Sir Perceval are engraved around the perimeter of the table.
Wikipedia

Doc. 6.38 This piece of tapestry dating back to the early 15th century represents King Arthur. Since it was he who introduced the principle of the Round Table, where all the knights were equal, Arthur has become a symbol of good government.

THE LEGEND OF ROBIN HOOD

Did you know that there are several versions of the legend of Robin Hood? The following is the version told in the 19th century by French author Alexandre Dumas in his two works on the subject: Robin Hood Prince of Thieves and Robin Hood the Outlaw. The story takes place in England between 1162 and 1217 during the reigns of Henry II, Richard the Lionheart and John Lackland. The country was then under the Normans and this created numerous conflicts with the Saxons, the local population.

From early childhood, Robin was a skilled Saxon archer who had been cared for by Gilbert, a fine woodsman. In fact, Robin was the heir to the County of Huntingdon.

One day, as they were crossing Sherwood Forest, Allan Clare and his sister Marian met Robin. Allan was going to the castle of the Sheriff of Nottingham to ask him for the hand of his daughter, Christabel. The Sheriff refused. Allan and Robin tried to kidnap the young girl, but the plan failed and Christabel was sent away to London. Upon learning the role Robin had played in this affair, the Sheriff became furious. He did everything in his power to make sure Robin did not get his inheritance and even complained to the King.

The Sheriff's hatred meant Robin was now an outlaw. So Robin hid in Sherwood Forest with some friends, Little John and Friar Tuck. To make sure his little band was taken care of, Robin imposed a tax on people who travelled through the forest. They paid according to how rich they were.

Allan finally married Christabel and Robin married Marian. Then the band decided to rob the rich Normans and the royal clergy and give the money to the poor. King Richard the Lionheart intervened to give Robin back his land in Huntingdon. Unfortunately, the King had to leave on a Crusade and Prince John reversed the decision. To the great dismay of the Normans, Robin and his friends intensified their activities. During a battle against them, Marian was fatally wounded. Inconsolable, Robin let his band go their separate ways. He died at the age of 55 following a betrayal.

Some history

DID ROBIN HOOD REALLY EXIST?

Robin Hood's character first appeared in a text written in 1377 called Piers Plowman, a work by William Legland. Even in the Middle Ages, his adventures were entertaining the public. Many outlaws of the time had last names taken from the legend, especially Robin and Little John.

In the 18th century, British historians tried to prove that Robin–who at the time was considered a national hero by many–did, in fact, exist. Nowadays most historians believe that this character was wholly invented from stories about several outlaws of the time. This said, some important elements of the legend actually did exist, for example, Sherwood Forest and Nottingham Castle.

TO KNOW MORE +

Doc. 6.39 Sherwood Forest is located in Nottinghamshire in England. It is known throughout the world as having been the home of Robin Hood, and is also known for its ancient oak trees. Some of these trees are more than 500 years old! In 1952, the British government declared this forest a protected nature reserve. It attracts some 500 000 visitors every year.

Outlaw: an individual acting outside the law.

The diversity of forms of religious expression in literature and the media

Synthesis

- The term "divine," when used as a noun refers to all things that come from God or the gods. Representations of the divine are infinitely diverse.

- Some representations of the divine are images, while others consist of allocating names or attributes to the divine, such as feelings, physical characteristics, proper names and labels.

- Symbols are also associated with the divine, like colours, forms, elements and plants.

- Of all the elements in nature, fire is without a doubt most often associated with divine power.

- In religious traditions that have image representations of the divine, the position of the hands is quite significant.

- Many of the symbols that come from religious traditions are used by marketing experts.

- In advertising, gods and goddesses are sometimes called upon directly to promote the sale of various items.

- Advertising terms often refer to the divine.

- Mythical beings are associated with myths. Supernatural beings have features that defy the laws of nature.

- Long before movies, we learned about mythical gods and heroes through literature. Literature and movies also introduced various heroes of their own.

- The quest for good is also depicted in modern video games, where superheroes abound.

- Among the mythical figures born of legends are many animals that have become works of art, found in novels, movies or cartoons, like the unicorn, the siren (or mermaid), Medusa, Pegasus, the dragon, the leviathan, the griffin, etc.

- Supernatural beings thrive in literature and the media. Some are taken directly from religious texts, for example, angels, spirits and the Devil. Others come from mythology like the various gods and goddesses.

- Some colours are associated with good and others with evil, like white, black and red.

- Supernatural beings are not only found in literature or movies. They are also abundant in advertising. In particular, angels and their associated elements, such as the sky, wings, halos and heaven, are used to sell a large variety of products.

- Whether it be literature, movies, the Internet, advertising or information media, most provide opportunities to delve deeper into basic religious elements: stories, rituals and rules.

- The stories contained in religious sacred texts are an inexhaustible source of inspiration for the fine arts and literature, or for media like movies, television, the Internet and advertising.

1 What ritual is associated with the story of the Last Supper? From which religious tradition is it taken?

2 What did the Transfiguration reveal about Jesus?

3 What is a griffin? Where does this representation come from?

4 What were the Druids to the Celts?

5 To which supernatural being is the colour red often attributed?

6 In India, why is the goddess Lakshmi used in advertising?

7 What is the divine?

8 In some publicity advertisements, what words are used and associated with religious facts to qualify products?

9 What does the flame in the sanctuary lamp represent in Catholic churches?

10 What are the characteristic qualifications for supernatural beings?

11 What is a halo and what does this symbol signify?

12 In any given era, what is the ultimate goal of heroes and superheroes?

13 What is the significance of the lotus flower in Hinduism?

14 What are Medusa's mythical features?

15 In what advertising context is the image of the hand of God giving life to Adam used?

16 What role do supernatural beings play?

17 What did Robin Hood defend? Did he really exist?

18 In the Jewish and Muslim religions, can supernatural beings be represented in the arts and in the media? Justify your answer.

19 Why are angels used in advertising?

20 What symbolism is attributed to white and to black?

21 Explain the use of religious representations in the popular ad for a brand of cream cheese.

22 What super powers are generally attributed to superheroes?

23 What does the OM sound symbolize in Hinduism?

24 What is the purpose of stories, rituals and rules of religious traditions?

Dialogue

Reflecting to improve communications or communicating to improve reflection?

SUMMARY

SECTION 1
Forms of dialogue   162
Tools 1 to 7

SECTION 2
Means for developing a point of view   178
Tools 8 to 12

SECTION 3
Means for examining a point of view   190
Types of judgments
Tools 13 to 16
Processes that may hinder dialogue
Tools 17 and 18

Conditions that foster dialogue
Tool 19

Table of different forms of dialogue

There are many ways to practise dialogue. The table below presents seven different forms of dialogue. In the "Context" column, you will find tips on the best way to use one or more forms of dialogue.

FORMS OF DIALOGUE	DEFINITIONS	CONTEXT	EXAMPLES
Tool 1 Conversation 	A verbal exchange to **share** ideas and experiences.	It is used in small groups when you want to share information or ideas on a subject of common interest.	During recess, you and Thomas talk in the schoolyard about your soccer team losing the last game.
Tool 2 Discussion 	An exchange of opinions or ideas for **examining** a point of view.	It is used when you want to know more about others' points of view and arguments on a particular subject.	You and your teacher talk about the need for a school dress code.
Tool 3 Narration 	A detailed account that **relates** facts or events in a written or verbal manner.	It is used when you want to describe facts or events in a **neutral** way without expressing your point of view.	You read a story to children.

FORMS OF DIALOGUE	DEFINITIONS	CONTEXT	EXAMPLES
Tool 4 Deliberation 	An analysis of different aspects of a question (facts, interests, norms, values, consequences, etc.) in order to **make a group decision.**	It is used when the purpose of the exchange is to reach a common decision.	Participants at a conference deliberate on a proposal to make the recreation centre more easily accessible for people in wheelchairs. The proposal is adopted.
Tool 5 Interview 	A meeting where one **questions** an individual on their activities, ideas, and experiences in order to gain knowledge of the individual or the subject of expertise.	It is used when you want to get to know someone better or to benefit from this person's experience to improve your knowledge of a specific subject.	A successful author of children's books is interviewed by a journalist on the qualities that make a good children's book.
Tool 6 Debate 	An **organized** exchange that is overseen by a moderator who times each speaker to ensure that different points of view are expressed on a given subject.	It is used when you want to have a moderator lead a discussion so that exchanges allow participants' points of views to be expressed.	As part of an election campaign for president of the student council, a debate is organized so that candidates can express their points of view.
Tool 7 Panel 	A meeting between **subject matter experts** who share their knowledge to shed light on a subject.	It is used when you want to gain specific knowledge from certain subject matter experts by discussing an issue with them.	Your school organizes a panel made up of a psychologist, a social worker, a police officer, a nurse and a student representative to discuss verbal abuse.

Tool 1
Conversation

What is a conversation?

- A conversation is a form of dialogue.

- Its purpose is to talk informally about facts, values and ideas.

- It is used when you are in a small group and you want to share your emotions, feelings and points of view about facts, values or ideas.

Proposed approach

Remain open to the ideas, values, emotions and points of view being expressed by the members of your group.

1. Listen attentively and respectfully to each person who speaks to you.

2. Actively participate in the conversation.

3. Keep a constructive attitude to encourage reflection, if necessary.

COMPLEMENTARY FORMS OF DIALOGUE
- Narration (**tool 3**)
- Interview (**tool 5**)

PITFALLS TO AVOID
- Not listening
- Talking non-stop
- Remaining passive, not engaging in the conversation
- Getting off topic

> **! WARNING**
>
> This is not a linear approach. You can skip to any of the steps at any time.

Model of a **conversation**

SHOULD WE ALWAYS TELL THE TRUTH?

Julian: Last week, during recess, my best friend, Thomas, accidentally hurt Anne-Marie. The head monitor didn't see anything. She asked who had hurt Anne-Marie. Thomas didn't say anything. She then threatened to punish the entire class if no one told her who did it. I felt really bad. If I told the truth, I would be betraying my best friend; if I stayed quiet and didn't tell the truth, the entire class would be punished.

Philip: I don't know what I would have done in your place. It's not easy to choose between friendship and the truth. I think you should forget about Thomas. He's not a true friend. The other day, he refused to help me with my English homework. Coming back to your story, I think that it's not always easy to know when to tell the truth.

Julian: I'll talk to Thomas about it. He must feel bad knowing that the class is being punished because of him. I don't think it's a good idea to cover up for him. In his case, telling the truth would have given him the chance to tell his side of the story and avoid having the entire class punished.

A conversation allows people to talk about facts.

Julian is becoming more reflective as the conversation progresses.

A title presented in the form of a question sparks interest and reflection.

A conversation allows people to talk about values and norms.

In a conversation, it is acceptable to stray off topic, as Philip did when he explained how he felt about Thomas.

Tool 2
Discussion

COMPLEMENTARY FORMS OF DIALOGUE
- Deliberation (tool 4)
- Debate (tool 6)

PITFALLS TO AVOID
- Not listening to the points of view and arguments being expressed by the other discussion participants
- Not being clear in expressing your point of view
- Using processes that create obstacles to dialogue

What is a discussion?
- A discussion is a form of dialogue.
- It is an exchange of opinion on facts, ideas and values.
- Its purpose is to examine different points of view.
- It is used when you want to share information and ideas on a subject of common interest in a small group.

Proposed approach
1. Identify the subject, state the problem being addressed by the discussion, as well as the questions related to the problem and the resulting issues.

2. Organize your information.
   - Put your ideas in order.
   - Clarify your opinion and arguments.
   - Prepare your questions so that you can find out more about the other discussion participants' points of view.

3. Discuss opinions based on facts, ideas and values:
   - by expressing your point of view and arguments in a clear and qualified manner
   - by listening to other participants in the discussion
   - by not hindering the progression of the discussion through harmful approaches that use other people (tool 17), such as a personal attack, an argument based on authority, or the use of a stereotype
   - by concluding the exchange with a return to the initial question to find out what has come out of the discussion

> **! WARNING**
> This is not a linear approach. You can skip to any of the steps at any time.

Model of a discussion

IS MY SCHOOL DRESS CODE AN OBSTACLE TO MY FREEDOM?

Remi: I'm against the new school dress code. The way I dress is no one's business but my own. I have the right to express my personality through the clothes that I like. We should be free to wear what we want. The school should not get involved; it's none of its business.

Stephanie: I don't agree with you, Remi. The school has a right to impose restrictions on our freedom. The purpose of a dress code is to ensure that certain common values are respected. "Belly shirts" are not allowed so that we can maintain a certain **decency** in how we are dressed; we don't allow any clothes that display violent words or symbols so that we can maintain **peace** in the school; we don't allow certain designer clothes to avoid bullying and to provide students with a **safe environment**.

Vanessa: I share Stephanie's point of view, but I think that the school administration should have spoken to the student council. We're old enough for our opinions to count. In my opinion, freedom is also the right to say what we think.

Remi: I'm not surprised by what you just said, Vanessa. Ever since you were elected class president, you want to decide everything yourself. I found Stephanie's arguments interesting. I didn't look at the dress code that way. I agree with not allowing designer clothes to avoid bullying. But I don't think that defending decency is a worthwhile cause in this day and age.

A title presented in the form of a question gives direction to the discussion.

Within the discussion framework, Remi states his point of view, and then provides four arguments against having a school dress code.

Stephanie uses values to support her point of view in favour of a school dress code.

Remi puts up an obstacle to the flow of the discussion by making a personal attack on Vanessa for discrediting his point of view (personal attack, tool 17).

At the end of the exchange, Remi's conclusion shows that he has reflected on the question asked in the title of this discussion.

Tool 3
Narration

What is a narration?

- A narration is a form of dialogue.

- A narration is a story that relates facts or events in written or verbal form.

- It is neutral in tone; therefore, it does not reflect the narrator's opinions or feelings.

Proposed approach

1. Identify the subject, and make sure that the subject is clearly stated in your title and introduction.

2. Organize your information.
   - Determine the order in which facts will be presented (chronological, order of importance, etc.).
   - Prepare an outline.

3. Relate relevant and essential facts:
   - by using precise vocabulary
   - by setting the context for the subject
   - by concluding the narration

COMPLEMENTARY FORMS OF DIALOGUE
   - Interview (tool 5)
   - Conversation (tool 1)

PITFALLS TO AVOID
   - Expressing your opinion or feelings about the events or facts that you are relating
   - Presenting facts in random order
   - Failing to conclude your narration

! **WARNING**

This is not a linear approach. You can skip to any of the steps at any time.

Model of a **narration**

A VISIT TO A MOSQUE

As part of our research on holy sites in Québec, last month, I visited a mosque during an open house organized by the Montréal Muslim community. The mosque's imam was the tour guide. I learned that he is the religious leader of the Muslims, as a priest is to Catholics, a pastor to Protestants, and a rabbi to Jews.

The first thing that caught my attention during this visit was the way that Muslims pray. It was particularly surprising to see that the entire floor of the mosque was carpeted. The imam explained that the carpet was used for prayer. Muslims prostate themselves on the prayer rug five times a day to say their prayers. They face Mecca, the Muslim holy city in Saudi Arabia. This city is sacred to Muslims because their major prophet, Muhammad, was born in that city.

The imam also showed us a fountain, which is found in all mosques. Muslims use it to purify themselves before saying prayers. I thought the fountain looked really old and ugly. He then took us to a platform, called a *minbar,* where he leads the congregation in prayer.
The tour ended with him offering us juice, tea and cookies from Morocco, his country of origin.

What I learned from my visit is that prayer is a very important part of Muslim life.

Tool 4
Deliberation

What is a deliberation?

- A deliberation is a form of dialogue.

- It is an exchange of opinions on different aspects of a question (facts, interests, norms, values, consequences, etc.).

- It is used when the purpose of the exchange is to reach a common decision.

Proposed approach

1. Identify the subject, state the problem being deliberated, as well as the questions and issues related to the problem and the compromises that would be acceptable solutions for all of the participants.

2. Organize your information.
   - Put your ideas in order.
   - Clarify your opinion and arguments.
   - Prepare your questions so that you can find out more about the other discussion participants' points of view.
   - Discuss the rules to be observed during the deliberation.

3. Adopt a positive attitude that seeks to find a group solution.

4. Discuss opinions based on facts, ideas and values:
   - by expressing your point of view and arguments in a clear and qualified manner
   - by listening to other participants with an open mind, by searching for solutions
   - by not hindering the progression of the deliberation through obstacles to dialogue (tool 17), such as a personal attack or an argument based on authority which might prevent the group from coming to a decision
   - by concluding the deliberation with a group decision that respects the points of views of all participants

> ! **WARNING**
>
> This is not a linear approach. You can skip to any of the steps at any time.

COMPLEMENTARY FORMS OF DIALOGUE
- Discussion (tool 2)
- Debate (tool 6)

PITFALLS TO AVOID
- Not cooperating to find a solution
- Taking a position without considering the points of view of all participants

Model of a deliberation

A UNITED SOCCER TEAM

John begins the deliberation by clearly stating the team's problem and appealing to others to find a solution.

John: We've lost our last three games. We need to find a solution to our problems; otherwise, we're going to end up in last place.

Anne-Marie: I think the solution is simple: we need to have our best players on the field as much as possible and have our weaker players on the field less often. We're the only team in the league that gives equal time to all players.

Louis: Your solution makes no sense, Anne-Marie! Soccer is a team sport. The problem is that we aren't playing well together as a team. I think that if we worked harder at practices, we could beat the other teams.

Louis has a closed mind. His criticism will not help the group find a solution.

John: If we want to keep giving equal playing time to all players, then the weaker players will need to improve. So I don't think we need to limit their playing time on the field; on the contrary, we need to have them play more often.

John's solution incorporates elements of Louis' and Anne-Marie's points of view.

Anne-Marie: John, I don't understand your solution. Could you please explain your idea to us?

Anne-Marie actively seeks a solution by asking John to clarify his idea.

John: We could have an extra practice every week for players that are having a hard time. The whole team would benefit.

Louis: Good idea. Not only would the team improve, everyone would get to participate.

Anne-Marie: I'd like to try your solution. We'll see if it helps us win our next few games.

Once the deliberation has ended, Anne-Marie shows her support for the solution found by the other members of her team.

Tool 5
Interview

What is an interview?

- An interview is a form of dialogue.

- An interview is a meeting where a person is questioned on topics such as activities, ideas and experiences.

- It is used when you want to get to know someone better or to find out more about a subject that this person knows well.

Proposed approach

1. Identify the subject, then state what you would like to learn about the person being interviewed: their personal life or work, particular skills, experience, etc.

2. Organize your information.
   - Do research on the person being interviewed.
   - Put your questions in order before the interview begins.

3. Question a person on topics such as activities, ideas and experiences:
   - by beginning the interview with ordinary questions, such as "Could you please tell us, in a few words, who you are?"
   - by asking questions clearly
   - by first asking general questions, then moving toward more specific questions
   - by listening to the person being interviewed to adjust your questions according to the circumstances
   - by concluding the interview by thanking the person for answering your questions

▌ PITFALLS TO AVOID
   - Not being sufficiently prepared, which prevents you from asking relevant questions to the person being interviewed
   - Straying away from the topic that you want to discuss with the person being interviewed and by dwelling on anecdotes
   - Not listening to the person being interviewed because you are too busy thinking about the next few questions that you plan to ask

---

! WARNING

This is not a linear approach. You can skip to any of the steps at any time.

▌ COMPLEMENTARY FORMS OF DIALOGUE
   - Panel (tool 7)
   - Narration (tool 3)

Model of an **interview**

AN ABORIGINAL CHIEF TELLS US ABOUT HIS RELIGIOUS BELIEFS

Saïd: Hello. In a few words, could you please tell us who you are and what your role is in your community?

Algonquin Chief: *Kwey wichkewan,* Saïd. In Algonquian, this means "Hello, my friend Saïd." You may not know it, but more than 3000 people in Québec and Ontario currently speak our language, Algonquian. I am from *Kipawa,* a community in the very lovely region of Abitibi-Temiscamingue. There are beautiful lakes in that area. And the word kipawa means "water" in Algonquian.

Saïd: Could you please tell us a bit about the religious beliefs of your people?

Algonquin Chief: Our traditional beliefs are based on nature. For Algonquins, the basic religious rule is to respect nature. Nature does not belong to us; neither does the Earth we live on. We are sometimes shocked by the lack of respect some White people show toward nature. In our tradition, nature was created by the Great Spirit, *Kitchi Manito,* to whom we pay the greatest respect. Algonquins have traditionally offered corn to the Great Spirit so that he will watch over us.

Saïd: Could you please tell us a bit more about what nature represents in the religious beliefs of your people?

Algonquin Chief: Nature does not belong to us, and nature will only provide for us if we approach her with a respectful attitude. Hunting or fishing must be done with respect for nature and the spirits of the animals. Animals have a spirit and that deserves to be respected.

Saïd: I'd like to thank you for this interview. Now we know a bit more about the religious beliefs of the Algonquin people.

Saïd begins his interview properly, by asking the interviewee to introduce himself.

Saïd first asks a general question related to the subject of the interview.

Saïd follows up with a more specific question. His interview moves from general questions to specific ones. He also shows that he is listening by asking for more details about an element in the Algonquin chief's answer.

The conclusion comes back to the main topic and tells the interviewee that the interview has ended.

Tool 6
Debate

What is a debate?

- A debate is a form of dialogue.

- A debate is an exchange of ideas where participants express their points of view.

- It is used when you want to organize a discussion led by a moderator so that exchanges allow participants' to express their points of view on a given subject.

Proposed approach

1. Identify the subject, specifying the topics to be discussed during the debate, the allotted time for each participant to speak, and the name of the person who will act as moderator.

2. Organize your information.
   - Meet with participants beforehand so that you can agree on the rules of conduct to be followed during the debate: respect, listening, etc.
   - Before the debate begins, prepare, in order, the questions that will be asked by the moderator.

3. Ensure that the moderator:
   - introduces the participants, the topics to be discussed, and the rules to be followed
   - asks questions that help participants to be clear on their position with regard to the topics being discussed
   - encourages exchanges between participants so that what transpires is a genuine debate of ideas

COMPLEMENTARY FORMS OF DIALOGUE
   - Discussion (**tool 2**)
   - Deliberation (**tool 4**)

PITFALLS TO AVOID
   - Failing to state clear rules for the debate before it begins
   - Failing to enforce the rules during the debate
   - Being satisfied with participants simply expressing their points of view without a genuine exchange of ideas

> **! WARNING**
>
> This is not a linear approach. You can skip to any of the steps at any time.

Model of a **debate**

ELECTION OF A CLASS PRESIDENT:
A DEBATE TO CLARIFY OUR CHOICES

Moderator: Hello. I'd like to introduce the three candidates running for election: Karine, Cristina and Mark. They will each have 5 minutes to explain their campaign platform. After that, they will have 10 minutes to debate amongst themselves. I would ask each participant to show respect for the others and to remain open-minded to what the other candidates have to say. After the debate, you may ask the candidates questions. The candidates' names have been randomly chosen to determine the order in which they will speak. Karine has been chosen to speak first. Go ahead, Karine.

The moderator states the rules of the debate.

Karine: I am running for class president because I would like to create a newspaper for students in Secondary 1 and 2. In my opinion, the school newspaper presently caters only to students in Secondary 5. If we had our own newspaper, we could have columns on items of interest to us, like fashion, perhaps...

Moderator: Thank you, Karine. Mark, it's your turn to speak.

Mark: If I am elected, I would like to organize a soccer league with the Secondary 2 classes. We could have a tournament at the end of the year to see who has the best team. I don't think Karine's idea would work. A fashion column would be of interest only to girls.

Mark does not follow the rules of the debate, which include a discussion after the candidates' platforms have been presented.

Moderator: Mark, you must present your platform without criticizing the positions of the other candidates. The discussion will take place after everyone has had a chance to speak. I will now turn the floor over to our final candidate, Cristina.

The moderator does her job properly and intervenes to remind Mark of the rules.

Cristina: Hello. I'm running for class president because I would like to set up a green committee. The committee could be in charge of recycling and cleaning the schoolyard in the spring. We need to do our part for the environment...

Moderator: I would like to thank our candidates. We will now begin the discussion period. We'll start with Karine's idea to create a newspaper if she is elected. Do you have any questions on Karine's platform?

After all of the platforms have been presented, the moderator introduces a new form of dialogue: a discussion.

The debate continues with a discussion of the three candidates' platforms. At the end of the discussion, the moderator concludes the debate.

Moderator: I would like to thank the candidates and congratulate them for showing respect and openness during this debate. It is now time for the candidates to answer any questions that the audience may have.

Tool 7
Panel

COMPLEMENTARY FORMS OF DIALOGUE

- Interview (**tool 5**)
- Discussion (**tool 2**)

PITFALLS TO AVOID

- Failing to meet with the panellists beforehand to establish rules for the panel
- Failing to enforce the established rules during the panel
- Failing to ask panellists questions after their presentation

What is a panel?

- A panel is a form of dialogue.

- It is an organized meeting, led by a presenter, during which subject matter experts share their knowledge on a particular subject.

- It is used when you want to gain specific knowledge from certain subject matter experts by discussing an issue with them.

Proposed approach

1. Identify the subject, specifying the topics that will be discussed during the panel, the time allotted to each panellist, and the name of the person who will act as presenter.

2. Organize your information.
   - Meet with panellists beforehand so that you can agree on how the panel will proceed: presentation time, order of presentations.
   - Prior to the panel, gather necessary information from the panellists about their lives and experience for a brief panel presentation.

3. Determine the panellists' points of view:
   - by introducing the panellists and the topics to be discussed, and following the established order of presentation
   - by remaining attentive while the panellists give their presentations
   - by asking questions that allow the panellists to explain their points of view on the topics under discussion

Model of a panel

CO-OPS: THE VALUES INHERENT IN THE SPIRIT OF COOPERATION

Presenter: Today, we have organized a panel to learn more about co-ops. There are many of them in Québec. As we will see, participating in a co-op means having certain values in common with other members of the co-op. Our panellists are co-op members; they will certainly be able to teach us a lot about different types of co-ops and the values that guide them.

I would like to present Mr. Pierre Lacombe, manager of our local Caisse Populaire, Mr. Andrew Levin, who heads a student co-op, and Ms. Lucia Barker who is a member of a farming co-op. I will now turn the floor over to Mr. Lacombe who will be our first speaker. Mr. Levin and Ms. Barker will follow. Once their presentations are over, you may ask our panellists questions.

Pierre Lacombe: I would like to talk to you about our Caisse Populaire. Do you have a savings account at our bank? If you do, then you are already a member of our co-op. When you opened your account, not only did you start saving money, you also became a co-op member. I would like to let you know that, as a member of our Caisse Populaire co-op, even though you may not have a lot of money in your account, you have as much power as any other member of the co-op. In a Caisse Populaire co-op, all members are equal, regardless of the amount of money they have in their account. They have the right to express their point of view on the bank, to vote for the bank executives, or to run for election if they would like to be part of the board of directors.

Presenter: Thank you, Mr. Lacombe. We will now turn the discussion over to Mr. Levin, who is a member of a student co-op.

Andrew Levin: Hello. Perhaps you weren't even aware that student co-ops exist! At my CEGEP, we have set up a co-op for books and school supplies. Students sell these items at the college bookstore. To become a member of the student co-op, all you have to do is buy a membership card for $10. In addition to offering textbooks and school supplies at a good price, the creation of our co-op turned out to be a very enriching experience. We learned how to work together, how to face challenges, and how to become more autonomous. Several of us work at the co-op to help pay for our studies. Later, when you go to college, I encourage you to become a member of a student co-op.

Presenter: Thank you, Mr. Levin. Ms. Barker, who works at a farming co-op, will now tell us more about her co-op.

Lucia Barker: Hello. You are no doubt aware that our ancestors were almost all farmers who lived in rural areas. They learned early on in life that it was good to help each other. At the end of the summer, several families would often get together to harvest the crops. The first farming co-ops were probably based on this tradition of helping each other. For example, in my farming co-op, we joined together to purchase farm equipment. Farmers who made less money would not have been able to buy such expensive machinery. Since it is purchased collectively by the group, the machinery belongs to everyone and is used by everyone when necessary—like at harvest time.

Presenter: I would like to thank Ms. Barker and our other panellists. Our panel discussion is now over.

The presenter states the topic, introduces the panellists, and states the order in which the presentations will be given.

Mr. Lacombe tells the students about his co-op's values.

Like Mr. Lacombe of the Caisse Populaire, Mr. Levin talks about other values related to his experience in the student co-op.

Another value associated with co-ops is mentioned by Ms. Barker.

At the end of the panel, the presenter forgets to ask the students if they have any questions or comments.

Table showing different means for developing a point of view

There are many means for developing a point of view while practising dialogue. The table below presents five different means. In the "Context" column, you will find tips on the best way to use one or more means for developing a point of view.

MEANS FOR DEVELOPING A POINT OF VIEW	DEFINITIONS	CONTEXT	EXAMPLES
Tool 8 Description 	A complete list of the specific characteristics of an ethical situation or a form of religious expression.	It is used when you want to make a note of ethical situations or forms of religious expression. It is prepared by answering a few questions likely to give a good description of the phenomena: who? what? when? where? how? why? how many? etc.	While giving a narration (**tool 3**) on the Catholic Church, you **describe** the local church.
Tool 9 Comparison 	A list that establishes the differences or similarities between two or more elements.	It is used when you want to describe and compare ethical situations or forms of religious expression. Comparisons may help you draw certain conclusions.	You **compare** the restrictions on freedom at home and at school.

SECTION 2

Means for developing a point of view

■ MEANS FOR DEVELOPING A POINT OF VIEW	■ DEFINITIONS	■ CONTEXT	■ EXAMPLES
Tool 10 Synthesis 	A structured and coherent summary of the key elements (ideas, facts, experiences, arguments, etc.) of a discussion, story or text.	It is used when you want to do the following: - organize your ideas or arguments - make a note of ideas and arguments expressed during a discussion, debate, panel, etc. - summarize, in a coherent manner, a chapter of a book, a newspaper article, information gathered from the Internet, etc.	At the end of a panel discussion (**tool 7**) on ethical values associated with teen sexuality, you present a **synthesis** of the ideas expressed by the panellists.
Tool 11 Explanation 	The development of an idea to better understand its meaning.	It is used when you want to do the following: - clarify ideas, a point of view or arguments by making them more explicit - add definitions and examples to a text so that it is easier to understand - provide further explanation for answers given to questions asked by participants in a debate	You discuss (**tool 2**) why Catholics genuflect (bend down on one knee in church as a sign of respect). In response to a question from a Muslim student, you **explain** the background behind this Catholic practice.
Tool 12 Justification 	A presentation of ideas and arguments in a structured and logical manner to support a point of view.	It is used when you want to elaborate on a point of view by presenting a relevant and coherent argument in order to convince one or more people.	In a debate (**tool 6**) on the values transmitted by electronic games, you **justify** your position against violence in these games.

Tool 8
Description

What is a description?

■ A description is a means for developing a point of view.

■ It is a complete list of the specific characteristics of an ethical situation or form of religious expression.

■ It is used when you want to make a note of ethical situations or forms of religious expression.

Proposed approach

1. Answer the following questions if they are relevant to what you want to describe:
   - ☐ Who? Founder, author, organizer, group, etc.
   - ☐ What? Work of art, gathering, event, fact, etc.
   - ☐ When? Year, era, season, etc.
   - ☐ Where? Location, environment, etc.
   - ☐ How? Process, means, etc.
   - ☐ Why? Motive, interest, need, etc.
   - ☐ How many? Frequency, number of people, etc.
   - ☐ Etc.

2. Ensure that the description is complete.
   - ☐ Did the answers to the questions above help you to fully describe your subject? If not, then complete your description.
   - ☐ Ask yourself the following question: "Did I only describe what is of interest to me?" If so, then correct the description by adding all of the characteristics.

3. Determine the order in which ideas will be presented in your description.
   - ☐ Prepare an outline for your description.
   - ☐ In your description, start with the most important elements, and then continue with the secondary elements.
   - ☐ Be sure to include a conclusion with your description.

! WARNING

This is not a linear approach. You can skip to any of the steps at any time.

■ COMPLEMENTARY WAYS OF DEVELOPING A POINT OF VIEW
- ☐ Synthesis (**tool 10**)
- ☐ Comparison (**tool 9**)

■ PITFALLS TO AVOID
- ☐ Creating a partial description that does not present all of the characteristics of the element being described
- ☐ Creating a subjective description that comes across as more of an opinion than a description
- ☐ Presenting facts in a random order

Model of a **description**

VISIT TO MY LOCAL CHURCH

As part of her research project on holy sites, Maria is asked to describe her local church.

The church in my neighbourhood is a Catholic church that was built in the 1960s. It has modern architecture and does not look like old churches in Québec at all. It has a really strange bell! Unfortunately, it does not have a bell like old churches; instead it has an electric bell. Personally, I like old churches much better than new ones. My church is near a park. It can hold around 300 people when it is full.

When you first walk in the door, you are in the nave. The walls on both sides are decorated with wooden sculptures that mark the Stations of the Cross within our church. The altar is the main element that you see at the front of the church. To the right is the pulpit where the priest addresses the congregation during religious ceremonies. On the altar, there is a lamp that continually burns to symbolize that God (the Holy Spirit) is present in the church.

At times, the church is decorated to mark religious celebrations. At Christmas, for instance, a manger is set up in the church to represent the birth of Jesus, the son of God.

In conclusion, I hope that this description of my church has helped you to better understand this important religious building in my neighbourhood.

Adding visual elements to a description makes it more interesting.

Maria added her opinion of the church bell in her description. An opinion does not belong in a description.

Maria answered the question "what?"

Maria answered the question "when?"

Maria answered the questions "what?" and "when?" as she stated the period during which her church was built.

Maria answered the question "where?" when she mentioned the park, and she answered the question "how many?" when she stated the number of people that the church can hold.

Maria ended her description with a proper conclusion.

Means for developing a point of view

181

Tool 9 Comparison

What is a comparison?

- A comparison is a means for developing a point of view.

- It helps to establish the differences or similarities between two or more elements with the goal of comparing ethical situations or forms of religious expression.

- It is used when you want to do the following:

  - organize ideas and arguments

  - synthesize ideas and expressed arguments in a discussion, debate, panel, etc.

  - structure a coherent summary of a chapter in a book, a newspaper article, Internet research, etc.

- The comparison may help you draw certain conclusions.

Proposed approach

1. Pick a topic of comparison and state the ethical situations or forms of religious expression that you want to compare.

2. Establish the differences and similarities between the situations or forms of expression.

3. If necessary, formulate your own conclusions.

4. Ask yourself the following questions:

   - Can I compare the situations or forms of expression that I have chosen?

   - Does my comparison include the main characteristics of the two situations being compared?

   - Does my comparison show a bias for one of the situations or forms of expression being compared?

5. Determine the order in which ideas will be presented in your comparison.

   - Prepare an outline for your comparison.

   - In your comparison, first describe the points that the situations or forms of expression have in common, and then describe the differences. If necessary, draw your own conclusion.

! WARNING

This is not a linear approach. You can skip to any of the steps at any time.

■ COMPLEMENTARY WAYS OF DEVELOPING A POINT OF VIEW

- Description (tool 8)
- Synthesis (tool 10)

■ PITFALLS TO AVOID

- Creating two descriptions without establishing a link between them

- Making a partial comparison that favours one of the elements and puts down the other in an exaggerated manner

- Drawing conclusions from a comparison based on our personal preferences rather than on logical reasoning

Model of a **comparison**

RESTRICTIONS ON MY FREEDOM,
AT HOME AND AT SCHOOL

To prepare for a class discussion about restrictions on freedom, John must make a comparison between the rules at school and at home.

It's not only at school that there are rules restricting our freedom. There are also rules in my family; some are similar to the rules at school, and some are different. Before examining the points that they have in common and what makes them different, I will describe the two situations.

In the first paragraph, John states the two situations that he wants to compare and the angle he wants to take for this comparison.

At school, there are several rules that restrict our freedom. We have to respect a dress code. We don't have to wear a uniform, but certain items of clothing are not allowed. By the way, I think it's ridiculous to ban certain designer clothes just to avoid bullying. We need to show respect for authority by using proper language and using "vous" when we speak to authority figures in French. Punctuality is also very important. We have to respect the school schedule or be punished.

John gives his opinion on the dress code; this is not the purpose of a comparison.

At home, we don't really have a dress code. I can wear whatever clothing I like as long as the price is reasonable. Manners are important, I don't have to speak to my parents formally, but I do need to show respect or I will be punished. My parents also expect me to speak properly. Punctuality is also important; my mother will not tolerate when I fall behind in homework or when I don't clean up my room.

John lists, point by point, the elements of his home life that correspond to the elements he has presented of his school life.

If I compare the two situations, I can see that I have more freedom at home in the clothes that I wear. With respect to manners, the two situations are similar; however, I have to use a formal manner with my teacher but not with my parents at home. Finally, my family is sometimes stricter than the school teachers about my punctuality.

In conclusion, I would say that both school and home impose restrictions on my freedom, but our habits at home and at school are not always the same. After comparing the two situations, I think that the school dress code is too strict.

The first part of John's conclusion is a logical result of his comparison; however, the second part is mostly a personal opinion.

Tool 10
Synthesis

What is a synthesis?

- A synthesis is a means for developing a point of view.

- It is a structured and coherent summary of the key elements (ideas, facts, experiences, arguments, etc.) of a discussion, story or text.

Proposed approach

1. Identify precisely what you want to synthesize.

2. Answer the following questions which will help you with your synthesis:
   - What is the fact, idea, experience, or argument that stands out most in what you have kept for your synthesis?
   - What are the secondary facts, ideas, experiences or arguments that you find important to include in your synthesis?

3. Ensure that your synthesis is complete and reflects what you want to synthesize.
   - Validate your synthesis by checking whether you have retained the essential elements. Did the answers to the above questions help you to describe your subject entirely? If not, then complete your description.
   - Ask yourself the following question: "Did I include all of the essential elements?" If not, then correct this by adding them to your synthesis.

4. Determine the order in which items will be presented in your synthesis.
   - The subject of your synthesis
   - The essential elements of your subject
   - The secondary elements that you feel need to be included
   - A conclusion

> **! WARNING**
>
> This is not a linear approach. You can skip to any of the steps at any time.

■ COMPLEMENTARY MEANS FOR DEVELOPING A POINT OF VIEW
- Description (**tool 8**)
- Comparison (**tool 9**)

■ PITFALLS TO AVOID
- Preparing a synthesis that only considers secondary elements without including the essential elements
- Not following the correct order of presentation which is to begin with the essential elements and then follow up with the secondary elements

Model of a synthesis for developing your point of view

PANEL
ETHICAL ISSUES RELATED TO TEENS' PREOCCUPATION WITH SEXUALITY

At the end of a panel (tool 7) on the ethical values associated with teen sexuality, the presenter, a student in the class, synthesizes the contributions of the various panellists.

Claudia: I would like to thank our panellists: Ms. Potter, our school nurse; Ms. Roberts, the sexologist at our local CLSC; Mr. Geraldo, our Ethics and Religious Culture teacher; and the students in the class who participated in the panel. Before we conclude, I would like to take a moment to synthesize our discussions.

Our panel discussed ethical questions regarding teens who may discover their sexuality earlier and earlier. It is a fact that we live in a highly sexual world and our adolescents can't help but be affected by this phenomenon.

Ms. Roberts spoke to us about teens' preoccupation with sex. She said that the sexy styles of clothing targeted at today's adolescents have an impact on the concept of sexuality. For some adolescents, this push toward sexuality is linked to other, more disturbing, phenomena, like Internet porn sites and cybersex. She concluded that, in the context of a sexually-driven society, sexuality can become a means of seduction to the detriment of other human values associated with sexuality, such as love, for example.

Ms. Potter continued on the same subject and insisted that this phenomenon is often linked to having sex at an increasingly younger age. In her opinion, adolescents are not prepared at such an early age to experience something as life-changing as their first sexual encounter. Ms. Potter feels that sexuality goes hand in hand with responsibility. She reminded us that many young teenagers get pregnant each year.

Finally, our teacher concluded the panel discussion by reminding us that sexuality is a new way for adolescents to experience freedom and autonomy, but it should be handled responsibly and with respect for certain rules. He also said that he was concerned to learn that violence and intimidation are often present in teens who are just beginning their sex life.

In conclusion, our panellists examined several ethical issues associated with teens' preoccupation with sexuality. Thank you all for your participation.

— Claudia begins her synthesis by reminding everyone about the panel subject and the overall statement made by the panellists.

— In her synthesis, Claudia emphasizes the panel subject, which is the ethical aspect of a phenomenon like teen obsession with sex.

— Claudia ends her synthesis properly with a brief conclusion.

Tool 11
Explanation

What is an explanation?

- An explanation is a means for developing a point of view.

- It is a development of ideas in order to better understand the meaning of something.

- It is used when you want to:
  - clarify ideas, a point of view or arguments by making them more explicit
  - add definitions and examples to a text so that it is easier to understand
  - provide further explanation for answers given to questions asked by participants at a debate

Proposed approach

1. Identify the subject that could use further explanation.

2. Find examples, definitions, or other information that would help to better explain certain aspects of your subject.

3. Ask yourself the following questions:
   - What aspects of my subject could use further explanation?
   - What would be the best means, definitions or examples to further explain my subject?

4. Determine the order in which your explanation will be presented.
   - Draw an outline of your explanation.
   - Begin with the more general part of your explanation, using a definition of what you want to explain, if possible.
   - Follow up with examples.
   - If necessary, end with special or exceptional cases.

! WARNING

This is not a linear approach. You can skip to any of the steps at any time.

COMPLEMENTARY MEANS FOR DEVELOPING A POINT OF VIEW
- Justification (tool 12)

PITFALLS TO AVOID
- Giving an explanation that complicates what you want to explain, rather than making it easier to understand
- Only providing secondary examples or exceptions to explain your subject
- Not defining terms that you want to explain
- Providing a description

Model of an explanation for developing your point of view

WHY DO CATHOLICS KNEEL?

During a class discussion on the rituals of different religions, someone asked what it means when Catholics kneel (get down on both knees) or genuflect (get down on one knee) under certain circumstances.

Aisha: I have noticed that Catholics get down on their knees—sometimes just one knee—on different occasions. I don't really understand what it means.

Aisha asks Samuel for an explanation.

Samuel: It is an act of humility, which shows that we recognize the existence of a higher being that we must worship. Catholics kneel on different occasions—to pray, for example, or at Mass during the Eucharist. There are also times when the priest or the congregation will get down on one knee. In those cases, genuflecting is an expression of the same religious feelings, but is limited to bending one leg only. My father told me that the congregation tends to kneel less often in church now. Some Catholics are fine with expressing their humility and adoration of God by bending their head slightly forward. In their private life, Catholics often pray on their knees to express their devotion. In the past, it was part of Québecois tradition for children to kneel before their father on New Year's Day to receive his blessing. That tradition has almost completely disappeared now.

Samuel's explanation helps to clarify the meaning of this ritual in the Catholic faith.

Samuel distinguishes between kneeling and genuflecting for which he provides a definition.

To make his explanation more concrete, he gives a few examples of times when Catholics kneel or just genuflect.

Do Muslims kneel to pray to God?

Aisha: We certainly do! Muslims prostrate themselves several times for each of the daily prayers. They generally do it on a rug that points toward Mecca, the holiest place on Earth for Muslims. For us, it is also an act of humility before God...

Aisha takes her turn to provide an explanation of the meaning of this ritual in the Muslim faith.

Tool 12
Justification

What is a justification?

- A justification is a means for developing a point of view.

- It is a presentation of ideas and arguments that are structured in a logical manner to prove or emphasize a point of view.

- It is used when you want to elaborate on a point of view by presenting a relevant and coherent argument in order to convince one or more people.

Proposed approach

1. Identify the point of view that you want to justify further in your subject.

2. Clearly state your point of view, your arguments and any objections that others could raise.

3. Ensure that your arguments are relevant, coherent and sufficient to convince other speakers that your point of view is correct.

4. Ask yourself the following questions:
   - Have I clearly expressed the point of view that I want to justify?
   - Are the arguments and examples in support of my justification relevant? Are my arguments good enough to convince others to share my point of view in a discussion? Have I presented my arguments coherently?
   - In my justification, have I taken into account any objections to my point of view that other speakers might raise?

5. Determine the order of presentation for your justification.
   - Clear presentation of your point of view
   - Presentation of your arguments and examples
   - Presentation and discussion of objections from other speakers

! WARNING

This is not a linear approach. You can skip to any of the steps at any time.

COMPLEMENTARY MEANS FOR DEVELOPING A POINT OF VIEW
- Explanation (tool 11)

PITFALLS TO AVOID
- Using non-relevant arguments that create an obstacle to dialogue (tools 17 and 18) rather than contributing, through justification, for developing a point of view
- Not including in your justification any objections that other speakers could raise

Model of a justification for developing your point of view

VIOLENCE IN VIDEO GAMES

In the classroom, the teacher launches a discussion with her students on the violence found in some video games. She asks her students the following question: Are students who regularly play violent video games more likely to develop violent behaviour?

Adolpho: I don't play video games. My parents won't let me because they think that the games could interfere with my studies.

Michelle: Adolpho, my parents let me play some video games, but they won't let me play the most violent ones because they are convinced that those games might have a bad influence on me. I don't agree with them. I think that young people are capable of telling the difference between a game and reality. For example, you can fly in some video games, but no one would ever think of jumping off a bridge to try and fly after playing one of those games.

Michelle begins to justify her position on violence in video games. She presents her main argument and supports it with an example.

She responds to her parents' objections. She provides a second argument based on the example of her friends.

I asked them if they had any proof that video games made people more violent. They didn't know what to say. For my part, I have friends who regularly play video games that are fairly violent and I've never noticed any change in their behaviour.

I think that adults should worry more about cyber-bullying. I read in the newspaper that it's a very widespread problem among young people who are just starting high school. I think that putting down another student or a teacher on the Internet is a lot more violent than playing with fictional characters in video games.

She concludes her justification by drawing attention to other widespread practices among youth that are, in her opinion, more likely to result in violence.

Teacher: Thank you for justifying your point of view, Michelle. I like your idea of looking into bullying and psychological violence on the Internet. But let's get back to our discussion on video games...

Types of judgments
Table of means for examining a point of view

Tool 13 Judgment of preference

DEFINITION	EXAMPLE	JUDGMENT IS BASED ON
A proposition that subjectively expresses personal preferences.	Hockey is my favourite sport.	Our tastes, our preferences

MEANS FOR EXAMINING A POINT OF VIEW

Examine your personal preferences and others' preferences so that in a dialogue you can better understand the reasons behind these preferences. For example, ask why hockey is someone's favourite sport.

Tool 14 Judgment of prescription

DEFINITION	EXAMPLE	JUDGMENT IS BASED ON
A proposition that conveys advice, a recommendation or an obligation that moves someone to take action.	End this inhumane war immediately!	Judgments of fact or judgments of value

MEANS FOR EXAMINING A POINT OF VIEW

Ask the person who is prescribing something on which fact or value they are basing their prescription. For example, you can't call for the end to a war unless you have the power to make both sides stop fighting.

TYPES OF JUDGMENTS

Tool 15 Judgment of reality

DEFINITION

A proposition that states a fact, an event or an eyewitness account.

EXAMPLE

According to the Catholic Church, God is composed of three entities: the Father, the Son and the Holy Spirit.

JUDGMENT IS BASED ON

Facts, testimonials

MEANS FOR EXAMINING A POINT OF VIEW

Ask the person who is making a judgment of reality on what they base their judgment since a judgment of reality is not necessarily true. For example, does the Catholic Church really state that God is composed of three entities? Where is this written in the Scriptures?

Tool 16 Judgment of value

DEFINITION

A proposition favouring one or more values over others.

EXAMPLE

I think that tolerance is indispensable to living in society.

JUDGMENT IS BASED ON

A reflection, an appreciation

MEANS FOR EXAMINING A POINT OF VIEW

Question a student about a judgment of value by asking them to explain the thinking that went into this judgment. For example, ask the following question: What personal reflection led you to become tolerant? Contrary to a judgment of preference, a judgment of value is generally based on personal reflection.

Tool 13
Judgment of preference

PITFALLS TO AVOID

- Wanting to impose your judgments of preference on others
- Not clearly expressing your judgments of preference
- Not asking other participants in the dialogue to clarify their judgments of preference
- Not expressing the underlying reasons for your judgments of preference
- Not examining the underlying reasons for the judgments of preference made by the other participants in the dialogue
- Drawing general conclusions from a judgment of preference

What is a judgment of preference?

- A judgment of preference is a means for examining a point of view.

- It is a proposition that expresses our tastes, interests and preferences for things or people.

- It is used when we want to express our preferences.

- In an argument, it could lead to a conclusion.

Proposed approach

1. Look for the judgments of preference used to develop your own point of view and those of the other dialogue participants.

2. Clearly state your judgments of preference. If necessary, ask for clarification on the judgments of preference made by the other dialogue participants.

3. Establish the underlying reasons for your judgments of preference and those of the other dialogue participants.

4. Find the conclusions that you, and the other participants in the dialogue, have drawn from your judgments of preference.

5. Ask yourself the following questions:
   - Are there any judgments of preference in my point of view or in those of the other dialogue participants?
   - What are my reasons, or those of the other participants, for supporting my judgments of preference and those of the other dialogue participants? Are these reasons good enough to justify my own judgments of preference or those of the other dialogue participants?
   - What are the implicit, unstated reasons underlying my judgments of preference or those of the other dialogue participants?
   - Are the conclusions drawn from my own judgments of preference, or those of the other participants, justified?

The use of judgments of preference for examining a point of view

MY FAVOURITE SPORT

A class discussion is being held on the values promoted in team sports. This gives Samuel and Thomas an opportunity to emphasize their preference for hockey and for soccer.

Samuel: My favourite sport is hockey. I think that in this team sport you can't win if you don't help each other and play together as a team.

Thomas: Samuel, I don't understand how you can like hockey. It's such a violent sport. I like soccer because it's the only sport where everyone helps each other; no one acts like a big shot and there are never fights on the field. Soccer is a much better sport than hockey.

Annie: Samuel, how did you come to prefer hockey?

Samuel: Because my father and mother watch the Canadiens' games on TV. Also, I find that it's a fast-moving sport. I don't agree with Thomas when he says that soccer is the only sport where the players help each other.

Annie: Thomas, how can you conclude that soccer is a better sport than hockey? Don't you find that you're generalizing a bit?

Thomas: You may have a point. I like soccer so much that I don't see the qualities of other team sports.

Thomas expresses his preferences when he has his turn. He justifies this preference through a series of arguments.

Samuel expresses disagreement with Thomas regarding the conclusion that he has reached based on his preference for soccer.

Samuel expresses a judgment of preference.

Annie questions Samuel on his preferences.

Annie points out a common error: drawing a general conclusion from a personal preference. This is a hasty generalization.

Tool 14
Judgment of prescription

What is a judgment of prescription?

- A judgment of prescription is a means for examining a point of view.

- It is a proposition that helps to state an order, an obligation or a recommendation. The judgment of prescription states the necessity to perform an act, modify a situation or solve a problem.

- It is used when you want to express a desire to get something done in order to change a situation or solve a problem.

Proposed approach

1. Look for the judgments of prescription used to develop your own point of view and those of the other dialogue participants.

2. Clearly state your judgments of prescription. If necessary, ask for clarification on the judgments of prescription made by the other dialogue participants.

3. Establish the underlying reasons for your judgments of prescription and those of the other dialogue participants.

4. Ask yourself the following questions:
   - Are there any judgments of prescription in my point of view or in those of the other dialogue participants?
   - What are my reasons, or those of the other participants, for supporting my judgments of prescription and those of the other dialogue participants? Are these reasons good enough to justify my own judgments of prescription or those of the other dialogue participants?
   - What are the implicit, unstated reasons underlying my judgments of prescription or those of the other dialogue participants?

PITFALLS TO AVOID

- Formulating judgments of prescription without sufficient justification
- Not clearly expressing your judgments of prescription
- Not asking other dialogue participants to clarify their judgments of prescription
- Not expressing the underlying reasons for your judgments of prescription
- Not examining the underlying reasons for the judgments of prescription made by the other participants in the dialogue

The use of judgments of prescription for examining a point of view

TEAMWORK

As part of their Ethics and Religious Culture course, the students are divided into groups of two and make a class presentation on the pioneers of Québec's religious heritage. After giving instructions to the class, the teacher asks the students to discuss among themselves how they plan to proceed with their presentations. Below is what she said to one of the teams:

Teacher: Your team must present the life and work of Marguerite Bourgeoys, a key figure in Québec society who stood in the forefront of Québec's religious heritage. You both need to participate in the presentation. You can't take more than 15 minutes total to present your subject and this includes a question period at the end of your presentation.

The teacher makes several judgments of prescription as she gives the instructions to follow for the class oral presentation. How many can you find?

Naïma: Why do we have only 15 minutes? That's not very long to present our subject!

Naïma questions the teacher's point of view by asking for the underlying reasons behind the judgment of prescription on the duration of each presentation.

Teacher: All of the teams need to give a presentation, and I don't want to give extra time to any team. It wouldn't be fair.

The teacher gives the reason behind her judgment of prescription.

Samuel: Naïma, you'll be the first to talk for our presentation.

Samuel then makes a judgment of prescription himself.

Naïma: Why?

As expected, Naïma asks Samuel to justify his judgment of prescription.

Samuel: You're more used to speaking in public than I am. I'm shy and I prefer being the last one to speak.

Naïma: Okay, but if I speak first, then you need to do the research on Marguerite Bourgeoys.

Can you recognize Naïma's judgment of prescription?

Samuel: Why?

Naïma: Because I hate doing research in books and on the Internet, I prefer speaking to people.

What type of judgment does Naïma use to justify her prescription? (judgment of preference, tool 13)

Teacher: There's no way that Samuel is going to do all of the research himself. You both need to prepare your subject.

The teacher corrects the situation by stating a new judgment of prescription.

Samuel: Okay, the instructions are clear and we'll be ready for our presentation.

Tool 15
Judgment of reality

PITFALLS TO AVOID

☐ Not checking judgments of reality made during a discussion

☐ Not questioning the other participants on the judgments of reality that they make during a discussion

☐ Drawing conclusions from judgments of reality that have not been verified

☐ Considering that something is true just because a person said it in the form of a judgment of reality

What is a judgment of reality?

■ A judgment of reality is a means for examining a point of view.

■ It is a proposition that allows you to make an objective observation and supports your position explicitly or implicitly with facts, events, eyewitness accounts, etc.

■ One or more judgments of reality can lead to a conclusion.

Proposed approach

1. Look for the judgments of reality used to develop your own point of view and those of the other dialogue participants.

2. Clearly establish the facts upon which you and the other participants have based your judgments of reality.

3. Go over the conclusions that you and the other participants have drawn from your judgments of reality.

4. Ask yourself the following questions:

☐ Are there any judgments of reality in my point of view or in those of the other dialogue participants?

☐ Are the judgments of reality stated in my point of view or in that of the other dialogue participants true? Can they be verified? Do they come from sources of scientific value? Are the eyewitness accounts credible?

☐ Are the conclusions drawn from my own judgments of reality, or those of the other dialogue participants justified?

The use of judgments of reality for examining a point of view

FOOD ALLERGIES

An information session has been organized with the school nurse to discuss food allergies at school. The meeting led to a discussion on the attitude needed toward students who suffer from food allergies.

Helen: At my elementary school, students weren't allowed to bring anything in their lunch and snacks that contained allergens like peanuts. Since I've been in secondary school, I've realized this restriction isn't in effect anymore. They just ask us to be careful and not to share our food with others. I think that's a better idea since it respects our freedom. I have no allergies and I don't see why I can't just eat whatever I want—like peanut butter, for instance.

Helen bases her point of view on judgments of reality about her primary and secondary schools. Are these judgments true? Can they be verified? How?

Matthew: I don't share your point of view, Helen. As the nurse said, someone who is allergic to peanuts could die from eating them. If, as you suggest, someone forgets to be careful, there could be very serious consequences.

Matthew jumps in with a judgment of reality about the danger of peanuts. Is his judgment of fact true? Can we verify what he said? How?

Philip: You're exaggerating, Matthew. No one at our school has ever had health problems due to allergies. I agree with Helen; the school is right to trust us. The proof is that there's never been a problem.

Philip makes a judgment of reality. Could you restate it in your own words?

Matthew: You say that there has never been a problem. Can you tell us who gave you that information on allergies at our school?

Philip: Everyone knows it, Matthew! I've never seen anyone sick at school because they ate something they were allergic to.

Matthew questions Philip about his judgment of reality in order to examine his point of view on peanuts.

Matthew: Your argument is good Philip, but you need to check your facts. The nurse might be able to tell us what she knows about the subject.

Nurse: Thank you, Matthew. Philip, it is possible that you have never seen a person having a reaction because of a food allergy, but there were five cases last year. One person had to be taken to the hospital. In three of the cases, the students had shared a lunch or snack with their friends.

The nurse steps in and helps Philip to establish the facts correctly by making more precise judgments of reality supported by statistics on cases of food allergy reactions over the past year.

Philip: Really! That's the first I've heard of it. Obviously, that changes my point of view somewhat. We really do need to make sure that students follow the rules and don't share their food. Otherwise, it might be best not to allow the more dangerous foods like peanuts.

Notice that Philip's conclusion is not as black and white after the nurse helps him to establish the facts more clearly in this discussion.

Tool 16
Judgment of value

WARNING

This is not a linear approach. You can skip to any of the steps at any time.

PITFALLS TO AVOID

- Not clearly stating a judgment of value
- Refusing to discuss your own judgments of value and those of the other participants
- Not explaining the underlying reasons behind your judgments of value
- Not asking other participants to clarify the meaning of their judgments of value and the underlying reasons behind their judgment
- Drawing conclusions that reflect personal preferences rather than ones based on logical reasoning

What is a judgment of value?

- A judgment of value is a means for examining a point of view.
- It is a proposition that favours one or more values in relation to others.
- It is used when you want to express your values.
- In an argument, it can lead to a conclusion.

Proposed approach

1. Determine the judgment of values used to develop your own point of view and those of the other dialogue participants.

2. Clearly state your judgments of value. If necessary, ask for clarification on the judgments of value made by the other dialogue participants.

3. Establish the underlying reasons for your judgments of value and those of the other dialogue participants.

4. Find the conclusions that you, and the other dialogue participants, have drawn from your judgments of value.

5. Ask yourself the following questions:
   - Are there any judgments of value in my point of view or in those of the other dialogue participants?
   - What are my reasons, or those of the other participants, stated in support of my judgments of value and those of the other dialogue participants? Are these reasons good enough to justify my own judgments of value or those of the other dialogue participants?
   - What are the implicit, unstated reasons underlying my judgments of value or those of the other dialogue participants?
   - Are the conclusions drawn from my own judgments of value, or those of the other dialogue participants justified?

The use of judgments of value for examining a point of view

WHY DON'T WE ALL EAT THE SAME FOODS?

At lunchtime, some students noticed that they were eating different foods as a result of certain values and religious convictions. A meeting was arranged with Ms. David, the school dietician, to discuss the matter.

Francesca: I love spaghetti with meat sauce, but I haven't had any since my mother convinced me to become a vegetarian. I think that it's cruel to kill animals just so that we have food to eat. I think that respecting animals is a very important value, a value that is more important than my personal tastes.

Francesca makes a judgment of value by saying that respect for animals is more important than her personal tastes.

Emilie: I don't agree with you, Francesca. The fact that you're a vegetarian has nothing to do with respect for animals. In nature, animals eat each other all the time. Why shouldn't we? It seems to me that we're just respecting the food chain, which means that we are respecting nature!

Emilie questions the underlying reasons for Francesca's judgment of value. She states her own argument in favour of respect for nature.

Saïd: I eat meat, but not all meat. In my religion, you're not allowed to eat pork because it is considered impure. My mother also says that it's better for your health if you don't eat it. I also fast for a month; it's called Ramadan. During that month, I don't eat anything between dawn and sunset.

Francesca: Why?

The judgments of value made by Saïd are based on his religious convictions and his family traditions.

Saïd: Because God asked us to fast and I have to obey him. Fasting teaches us perseverance and helps us to better understand the suffering of the poor.

Francesca: That's funny—my mother told me that when she was young, she had to give up certain foods for 40 days before Easter. If I remember correctly, she called it Lent. I think that Catholics fast for basically the same reason as Muslims do.

Francesca questions Saïd on his point of view so that he can further justify the value of fasting.

Emilie: At my house, we eat everything—even fries and pizza. While we're on the subject, I don't agree with the school's decision to stop selling junk food in the cafeteria. I don't think the school should tell us what we can or can't eat with the excuse that it's for our own health. We are free, after all!

Emilie states her preference for the value of freedom over the value of health.

Francesca: Ms. David, why did the school decide to ban junk food?

Ms. David: As you can see, the subject of food raises a lot of discussion around our values. As for junk food...

By appealing to the dietician, Francesca wants to get back to facts (judgment of reality, tool 15) to better support the judgments of value being made.

Obstacles to dialogue

Table of processes that may hinder dialogue created by appealing to others

PROCESSES THAT MAY HINDER DIALOGUE	EXAMPLES	DEFINITIONS	WHY IS THIS AN OBSTACLE?	HOW CAN I RESPOND TO AN OBSTACLE?
Personal attack	You'd like to convince us to be pacifists when you spend your days playing really violent video games.	It is designed to ruin someone's credibility in order to weaken their point of view while strengthening your own.	In a dialogue, respect for others is essential. When you make a personal attack, you get off topic. You can, for example, discuss a value like pacifism without making a judgment about the people participating in the dialogue.	By proposing that you get back to the topic of discussion and put personal attacks aside. In our example, we could remind everyone that the discussion is not about video games but rather about a value—pacifism.
Appeal to the people	You're the only person who is opposed to the school dress code. You should know that everyone in your class agrees with the code.	Its purpose is to lead someone to believe that something is true or false by claiming that a large group of people agree with what you're saying without checking whether they do or not.	In a dialogue, when you rely on a group majority to support your point of view, you seek to isolate the person who thinks differently. However, we know that taking a minority position can also be correct. For example, you can't conclude that the school dress code is good just because the majority of students support it.	By reminding people that the value of a point of view does not depend on the number of people who support it. Some very popular opinions can be wrong. In our example, even if I am the only one opposed to my school's dress code, my arguments are still worth hearing.
Appeal to the crowd	How can you waste your time listening to boring classical music when all of your friends listen to rock music?	It serves to support a point of view using the opinion of a highly-valued group, such as a group of friends, for example.	When we put a high value on the opinion of groups that matter to us, like our family and friends, we manipulate the feelings of the participants in the dialogue. Our convictions should not be based on the opinions of our friends or relatives.	By reminding people that every individual in a group has a valid personal point of view, even if the group has a different opinion. In our example, we could explain that tastes in music are personal, and we can fully appreciate our group of friends without necessarily liking the same music.

PROCESSES THAT MAY HINDER DIALOGUE	EXAMPLES	DEFINITIONS	WHY IS THIS AN OBSTACLE?	HOW CAN I RESPOND TO AN OBSTACLE?
Argument from authority	You're totally wrong in thinking that dialogue is not constructive. The teacher said the opposite in our last class.	Its purpose is to seek support from authority to back up a point of view or to criticize the points of view of others.	A discussion is cut short when someone seeks to impose their point of view through the use of authority. In this example, the teacher may have been right in pointing out the importance of dialogue in class, but using authority to support or criticize a point of view can put an end to dialogue rather than encourage it.	By reminding people that the value of a point of view does not depend on the support of any authority. It is more important to come up with relevant arguments that defend a point of view. In our example, we could ask why we need to believe in the value of dialogue rather than just deferring to the teacher's authority.
Conspiracy	It's because of you skateboarders that they told us we can't play soccer in the schoolyard. Ever since, you've had the schoolyard to yourselves.	It is designed to lead people to believe that those who profit from a situation to the detriment of others are responsible for the situation.	Dialogue is hindered whenever a speaker uses an accusatory tone or infers a conspiracy to denounce a situation. For example, we cannot conclude that a conspiracy is behind the fact that the skateboarders get to enjoy the schoolyard while the soccer players don't.	By reminding people that the value of a point of view does not increase when you trick people into believing that you are a victim of a conspiracy. In our example, we could ask the soccer team to find out why school authorities decided to ban them from the schoolyard.
Appeal to stereotype	The reason why there is so much theft and violence in your neighbourhood is because there are more and more Black people moving in.	It is designed to create a negative, rigid and demeaning image of a group of people to support or criticize a point of view.	In a dialogue, you stigmatize and offend participants when you present arguments based on stereotypes. For example, you sidetrack the discussion on the causes of violence in the neighbourhood when you reduce the neighbourhood's Black residents to nothing more than a bunch of violent, thieving hoodlums.	By reminding people that negative, and often rigid, images are not beneficial to a discussion but rather serve to maintain stereotypes. In our example, we could suggest to this participant that the local authorities be contacted to determine the real causes of the increase in violence.
Straw man argument	What you're saying makes no sense at all. Giving students more freedom at school would mean letting them arrive whenever they felt like it, hand in their homework whenever they felt like it, etc.	It serves to ridicule the position of a participant by making the position appear simplistic and non-credible.	In a dialogue, you discredit a participant's point of view when you describe it in overly simplistic terms. For example, wanting greater freedom at school does not mean that the school should have no rules at all and that students should no longer show any respect. A caricature like that falsely associates freedom with irresponsibility.	By reminding people that ridiculing a point of view through caricature does not bring a valid argument to the discussion. In our example, we could propose that the Straw man argument be corrected by being more specific about the freedoms that students should have at school.

Tool 17
Processes that may hinder dialogue created by appealing to others

PITFALLS TO AVOID

☐ Using authority, or the brash remarks of a majority or a group: classmates, friends, family to support your own point of view or to discredit someone else's point of view

☐ Drawing incorrect conclusions from false arguments that are obstacles to dialogue

☐ Not reacting to a discussion when someone is negating your point of view using different types of obstacles to dialogue

What is a process that may hinder dialogue created by appealing to others?

- An obstacle to dialogue is a judgment that prevents the thorough development of a point of view.
- A personal attack, an appeal to popularity, an appeal to the crowd, an argument from authority, a conspiracy, an appeal to stereotype and a caricature are all obstacles to dialogue that unduly appeal to others to support or contradict a point of view.
- The use of these techniques often shows a lack of ethics in the practice of dialogue. Respecting others in a verbal exchange should lead us to refrain from discrediting what they have to say using any of these obstacles to dialogue.

Proposed approach

1. Pay attention to your own words and to those of the other participants in a discussion, so you can discern obstacles to dialogue that appeal to others in an inappropriate manner.

2. Change your wording; replace these obstacles to dialogue with thorough and respectful arguments or points of view.

3. Question other participants who use such obstacles; your goal should be to lead them to restate their point of view in such a way that they become aware of how these techniques can harm dialogue.

4. Point out and criticize logical conclusions that are derived from arguments based on such obstacles to dialogue.

5. To assist you in this process, ask yourself the following questions concerning your own words, or those spoken by other dialogue participants:

   ☐ Do my words contain a personal attack aimed at promoting my own point of view or discrediting someone else's point of view?

   ☐ Am I incorrectly relying on a majority opinion to promote my own point of view or discrediting someone else's point of view?

   ☐ Do my arguments contain stereotypes that bring to mind negative and incorrect images of certain people or groups?

   ☐ Do I tend to overuse references from certain groups, such as family and friends, to support my arguments?

   ☐ Do I appeal to authority without justification in my arguments?

   ☐ Do I invent conspiracies to discredit the positions of others?

Processes that may hinder dialogue

SHOULD STUDENTS BE GIVEN MORE FREEDOM AT SCHOOL?

Francesca creates an obstacle to dialogue by making a racial slur to support her argument that students should be free to choose where they sit in the classroom.

The students are having a classroom discussion about the amount of freedom that should be given to youth at school.

Francesca: I am in favour of more freedom in the classroom. For example, we should be able to choose who we want to sit with. I don't want to be racist, but I don't want to be forced to sit beside Black people.

Michelle: I understand you want to sit wherever you like, but there's no reason to back up your request with a racial slur. I don't think it's a good way to encourage other students to continue the discussion. You should look at the rest of the class. You would see that no one thinks like you do; we should be able to choose where we sit.

Louis: I agree with Michelle. Francesca, imagine what the classroom would look like if we used your idea: a real circus, where everyone would be constantly changing places! The teacher would always be disciplining us and wouldn't have any time left to teach.

Francesca: Louis, making a mockery of my position is not helping out the discussion. We're supposed to be discussing freedom, but up until now no one has really talked about it. Perhaps we should get back to the topic.

Louis: You're right. Let's put aside any arguments that attack other people and get back to discussing freedom at school. . .

Michelle steps in to make Francesca aware that her racial remark is harmful to the discussion. Here, Michelle wants to convince Francesca by appealing to a group (their classmates). Her argument pointlessly seeks to isolate Francesca in her position.

Louis pointlessly caricatures Francesca's position; as a result, she might react badly as the dialogue continues.

Francesca and Louis want to move the discussion forward by putting aside any obstacles to dialogue and switching over to a more productive discussion of restrictions on freedom in the classroom.

Table of processes that may hinder dialogue created through errors in reasoning

PROCESSES THAT MAY HINDER DIALOGUE	EXAMPLES	DEFINITIONS	WHY IS THIS AN OBSTACLE?	HOW CAN I RESPOND TO AN OBSTACLE?
Hasty generalizations	You've noticed that Samuel and Vanessa are at the top of the students in their class and don't play any sports. It's well-known that top students spend all their time studying and don't play sports.	It consists of drawing a general conclusion from a small number of non-representative cases.	In a dialogue, you mislead others when you jump to conclusions based on just a few cases. Likewise, you may criticize other people's positions by drawing unjustified conclusions from their position. For example, basing a conclusion that top students don't like sports on two cases is a hasty generalization that would mislead others.	By reminding people that you can't draw a general conclusion from a particular case. In our example, Vanessa and Samuel are far from being the only top students in the class, and it would be worthwhile to investigate further before concluding that all top students do not play sports.
Appeal to prejudice	We shouldn't allow girls on our hockey team because they aren't any good at sports.	It consists of stating a favourable or unfavourable preconceived opinion that is often heavily influenced by the person's social environment.	You hinder a discussion when you make a prejudicial comment that you refuse to discuss because it seems so obvious to you that you don't feel it's worth discussing. In this example, the boys' prejudice against the girls' ability in sports is an obstacle in this discussion to the possibility of creating mixed hockey teams.	By reminding people that it is always a good idea to stop and think before repeating set ideas that you've often heard in your social environment. In our example, it would be good to ask the boys where they got the idea that girls are no good at sports.
Two wrongs don't make a right	I'm not going to wash the dishes even though it's my turn because my two brothers didn't do it yesterday.	It consists of justifying behaviour by stating that others did the same thing or worse.	When you cite someone else's wrongdoing to excuse your own behaviour, you create an obstacle to dialogue by evading responsibility. In this example, the parents will have a hard time continuing the discussion on household chores because one of the family members is evading his responsibilities.	By reminding people that our behaviours cannot be excused just because someone else did the same thing. In our example, it would be good to remind the third brother that the wrongdoing of the first two does not excuse him from doing the dishes since it is his turn.

PROCESSES THAT MAY HINDER DIALOGUE	EXAMPLES	DEFINITIONS	WHY IS THIS AN OBSTACLE?	HOW CAN I RESPOND TO AN OBSTACLE?
False dilemma	I know that you don't want to go skiing this weekend, so I'll let you decide if you want to go tonight or Saturday.	It consists of forcing a person to choose between two possibilities, one of which is so undesirable that the person has no choice but to pick the second one.	A false dilemma creates an obstacle to dialogue by detracting from the subject through the presentation of a false choice that only benefits the person proposing the choice. In this example, the person who does not want to go skiing on the weekend is trapped by this false dilemma and cannot express his or her own point of view.	By reminding people that you should never present a choice that traps another person. In our example, you would need to insist that both proposed ski dates were viable alternatives rather than a false dilemma.
Causal fallacy	Obviously, the reason why it's so hot today is because of global warming caused by greenhouse gases.	It consists of establishing an incorrect cause and effect relationship between two phenomena.	A causal fallacy can mislead participants and hinder the progression of a dialogue. In this example, if the temperature is cooler the day after the discussion, then a participant might erroneously conclude that global warming due to greenhouse gases is now a thing of the past.	By reminding people that a connection between two phenomena is not necessarily one of cause and effect. In our example, you would need to ask the person to base findings on more complete scientific observation before concluding that there is a cause and effect relationship between the increase in temperature that day and the increase in greenhouse gases.
Slippery slope	If you don't do your homework tonight, you'll fail your school year, you won't finish high school, you'll never find a job and you'll probably end up your life as the worst of criminals.	It consists of exaggerating the consequences of an action by saying that it could have insurmountably disastrous effects.	Exaggerating the consequences of an action can create an obstacle to dialogue by shifting the topic of discussion to distant and unlikely issues. In this example, it seems exaggerated to conclude that not doing homework one night could result in a person ending up becoming a criminal. If that were true, there would certainly be a lot of criminals in society!	By reminding people that the consequences of an action must be considered carefully and thoroughly. In our example, it would be good to remind the speaker that the simple act of not doing homework one night of the year will not necessarily result in such catastrophic consequences.
False analogy	All secondary-level students should pay for their courses just as university students pay for theirs.	It consists of drawing a conclusion from an analogy between two things that are not similar enough to be compared.	Making a false analogy harms a discussion by introducing false evidence based on a comparison of elements that are too far removed from each other. In this example, secondary-level education and university education target different types of students: in one case, the students are adults, somewhat financially independent, and in the other case, the students are adolescents who are still financially dependent on their family.	By reminding people that comparisons must be made carefully, and, as the saying goes, you must never compare apples with oranges. In our example, you would need to remind the speaker that the financial situation of secondary-level students and university students is so different that it is difficult to conclude that secondary-level students should pay for their courses like university students do.

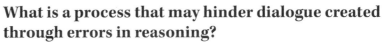

Tool 18
Processes that may hinder dialogue created through errors in reasoning

What is a process that may hinder dialogue created through errors in reasoning?

- An obstacle to dialogue is a judgment that prevents the thorough development of a point of view.

- Making hasty generalizations, appealing to prejudice, forgetting that two wrongs don't make a right, or introducing a false dilemma, a causal fallacy, the slippery slope or false analogy are ways to create an obstacle to dialogue through errors in reasoning when it comes to supporting or contradicting a point of view.

- The use of these techniques often shows a lack of integrity and, at times, a lack of ethics in the practice of dialogue. Respecting others should lead us to refrain from using any of these obstacles to dialogue.

Proposed approach

1. Pay attention to your own words and those of others so that you can detect obstacles to dialogue that are based on errors in reasoning.

2. Change your wording; replace these obstacles to dialogue with more valid arguments.

3. Question other participants who use these types of obstacles, with the goal of making them aware that these techniques have no place in a dialogue.

4. Point out and criticize logical conclusions that are derived from arguments based on such obstacles to dialogue.

5. To assist you in this process, ask yourself the following questions concerning your own words or those spoken by other dialogue participants:

   □ Do I tend to over-generalize based on a single or a few cases?

   □ Do I question the value of certain ideas that come from my social environment to ensure that they are not prejudiced?

   □ Do I tend to justify myself by putting others at fault?

- Are the choices that I offer other dialogue participants genuine alternatives for them? Are my preferences clearly seen when I suggest choices to others?
- Is the cause that I have determined really the cause of the phenomenon that I want to explain?
- Does my comparison include elements that can actually be compared? Is the conclusion that I draw from the comparison based on logic?
- Do I exaggerate the consequences of positions taken by other participants in the dialogue? Do I tend to present consequences as being more horrific and serious than they are in reality?

PITFALLS TO AVOID

Be careful not to make errors in reasoning by:

- Making hasty generalizations
- Making a participant responsible for certain actions to reduce or deny your own responsibilities
- Proposing false choices to others in order to promote your own preferences
- Not verifying whether the cause identified is truly the cause of the phenomenon
- Not paying attention to inappropriate comparisons from which conclusions might be drawn
- Jumping in with catastrophic consequences for positions taken by other dialogue participants
- Criticizing the position of other participants using erroneous logic that creates obstacles to dialogue
- Weakening your own position by making errors in reasoning that render your point of view less convincing

! WARNING: DO NOT CONFUSE

Several forms of reasoning are welcome in a dialogue and are not necessarily obstacles to communication.

- Generalizing on the basis of particular cases is a good thing. You simply need to make sure that the generalization is based on a sufficient number of cases.
- Establishing a cause and effect relationship between different phenomena can move a dialogue forward if you are sure that the cause is correct.
- Establishing consequences of an action or decision can move a discussion forward provided that the consequences are realistic and reasonable.
- A comparison or analogy can help to better understand a situation provided that the elements being compared are genuinely comparable.

Processes that may hinder dialogue created through errors in reasoning

When it is her turn to speak, Myriam makes two errors in reasoning that could prevent the dialogue from moving forward: she makes a generalization based on a single example and comes up with exaggerated and somewhat catastrophic consequences for climate change.

After moving the dialogue forward by supporting Lukanu's argument, Pablo comes up with a false dilemma that only serves to support his point of view in the discussion.

Myriam does not fall for Pablo's false dilemma. She redirects the discussion by suggesting that there are different ways of fighting pollution.

WHAT CAN WE DO TO PREVENT THE EARTH FROM OVERHEATING?

The students are discussing climate change and ways we can help to stop it.

Pablo: Global warming is something that ecologists invented. Our planet may be getting warmer, but it's not that big a deal.

Myriam: It was very hot this week. It's proof once again that the Earth's temperature is increasing quickly. If we don't do something to stop it now, all of the big cities like New York will be submerged by a tsunami next year and we won't be able to go on vacation to the United States!

Lukanu: I've also heard about global warming, Myriam, but if we want to understand it better, I think we should trust scientists' judgment rather than the weather this week! We really need to do something to prevent it. The problem is the Americans with their huge factories that are polluting the planet.

Pablo: I agree with you, Lukanu, we should find out what scientists have to say before we go any further in our discussion. But when you put the blame on large American factories, you are forgetting that those same factories have made the United States rich. I think we have only two choices: live in extreme poverty after closing all of the factories that contribute to pollution, or live in a world that is a bit warmer than before. Which would you choose? I prefer taking the risk of the planet getting a bit warmer so that I don't end up living in poverty.

Myriam: I'd like us to do more research on the subject. Pablo's choice isn't really a valid one. It's as if we have to choose between two different diseases. There are many other choices and we need to take a closer look at what we can do to reduce pollution and greenhouse gases.

Pablo expresses a prejudice against ecologists. He has states, without proof, that global warming is something invented by ecologists.

Lukanu reminds Myriam that we should rely on the opinion of scientists rather than this week's weather to predict what will happen to the Earth's climate in the long term. But she commits an error in logic by making large American factories the only ones responsible for climate changes. She also places the responsibility on another country rather than looking at our own society's responsibility for global warming.

3 SECTION

Conditions that foster dialogue
Tool 19
Attitudes that foster dialogue

What is an attitude that fosters dialogue?

- An attitude that fosters dialogue promotes an exchange of ideas between participants in a dialogue.

- Attitudes that foster dialogue include:
  - Following the rules
  - Expressing feelings in an appropriate manner.
  - Listening attentively
  - Paying attention to the attitude that others have in response to what you say
  - Remaining open and respectful
  - Showing concern for others by respecting their ideas, their feelings, etc.
  - Showing concern for moving the dialogue forward by proposing a review of what has been said or reminding everyone of the topic being discussed if the participants go off topic
  - Speaking in qualifying terms and listening for qualifying terms in what others have to say
  - Showing that you are open to the ideas of others
  - Asking yourself questions rather than jumping to conclusions
  - Thinking before speaking
  - Checking with other participants to see if you fully understood what they said

Proposed approach

1. Prepare to participate in a dialogue by structuring your ideas and arguments.

2. Consider the dialogue as a means for expressing your point of view and also as an opportunity to develop it.

3. Be aware of your attitude during the dialogue by asking yourself the following questions:
   - Is my point of view qualified enough?
   - Does my point of view take into account what the others have contributed?
   - Have I been aggressive or receptive toward the points of view of others?
   - Could I reword the last speaker's point of view?
   - When someone is speaking, am I listening or thinking about what I want to say next?
   - If asked, could I summarize what has been said in the dialogue?

> **! WARNING**
>
> This is not a linear approach. You can skip to any of the steps at any time.

▌ PITFALLS TO AVOID

- Not following the rules established by the participants in the dialogue
- Not reflecting on your attitude and its consequences on others
- Not listening to others
- Not showing empathy for the ideas and feelings of others
- Not feeling responsible for the success of the dialogue

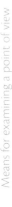

Means for examining a point of view

Attitudes that foster dialogue

WHY DO WE NEED TO ENGAGE IN DIALOGUE?

In class, the students wonder why dialogue is so important and what attitudes they should adopt to foster the best possible communication between participants.

Christina: I think that the most important thing in a dialogue is to take turns speaking. Students often talk at the same time without raising their hands. We need to establish rules and follow them; otherwise, it's always the same people talking.

Christina insists on the importance of setting rules in a dialogue.

Alex: You're right, Christina, but we also need to listen. Have you ever heard of the expression "talking to a brick wall"? I often find myself thinking about what I want to say next, rather than paying attention to what other people are saying. When I do that, I am not contributing to the dialogue. It's as if everyone were on parallel tracks that never meet.

Alex is able to criticize himself. He is humble enough to admit his mistakes. He insists on the importance of listening to others.

Miguel: Alex, I hate discussing things with you. You never listen to anyone else; you just do what you want. Personally, I think that to have a good dialogue, you need to set rules like giving each person a chance to speak.

Miguel's aggressive tone hinders the dialogue. His last comment also shows that he was not listening to what Christina had to say.

Annie: Miguel, you might have things against Alex, but you should speak to him respectfully, and I believe that Christina already suggested that everyone be given a turn to speak. Were you paying attention?

Annie criticizes Miguel so that he can contribute to the dialogue by speaking more constructively.

Miguel: You're right, Annie; I got carried away for no reason. I could have been more polite in my comments to Alex. So let's review: to have a good dialogue, we need to set rules, listen attentively to what others have to say and show respect for each other. What do you think of my summary? Do you have any points to add to our topic?

Miguel calms down and shows that he is capable of accepting criticism. He also moves the dialogue forward by proposing a synthesis of the ideas presented up to that point.

SECTION 3

Glossary

Ablution : the act of washing to purify oneself.

Abolish: putting an end to a custom or practice.

Abusive control: excessive control that is likely to cause harm to someone.

Age of Enlightenment: intellectual, cultural and scientific movement dating back to the 18th century.

Altruism: a tendency to love and a desire to help others.

Ambrosia: food for the gods.

Anonymity: the state in which a person's identity is not made public.

Anti-globalization: term used to describe opposition to economic neo-liberal globalization where the state intervenes very little.

Apostle: each of Jesus' twelve companions and other disciples who preached His teachings.

Ash Wednesday: the first day of Lent.

Autonomy: the ability to make a decision, without consulting an authority, to determine independently which rules to live by.

Baby-boomer: generation of people born after World War II (1945-1964).

Ban: to exclude permanently.

Blasphemous: that which bears outrage upon the divine, the sacred or on religion. Blasphemy can also be an insult toward someone who is respectable.

Broadcaster: an organization that transmits television programs or radio shows.

Censorship: control held by a government or an authority over the press.

Charisma: the quality that gives an individual a great deal of influence, a magnetic power over others.

Charter: a law established by a monarch or a pope.

Code of ethics: the rules and duties imposed on the members of a profession.

Common good: the material and spiritual conditions which provide a group's well-being and which help in the development of individuals making up the group.

Communion: the part of the Catholic and Orthodox mass or Protestant service during which the faithful receive consecrated bread.

Confederation: the association of several states that maintain a certain degree of autonomy in relation to a central government.

(to) Confess: in Catholicism, the confession of one's sins to a priest to obtain forgiveness.

Consecrate: to make sacred.

Consent: to accept that something should take place.

Constraint: that which obliges us to, or prevents us from, doing something.

Contract: agreement between individuals.

Cooperative: an enterprise whose partners share equally in the work, in its management and its profits.

Corruption: the means taken to provoke individuals to act contrary to their conscience or duty.

Crusade: a campaign undertaken to mobilize public opinion on a specific subject.

Defame: to discredit someone's reputation by saying or writing things that are unfounded.

Democracy: a type of political organization where the people hold the power and freely elect representatives to exercise it on their behalf.

Dictator: a leader who seizes power and exercises it in an authoritarian manner.

Discriminate: the act of separating one group of human beings from another and treating this group differently.

Divination: attempting to foretell the future by interpreting signs or omens.

Divining: as related to divination.

Ethnic group: a group of people who speak the same language and share the same culture.

Faith: a belief or conviction.

Foundation: a gift of money to be used as the donor sees fit.

Governmental apparatus: a combination of institutions, structures and mechanisms held by a government to fulfill its functions.

Halo: a ring of light or a coloured circle that surrounds the head of holy figures in Christian pictorial art.

Hell: In Christian traditions, a place of pain and turmoil for the damned.

Heritage: art work (paintings, sculptures, stained glass windows, monuments, buildings, etc.) that is part of our past.

Holocaust: the systematic extermination of Jews by the Nazis.

Ideal: a model of perfection toward which we strive.

Identity: all of the aspects of a person or group which constitute their individuality or uniqueness.

Ideology: a collection of philosophical, social, political, moral, religious and other ideas that are specific to a given period or social group.

Inclement weather: bad weather.

Infrastructure: the large-scale public systems, services and facilities that are necessary for economic activity (e.g. power and water supplies, roads, telecommunications, schools).

Inquiry commission: a commission mandated by the government to seek the opinion of the public on a given topic or to shed light on a specific event. Most of the time, the name of such a commission is abbreviated by giving them the name of the person in charge. For example, the Gomery Commission, or the Bouchard-Taylor Commission.

Interdependence: dependence on each other.

Interference: an obstacle that prevents something from taking place.

Judeo-Christian: that which falls within both Jewish and Christian spriritual values. Catholic, Protestant and Orthodox churches are all Christian churches.

Judicial incapacity: the inability of a person to exercise his or her rights.

Legislative competence: an authority's power to make laws in a given area.

Lent: in Catholic and Orthodox Churches, as well as in Anglican Churches, the 40-day period preceding Easter. During Lent, Christians are asked to pray more and to abstain from eating certain foods (meat and sweets).

Maghreb: the Maghreb is made up of various countries in northwest Africa: Libya, Tunisia, Algeria, Morocco and Mauritania.

Mardi Gras or Shrove Tuesday: a holiday related to the carnival that precedes Ash Wednesday.

Mass: a ritual ceremony of the Catholic religion, celebrated by a priest who offers God some bread and wine that, through consecration, becomes the body and blood of Christ.

Media: a collection of means for distributing information to the public (press, radio, television, movies, advertising, notices, the Internet).

Moral rule: a moral norm that indicates how a moral principle or value must be applied in a given situation.

Morals: customs and codes of behaviour common to a society, a people and an era.

Municipal: that which concerns a given city or territory.

Mythical: that which comes from the supernatural, the imaginary.

Native: said of a people that have always lived in a given country. The Amerindians and the Inuit are Canada's Aboriginal Peoples.

Need: a natural or social requirement that results in human beings performing actions that are necessary to them.

Norm: rule, law or moral requirement that serves as a criterion to determine behaviour.

Ordain: to grant someone the sacred order of a particular Church, that is, responsibility for a ministry.

Order: that which has been specified.

Organ builder: someone who makes or builds musical instruments.

Outlaw: an individual acting outside the law.

Peer: a person in the same social situation, having the same standing.

Philanthropist: a person who contributes through personal deeds, through donations of money, through the founding of organizations, to help improve the plight of the less fortunate.

Phonetics: a written representation of the sound of a word.

Piety: a feeling of devotion and respect for God and all religious things.

Principle: a rule of conduct that is based on values that influence a person's or a group's behaviour.

Propaganda: an action taken to provoke the public to adopt certain ideas.

Public funds: sums of money belonging to the State and subject to specific laws (income taxes, etc.).

Purgatory: for Catholics, a place or state for temporary suffering where souls finish atoning for their sins before going to heaven.

Puzzle: a series of words, signs or drawings that evoke the sound of a word or an expression that the receiver must guess.

Repression: using violence to stop protests and revolts.

Reprisals: violent measures taken against someone because of their acts of retaliation.

Secularization: the action of secularizing, of making secular, of removing the religious aspect. A secular person (or layperson) is someone who is not part of the clergy.

Self-denial: devotion and voluntary self-sacrifice.

Senate: assembly where senators sit in the Parliament of Canada.

Service: a ceremony of worship in a given religion.

Sikh: someone who practises Sikhism, a religion that originated in India. Among other things, Sikh men must wear a turban.

Sin: a transgression of a divine law.

Slogan: a short phrase used to spread an idea.

Social success: a person's success in their relationships with others.

Sponsorship: the financial support given to an organization or an event.

Stenographer: a person who practises shorthand, that is, a much simplified writing process that makes it possible to write a text as quickly as the words are spoken.

Suffragette: someone who fought for women's right to vote in the early 20th century.

Sulphur: a chemical element that smells like rotten eggs.

Sunday: from Latin, *dies solis*, which means "day of the sun."

Swear word: a blasphemous or rude expression.

Tenet (precept): a statement that expresses a teaching, a rule or a way of doing things.

Transgression: the act of not obeying an order, law or rule.

Transparency: the quality which expresses reality without changing it.

USSR: the Union of Soviet Socialist Republics, a state whose territory extended to Europe and Asia from 1917 to 1991. The USSR has since been divided into several countries, including Russia.

Value system: a consistent and prioritized set of values.

Value: the importance attributed to things, to behaviours or attitudes that are more or less highly regarded or desired by people or groups of people who use them to make judgments to base their conduct.

Ward off: to get rid of an evil power.

Weekly: takes place every week.

Photo credits